AS SILVER REFINED

*Learning to Embrace Life's
Disappointments*

As
Silver
Refined

KAY ARTHUR

WATERBROOK
PRESS

COLORADO SPRINGS

As Silver Refined
Published by WaterBrook Press
5446 North Academy Boulevard, Suite 200
Colorado Springs, Colorado 80918
A division of Random House, Inc.

ISBN 1-57856-064-0

Printed in the United States of America.

2000—First Trade Paperback Edition

10 9 8 7 6 5 4 3

This book is dedicated to my precious husband, Jack,
who shakes his head and says,
"I don't know how you do it all,"
and to whom I say,
"Without your heart for ministry,
without your support and encouragement,
without your prayers,
and without your selfless sharing of me,
I never could."
How well Jack and I have come to understand and rest
in the sovereignty of our omnipotent Father
in giving us children who now share our love
for the Lord and His Word,
and in giving us a ministry and a godly staff
that is far beyond us as two very ordinary human beings.

Contents

Acknowledgments

I WANT TO THANK my dear brothers and sisters who over the years have entrusted to me, as a friend, their stories—testimonies to the faithfulness of our gracious, sovereign God. Thank you, beloved ones, for believing God, for taking Him at His Word. You have believed that He is who He says He is and that He is a rewarder of those who diligently believe in Him. Your faith is pleasing to God, as you know from Hebrews 11:6. And it is also a joy and encouragement to me as a teacher of His inerrant Word.

Of all my books, this is the first of its kind in the way it captures my teaching in print. Therefore, I also want to thank Rebecca Price, Thomas Womack, and Dan Rich of WaterBrook Press, who caught the vision for *As Silver Refined* after reading transcripts of my teaching on these subjects. What a blessing it has been to work with them. With their servant hearts, they made this book happen when I wondered if it ever could or would. Their encouragement, help, and belief in this book's value to the precious body of Christ (and to those who later will come to know Him) have spurred me on through the challenges in the midst of a busy ministry.

Our collective and fervent prayer has been that it would all be of God—"from Him, through Him, and to Him. . . . To Him be the glory forever" (Romans 11:36).

I am grateful to Dr. Joseph Carroll of the Evangelical Institute of Greenville in South Carolina for introducing me to the "Five Deadly D's" concept.

The authors of the poems "The Refiner's Fire," quoted partially in the introductory chapter, and "Disappointment: His Appointment," quoted in chapter 2, are unknown.

Words for the Peggy Lee song "Is That All There Is?" as quoted in chapter 2 are by Jerry Leiber (1966), with music by Mike Stoller.

The exciting story of captive missionary Bruce Olson in chapter 8 and the accompanying quotations are from the two-part article "Bruce Olson's Nine-Month Colombian Captivity" in *Charisma & Christian Life*, November and December 1989.

The story in chapter 9 about Marie Monsen, missionary to China, is from her book *A Wall of Fire*.

The story of faithful Mae Louise Westervelt in chapter 11 is from "The President's Letter," April 1982, by Robertson McQuilkin, president of Columbia Bible College and Columbia Graduate School of Bible & Missions

Information and statistics on depression in chapter 13 are from The Harvard Mental Health Letter, October 1994 (© 1994 by the President and Fellows of Harvard College, and © 1995-1996 by Philip W. Long, M.D.).

The story of John Sung in chapter 15 is adapted from Leslie T. Lyall's *John Sung: Flame for God in the Far East* (Chicago: Moody Press, 1964).

THE REFINER AND HIS FIRE

⟨≈⟩

COME, LET ME TAKE YOU BACK to a Judean village in ancient days.

Inside a small, walled courtyard under a blue and blazing sky, there stands a refiner of metals. In his hands, gnarled with age, he is rolling and fingering a lump of ore. He watches the sun play on the streaks and veins of lead and other minerals running through this bit of rock chiseled from the bowels of the earth.

His experienced eye knows that, intermingled within this ore, there is silver.

He lays the ore on his worktable then builds his fire with care and the wisdom of years. Soon the flames are rising in the pit situated against the courtyard's stone wall.

At the worktable he picks up his hammer and begins crushing the lump into smaller pieces.

He pauses occasionally to stare at the fire, as if in study. From time to time he places more fuel upon the already-blazing coals and works his bellows until the flames are in a frenzy.

When the fire is right, he gathers the hammered bits of ore from the place of their crushing and lays them in a small, sturdy container of tempered pottery—his crucible.

He places the crucible in the fire and sits down beside it. A long day is before him, and this is where he will stay for as long as the metal is subject to the flames. Silver is too precious to be forsaken in the furnace, too valuable to be ruined through inattention.

Carefully he watches the fire. It must be maintained at exactly the right temperature for the right duration of time to accomplish its purpose. Slowly the ore softens. The silver, with its greater density and lower melting point, liquefies first, hissing and bubbling as oxygen is released. The still-solid impurities rise to the top of the molten metal. This is the dross, and the refiner skims it off.

Now he adds bits of charcoal inside the crucible. He knows this will enhance the sheen of the silver. The carbon of the charcoal will keep the refined metal from reabsorbing oxygen from the air, which would only dull its finish.

He tends the fire, adds more fuel, and applies more air from the bellows.

Amid the relentless heat surrounding the crucible, more dull impurities, newly revealed, rise to the surface of the mixture.

Again the refiner carefully skims away the murky, smudgy metal floating at the top of the crucible. Gazing down upon the molten surface, the refiner sees at best but a dim reflection of himself.

The refiner works and watches and waits. The heat and its effect continue. More impurities rise to the surface, and again he skims them off.

He never leaves the crucible unattended, never steps away from the fire he has formed to do its work. The finished product he cherishes demands this process. Only his guided and guarded refinement will yield the promised and precious metal.

And he is not yet satisfied.

He lets the fire cool. Eventually he sets the crucible aside.

Then once again he builds up the fire, and the process begins all over. This time the skilled refiner makes the fire hotter. Within the crucible, new impurities are released, brought to the surface, exposed for what they are, then skimmed off.

Finally his leathery face breaks into a smile, for now as he gazes into the liquid silver his reflection is apparent—not yet sharp, but more distinct than before.

More hours pass as he perseveres in his anxious and delicate work.

And then . . . once more he bends over the crucible, and this time he catches his breath. There it is! In the silver he sees what he has waited for so patiently: a clear image of himself, distinct and sharp.

Delight banishes his frown. His task is done. The impurities are gone. The silver is refined.

He has his treasure.

He has "choice" silver, the most lustrous of all metals, beautiful and highly valued. It's as pale and shining as the wings of a dove, as brilliant and splendid as the moon, worthy to become coin or trumpet or ornament, worthy to grace the king's table or to reflect sunlight in a crown upon his head.

The refiner has taken what was impure and made it pure.

He has taken what was dull and made it beautiful.

Potential value has become actual value.

And the fire—the guarded, guided, relentless fire—made the difference. The fire allowed ordinary ore from the earth to be transformed into treasure.

All under the refiner's watchful care, for all the while he never left it unattended.

WE ARE HIS SILVER

You and I are more than observers in this picture, beloved. This image of refinement is something God touches on again and again in His Word. He is the true Refiner. We are His silver.

And the fire is the fire of His making, for through His fire our Refiner will perfect an awesome work, a divine work. He will take what is impure and make it pure. He will take what is dull and make it beautiful. He'll take what is of potential value and reveal its actual value.

He will transform us into treasure.

He'll refine us in the crucible so that He can see *Himself* in the silver—in you and me. And so the world, as well as the principalities and powers and hosts of Satan, can behold the triumph of the Redeemer.

The fiery flames—the array of disappointing situations in our lives, from minor irritants to major tragedies—will make the difference.

Different flames, different fires will come and go. In the pressure of their heat we'll see the impurities in our lives being released and rising to the top. Then He'll skim them off, purifying us, refining us.

He'll make the fire a little hotter, causing new impurities to rise and be released, exposed for what they are. These, too, He'll lift away.

Early in our Christian lives He may see only a very dim image of Himself as He looks into our crucible. But as time goes on, His image becomes clearer, more lustrous, more beautiful.

And all the while, He never leaves or forsakes His treasure.

Our Refiner never leaves the crucible, never steps away from the fire.

He is always there to make sure every flame that reaches us is exactly the right temperature—not too hot!—to accomplish its work in our lives. He knows the precise temperature to maintain so we don't face more than we can bear. He tests and proves our faith, not to discredit us, but to show us how far we've come. He perfects our perseverance.

Years ago I filed away a copy of a poem called "The Refiner's Fire." Now is the time to share it with you. Instead of silver, the metal here is gold, as in 1 Peter 1:7—"that the proof of your faith, being more precious than gold which is perishable, even though tested by fire, may be found to result in praise and glory and honor at the revelation of Jesus Christ." But the process—and the Refiner's attitude—is just as we have seen, as the last two stanzas of this poem testify:

Can we think it pleases His loving heart
　　To cause us a moment's pain?
Ah, no, but He sees through the present cross
　　The bliss of eternal gain.

So He waited there with a watchful eye
　　With a love that is strong and sure,
And His gold did not suffer a bit more heat
　　Than was needed to make it pure.

A CHERISHED PICTURE

The Refiner's fire is a picture of great worth and importance to God, one He refers to often in His Word. Let me share a few of these verses with you as we begin our study of how to handle the disappointments and difficulties God uses to refine us.

"The refining pot is for silver . . . ," He says, "but the LORD tests hearts" (Proverbs 17:3).

"The crucible is for silver and the furnace for gold, and a man is tested by the praise accorded him" (Proverbs 27:21). Even the praise we receive can be a refining and testing fire.

"The tongue of the righteous is as *choice silver*" (Proverbs 10:20).

He even uses this image as a picture of His own Word: The words of the LORD are *pure words; as silver tried in a furnace* on the earth, *refined seven times*" (Psalm 12:6). Seven is the number of completion, perfection— God's Word is perfect and complete. And you will be too as you learn to respond to the fires in a way pleasing to God.

The Lord promises to bring His people *"through the fire,"* and to *"refine them as silver is refined,* and test them as gold is tested. They will call on My name, and I will answer them; I will say, 'They are My people,' and they will say, "The LORD is my God' " (Zechariah 13:9).

We can all tell the Lord what the psalmist acknowledged, "For Thou hast *tried* us, O God; Thou hast *refined us as silver is refined*" (Psalm 66:10).

REJECTED SILVER

Yet unfortunately, there are times when God's refinement fires are of no avail.

Why? Because you and I can resist and ruin God's refining process. Jeremiah 6:29-30 describes this very situation as God speaks of His people Israel:

> The bellows blow fiercely,
> > the lead is consumed by the fire;
> in vain the refining goes on,
> > but the wicked are not separated.
> They call them rejected silver,
> > because the LORD has rejected them.

The fire burns and burns. But the dross—the wickedness, the impurities—is not allowed to be released and removed. Instead it's held on to, stubbornly clung to, no matter how hot the Refiner's fire.

So the silver becomes rejected silver or, as the King James Version puts it, "reprobate silver."

Therefore the Refiner must reject it. It is impure and unusable and unattractive.

God will send the fire several times and with increasing heat to get rid of those impurities, those un-Christlike things in your life and mine, beloved. But if we insist on hanging on to them, then God must set us aside. He'll call us reprobate silver—rejected for His use.

Could there be any more tragic and fearful condition for a Christian than to hear God say, "I cannot use you"?

PROVEN AND QUALIFIED

Paul abhorred the possibility of becoming God's castaway. In 1 Corinthians 9:27 he spoke of his fear that "after I have preached to others, I myself should be disqualified." This word for *disqualified* is *adokimos,* meaning "without approval"—unfit for the Master's use. *Adokimos* is the negative form of the Greek word used in James 1:3 for the "proving" or "testing" *(dokimos)* of our faith, the proving that happens as we "consider it all joy" (James 1:2) when we encounter various trials.

If we respond correctly to the Refiner's fire, we find our proven faith producing endurance in our lives. We will exercise the self-control in "all things" that Paul mentioned in 1 Corinthians 9:25—the self-control that brings our flesh under subjection to the Holy Spirit, delivering a blow, a technical knockout to "self."

It means running in such a way as to win the prize, as Paul also said in that passage.

But if we respond wrongly to the Refiner's fire, we will find ourselves unproven and disqualified. This is the consequence—the awful, wasteful consequence—of failing to let God complete His purifying work in our lives.

I can't use you.

Oh, my friend, there is nothing greater in all this world than being used by God . . .

Nothing greater than knowing you've been obedient to what God has called you to be . . .

Nothing greater than hearing from the lips of the Father, "Well done, My good and faithful servant" . . .

Nothing greater than knowing you have pleased the One who gave His all so that we who were nothing might know the greatness of being reformed into His image . . .

Nothing greater than being used by God to do the work of God, to reach out and introduce others to Him, to His family, to His life.

There's *nothing* greater.

How my heart aches for those so self-centered, so wrapped up in themselves and their own world, in their own happiness and fulfillment and success, that they won't bend their knees and bow their heads and find out from God why He put them on this earth.

Beloved, we have much to explore about all of this.

We'll look at what it means to respond to the Refiner's fire so that *refinement* truly happens.

And we'll look at the dangerous alternative, which triggers a process of downward degeneration in a deadly, depressing spiral.

We want to understand all this well—because the good fire of our loving Refiner is burning. It burns for your good and His glory. You need not fear, for He never leaves the fire unattended or attended by someone else. He is always there . . . the perfect Refiner watching over you—His redeemed silver.

Therefore, take up the full armor of God.

EPHESIANS 6:13

CHAPTER ONE

WHEN YOU FEEL YOU'RE A FAILURE

Resisting the Spiral of Defeat

I WAS A FAILURE. I was convinced of it. I had failed God, and there was nothing I could do about it. I was impotent to change my circumstances. Disappointment overwhelmed me.

My dreams for being a missionary had been shattered. We were home in a small, rented, three-bedroom house after just three and a half years in Mexico, and Jack didn't even have a permanent job.

I was only about four and a half years old in the Lord, but I'd wanted to serve Him ever since I was saved at the age of twenty-nine. My first husband had committed suicide not long after I became a child of God, but I was convinced (even before I remarried) that the mission field was for me— even if for some reason God didn't give me a husband and father for my two sons.

Then along came Jack, the seasoned missionary whom God had told me I would marry before I ever met him face to face. Before we met, Jack had served with the Pocket Testament League in more than thirty countries in Africa and Latin America. Except for a few months, we had spent almost our entire four years of married life in Guadalajara. Jack assisted other missionaries in Mexico through film evangelization and literature distribution. Meanwhile I worked with English-speaking teens in Guadalajara. And that was very fulfilling for me as I saw many of them come to the Lord. Seldom did a day go by without one or more of the teenagers visiting in our home. Our house became their Bible school—and mine—as I spent hours in the Word, studying diligently and then teaching the teens what I learned. Those were wonderful days.

At times I traveled with Jack to remote villages, where I used my nursing skills to minister to people who were in need—spiritually and physically.

I absolutely loved being a missionary.

And I loved Mexico. As I drove the streets of Guadalajara, shopped in the open *mercado,* and tried talking to the warm-hearted Mexican people in my limited Spanish, I felt I was home—exactly where I belonged. I loved the people. I loved the country. I loved serving God there. I thought, *This is where I'll be when Jesus comes.* Little did I know that the onset of chest pains would keep my dreams from coming true.

The chest pains began without warning and kept getting worse. Often I found myself nearly out of breath.

Jack insisted I see a doctor. The examination and cardiogram revealed that I had pericarditis, an infection in the lining of my heart. I was confined to bed, allowed out just once a day and then only as far as the bathroom.

Jack put a halt to all the visits from teenagers. When I was able to travel, he sent me to the States to be examined by a cardiologist I once had worked for. Dr. Mullady's recommendation to leave Mexico was all it took for Jack to pack us up and move us back to the U.S.

I wept. I grieved. I agonized in prayer, crying out to God in my sense of failure. I mourned the fact that I had taken a much-needed man off the mission field. Through my physical weakness I had brought Jack's thirteen-year missionary career to a halt. Now Jack was helping some friends in their Christian bookstore and had applied for a job with a Christian radio station, but no other work had materialized. Before becoming a missionary Jack had sold insurance, but that had been so long ago, and I wanted a husband in some sort of full-time ministry . . .

For weeks I lived in torment of mind and heart, until the morning I rolled out of bed onto my knees and prayed, "Father, *whatever You want.* If You want Jack to sell insurance again, it's okay; I will accept it." God could do as He pleased. He was the Potter—I the clay.

That morning on my knees I surrendered my expectations, my desires, and my evaluations to my God. And in my submission came my peace.

TO BE SIFTED LIKE WHEAT

Oh my friend, has there been a time in your life when disappointment in your circumstances or your relationships sent you into an emotional tailspin? Did clouds of defeat and depression blow in, obliterating the joy you felt even on a breezy, bright, sunshiny day?

What did you do? How did you handle it? Did it throw you for the proverbial loop?

And what if a crushing disappointment came your way today or tomorrow—do you have the assurance that you could face it in such a way that it would become a steppingstone toward greater godliness rather than a stumbling block to plummet you into defeat, depression, and despair?

Surely by now you realize that if you are going to live for God you will not go unopposed.

Just before Jesus was betrayed and arrested, He turned to Peter and said, "Simon, Simon, behold, Satan has demanded permission to sift you like wheat" (Luke 22:31).

Peter was but the first! The devil—that serpent of old—wants the same opportunity to sift you and me. Once you come out of the kingdom of darkness into the kingdom of God, then want it or not it's war—warfare with the prince of this world. And although you can never be snatched from the Father's hand, the devil of darkness will do everything he can to keep you from being an effective witness for our Lord Jesus Christ.

Yes, warfare is inevitable.

Therefore one is very wise to learn the strategy of the enemy of our souls.

Our enemy has at least three major strategies for weakening us before the major battles come. One of them is simple *distraction*. He wants us to focus on anything except what is truly important. How often are you and I like Martha, drawn away and distracted from *the one thing that is needful* (Luke 10:40-42, KJV)?

The one thing "needful" is to sit at His feet and learn of Him; yet the pressures and pleasures of life can so easily distract—as do the pressures of ministry, the busyness of serving the Lord. And believe me, the more your ministry broadens, the greater will be the distractions! I think this is why we've seen so many Christian "celebrities" fall. The dangers of our time should put a holy fear within us. This is a day when Christendom focuses more on the messenger than on the message or on the God of the message and the Book of the message. (We could discuss this one for quite some time, couldn't we?)

Another strategy of the enemy is *deception,* which can often be the result of distraction. When we don't have time to stay in the Word, we're far more easily deceived. Deception looms large in the portrait God's Word gives us of our enemy. Jesus said the devil "does not stand in the truth, because there is no truth in him. Whenever he speaks a lie, he speaks from his own nature; for he is a liar, and the father of lies" (John 8:44). This "father of lies" has always challenged the authenticity of God's Word, right from the beginning. And any lie he can convince us of will have a negative effect on how we think and act and respond in various situations.

Distraction and *deception*—these are "Deadly D's," and to understand

and overcome these strategies we would do well to study them carefully. But that's another book. In this one I want to move from guerrilla warfare to the major battles of five other Deadly D's: disappointment, discouragement, dejection, despair, and demoralization. They represent another strategy of the enemy, a strategy with several layers. Together they form a downward spiral of deepening defeat and disorder. They're part of a devastating plunge that's triggered when we respond wrongly to the disappointments that God in His loving sovereignty allows in our lives.

I was first introduced to the concept of these five Deadly D's by Dr. Joseph Carroll of the Evangelical Institute of Greenville in Greenville, South Carolina. Over the years as I've pondered and dug deeper into these strategies of the enemy, God has used what He taught me to lead me and others in glorious victory when we could have suffered a shameful and needless defeat.

The downward spiral begins, as I mentioned, with *disappointment*. Disappointment comes when our expectations aren't met. Consequently we're not happy about it—we're disturbed.

When this happens and we don't conquer that disappointment in God's way, then we spin downward into *discouragement*. We're without courage. We want to give up. We want to quit because we're disheartened. We're ready to run rather than deal with the situation. Isn't this evident today as we see many who, in the face of adversities, name the name of Christ while throwing up their hands or shoving them into their pockets? They walk out; they run away. Their fighting spirit—their spunk—is gone.

And what follows discouragement? Depression in its various degrees.

The first "degree" of depression is *dejection*—a lowness of spirit, a feeling of spiritual and emotional fatigue.

If not reversed this dejection takes us down even further, plunging us into *despair* and finally into utter *demoralization*. At this stage of descent, hope is entirely abandoned and is replaced by apathy and numbness. Fear becomes overwhelming and paralyzing and can degenerate further into disorder and reckless action that is heedless of consequences.

When you pause to think about all this, can't you see that these are the tactics Satan is using to defeat so many of God's children today?

The question is, How well do you understand them? How quickly can you recognize them in your own life or in the lives of others around you? How quickly and confidently can you blast them out of their strongholds with the ammunition of God's truth?

Let's pause for a minute while you reflect on the last time you encountered a disappointment. How did you handle it? Where did it lead?

When was the last time you were truly discouraged, lacking in confidence, ready to give up on something when God wanted you to keep going? What triggered your discouragement? How did you respond?

And what about the degrees of depression—dejection, despair, demoralization? Have you had to deal with these paralyzing feelings when they felt so real they seemed truer than anything the Word of God has to say? What led to this state?

Have you ever felt hopeless, as if you'd fallen into an old, abandoned well in a wilderness with no way to climb out and no one to hear your plea for help? What did you learn from that situation?

Or could it be, beloved, that you're still there?

If you are, your cry has been heard. Help is here!

If in any way you've tasted the wretched awfulness of these Deadly D's—or if you have friends or loved ones (or recently turned enemies) who are in the heat of this warfare—I believe you'll find great help in this book in the form of insights from the Bible and from the instructive experiences the Lord has graciously given me and others. If I didn't believe this, I would never have taken the time to write this book. But as I've taught these things, a great many listeners have later caught my hand to say, "It saved my life, Kay, and I mean that literally." Lives, relationships, marriages—and minds—have been "saved," rescued from the enemy's prison camps simply because truth sets us free!

My goal is that no matter how fierce or long the battles we face, you and I together will be able to say, "But in all these things we overwhelmingly conquer through Him who loved us" (Romans 8:37).

PRINCIPLES OF WARFARE

Now let's look at some principles of warfare that hold true in the spiritual as well as the physical realm.

Throughout the New Testament (and with a concentration of teaching in Ephesians) God reminds us that *we are in a conflict*—not with flesh and blood but with principalities and powers and spiritual wickedness in high places. Therefore it's essential that you understand the tactics of the enemy so you won't be caught off guard. If you don't recognize your enemy for what he is and if you aren't aware of his tricks and devices (which God warns us about through the apostle Paul), the prince of the realm of darkness will establish a beachhead that will make it easier for him to push his way into your life until he holds you captive in his stronghold.

One reason for Israel's years of dark defeat, which are described in the book of Judges, was that after the passing away of Joshua's generation—those who had conquered and occupied the Promised Land—"there arose another generation after them who did not know the LORD, nor yet the work which He had done for Israel" (2:10). So what did the Lord do to strengthen this unknowing and unproven generation? He left some of Israel's enemies in the land of Canaan "*to test Israel . . .* that the generations of the sons of Israel *might be taught war*, those who had not experienced it formerly" (3:1-2).

We need to be "taught war"—and to know and understand our enemy. Our enemy is not just the devil but the entire world system that's opposed to God. How does this enemy wage war? What are the tactics and the weapons we face? And what do we have to counteract them?

We dare not go into battle unprepared!

War movies have always fascinated me. Years ago when I was leading our ministry's summer "boot camp" for teens, I used the old movie *Battle of the Bulge* to visually engrave in the minds of our young people some principles that hold not only in military battles but also in spiritual warfare.

Paul did something similar in his day when he used the Roman soldier and his armor as visual illustrations to strengthen God's people for their spiritual battles. In his last letter to his beloved son in the faith, he admonished Timothy to "suffer hardship with me, as a good soldier of Christ Jesus" (2 Timothy 2:3). Paul was adamant that Timothy not entangle himself in the affairs of this life so that he might please the One who had called him to be a soldier.

My goal for you, beloved, is the same—to prepare you to be a good soldier for the Lord Jesus Christ. (By the way, I want you to know I call you "beloved" because that's what God calls you time and again in the New Testament books written by Paul, Peter, and the boys. It's a manly term!) To help us understand the principles of warfare, let's explore a particular event in history. In 1944, the Second World War was in its fifth year in Europe. German troops still controlled most of the Continent. But on June 6, Allied forces under Gen. Dwight Eisenhower crossed the English Channel in five thousand ships and invaded Normandy in northern France. It was the long-awaited D-Day, the result of months of careful planning, with due respect to proven principles of war: the concentration and economy of forces, careful intelligence, and offensive action incorporating the element of surprise.

By August, the Allies had liberated Paris from the Germans. But then the Allied advance into Europe's interior was in danger of being halted. Supplies, which had to be hauled hundreds of miles inland from the coast, became seriously depleted.

Another problem facing Eisenhower was the strong rivalry between his most famous generals, Patton, the American, and Montgomery, who was British. Both wanted to be the first to capture and enter Berlin. However, both needed supplies—Patton in the south and Montgomery in the north—and there was not enough for both.

In September, Montgomery devised a spectacular plan to shorten the war by transporting thirty-five thousand men some three hundred miles behind enemy lines into Holland. Under pressure from his superiors, Eisenhower approved the plan, and Operation Market Garden was born. The time seemed right, especially because the German military effort was becoming increasingly disorganized.

"Market" was the code name for the airborne operation, "Garden" for the ground advance. Airborne troops were to be dropped astride three major Dutch rivers. The plan was to seize and hold seven key bridges. The Allies would then be in position to outflank the enemy and drive into Germany itself across a relatively open plain. From there they would turn into Germany's industrial heartland.

This was the biggest operation since D-Day. But it was not planned or executed nearly as carefully as the Normandy invasion had been. In the rush to conquer, basic combat principles were bypassed. As a result, Operation Market Garden was a failure that cost the lives of thousands of Allied troops.

You cannot ignore basic warfare principles and expect to win battles. Therefore warriors in training for military service are taught the following basic principles, which remain consistently true.

One of them is that of *concentration*, the ability to mass one's forces at a critical time and at a critical place for a decisive action.

In a war there are always battle lines dividing the territories held by opposing forces. Your enemy tries to break through the line and take territory that you hold. His best way to make a breakthrough is to amass his forces at a critical time and place.

Imagine the situation: After discovering a weak spot in your defensive line, the enemy lines up an arrowhead formation against it. He strikes suddenly with the steel tip of his arrow—one hundred tanks. Once this strategic penetration is achieved, a bigger enemy force of five hundred tanks follows right behind, widening the breach in your line. Behind that force is yet a bigger wave of a thousand tanks followed by twenty thousand infantry ready to devour your collapsing defense and then to occupy and hold the newly conquered territory.

Another key principle of warfare is that of *offensive action*. As one military historian puts it, going on the offensive allows the attacker "to exercise initiative and impose his will upon the enemy; to set the pace and determine the course of battle, to exploit enemy weaknesses and rapidly changing situations, and to meet unexpected developments."

The enemy of our souls—who's a master of warfare—understands these principles well. He's on the offensive, ready to invade. He's a roaring lion seeking whom he might devour, as Peter says. When a disappointment comes our way (and in this life disappointments will always keep coming), our failure to respond in a biblical way will produce a weak spot in our mental and emotional defensive line. The enemy will take advantage of our weakness to cross that line with more wrong thoughts and feelings that take us down into discouragement.

The breach is then opened. To conquer and hold more territory in our thought life and emotional being, this deceiver needs only to bring in more and more forces, dragging us down into dejection and despair. He has established his stronghold.

The razor-sharp point of a steel-tipped arrow is small and penetrates flesh quite easily. If only the tip has entered, it can be pulled out easily. But once the full arrowhead has penetrated into the underlying muscle, it can only be cut out or pushed on through; it cannot be pulled out.

If the enemy's first attack against a certain area of your life succeeds in achieving a penetration, he'll bring more and more and more of his might against you until you are demoralized—flattened, unable to get up, your face buried in the dirt and held there by the pressure of the enemy's combat boot.

And where is this struggle fought? On what front?

YOUR MIND IS THE BATTLEGROUND

The front line is always the mind. Never forget that principle, for understanding it is the key to winning the war.

Listen to what Paul said in 2 Corinthians 10:3-5:

> For though we walk in the flesh, we do not war according to the
> flesh, for the weapons of our warfare are not of the flesh, but

divinely powerful for the destruction of fortresses. We are destroying speculations and every lofty thing raised up against the knowledge of God, and we are *taking every thought captive* to the obedience of Christ.

We war, but not according to the flesh. With our divinely powerful weapons, we are able to take every *thought* captive to the obedience of Christ. *We are able*—but whether we *do it* is another story!

Just don't forget—*never* forget—that your mind is the battleground!

Satan will attack your mind with imaginations and thoughts that are contrary to what God says in His Word. These ideas and perceptions will be a perversion of His truth about you. These thoughts will be nothing more than disinformation and distortion.

Therefore we don't war after the flesh. Remember what God said: "The weapons of our warfare are not carnal [or fleshly], but mighty through God to the pulling down of strong holds; Casting down imaginations, and every high thing that exalteth itself against the knowledge of God, and *bringing into captivity every thought* to the obedience of Christ" (2 Corinthians 10:4-5, KJV).

At any moment, if you are experiencing anything but victory, if your thoughts are anything less than obedient to Jesus Christ, stop and ask yourself: *Why* am I feeling this way? *Why* am I thinking these thoughts?

Do you realize that *how you think* really determines how you behave? So consider your thought patterns. Ponder how they affect you. "Ponder the path of thy feet" (Proverbs 4:26, KJV). We so seldom stop and do this! We just react instead of taking a cognitive plan of action.

"*Consider* your ways!" the Lord told His people (Haggai 1:5,7).

Jesus called upon His followers *to think*. Do you recall how before telling a parable to His disciples He sometimes asked, "What do you think?" (Matthew 18:12, 21:28). He wanted them to *think* rightly, to reason correctly. "What do you think about the Christ?" He asked them (Matthew 22:42). He said to Peter, "What do you *think*, Simon?" (17:25).

Beloved, what do you *think*?

Satan chooses the mind for his battleground because he understands so well the principle laid down in the Word, that as a man thinketh so he is (see Proverbs 23:7, KJV). Satan knows if he can capture your mind he can capture your body. Isn't this the purpose of brainwashing prisoners? Brainwash them, and you can do with them as you please! (This is illustrated strongly, by the way, in another good war movie, *The Manchurian Candidate*.)

Therefore, either you must learn to take your thoughts captive—or the deceiver will take you captive with your thoughts!

And what kind of thoughts does he attack your mind with? Paul described them in 2 Corinthians 10:5 as thoughts that are "raised up against the knowledge of God." Satan will attack your mind with imaginations or with thoughts that are contrary to or a perversion of God's Word.

I think of David when he went forth against Goliath and shouted, "Who are you who comes against the armies of the living God!" David's mind-set wasn't on how big this guy was—no, it was "Who do you *think* you are?"

That's why we're told, "Be transformed by the renewing of your *mind*" (Romans 12:2).

Your mind is all-important. What is yours dwelling on? Scripture tells us, "Finally, brethren, whatever is true, whatever is honorable, whatever is right, whatever is pure, whatever is lovely, whatever is of good repute, if there is any excellence and if anything worthy of praise, *let your mind dwell on these things*" (Philippians 4:8).

Be careful, beloved, about what you let into your mind. As Jesus said, "Therefore *take care how you listen*; for whoever has, to him shall more be given; and whoever does not have, even what he thinks he has shall be taken away from him" (Luke 8:18).

Never a Foothold

You and I cannot prevent the enemy from directing his fiery arrows of wrong thoughts toward our minds. But we can keep him from achieving victory with these Deadly D's *by never permitting a penetration.*

This is the secret of victory: Never allow a penetration. Have you got that? This is imperative, and you may want to underline it here: *Never allow a penetration.* Don't allow the enemy to get his foot in the door. If you do, he'll have the leverage to push his way far deeper into your life.

These are our commands from General Headquarters: "Do not give the devil an opportunity" (Ephesians 4:27) and *"Be on the alert.* Your adversary, the devil, prowls about like a roaring lion, seeking someone to devour. *But resist him,* firm in your faith" (1 Peter 5:8-9).

Our enemy cannot be seen: "For our struggle is not against flesh and blood, but against the rulers, against the powers, against the world forces of this darkness, against the spiritual forces of wickedness in the heavenly places" (Ephesians 6:12). Yet God has given us spiritual armor, all of it having to do with God Himself and His Word, including our two-edged sword, the Word of God (6:17). We also have the belt of truth, the breastplate of His righteousness, the helmet of salvation, and the shield of faith by which we're able to quench all the fiery darts of the enemy.

We *do* have *all* the armor we need to keep him from making a penetration.

We also have the principles of warfare that can work *for* us even more than our enemy uses them against us.

Communication, for example, is a critical principle in warfare. Lines of communication must be kept open. How well this is illustrated in the movie *A Bridge Too Far,* which tells the story of Operation Market Garden. Some of the Allied soldiers who had parachuted behind enemy lines were issued inadequate radio equipment and later were unable to communicate that they weren't where they were supposed to be. Then Allied supply planes flew over and unknowingly dropped their supplies into German-held territory. Watching the planes fly over, the Allied soldiers lit fires, waved their clothing, screamed, and jumped up and down to try to get the attention of their pilots. But the pilots were trained to ignore such activity lest it be a ruse of the enemy.

That brings up another vital principle, that of *supply*. A war cannot be won without weapons, ammunition, food, and all kinds of gear and equipment. Therefore one of the enemy's primary tasks is to cut off supply lines.

Remember, my fellow soldier, to stay in communication with General Headquarters so you can receive His rich supply of everything you need. When our Lord tells us to "be strong in the Lord, and in the strength of His might" and to "put on the full armor of God that [we] may be able to stand firm against the schemes of the devil" (Ephesians 6:10-11), you and I can rest assured that everything we need in order to be more than conquerors is ours.

So let your requests be made known to God. Your Commanding General has said, "Ye have not, because ye ask not" (James 4:2, KJV) and, "I chose you, and appointed you, that you should go and bear fruit, and that your fruit should remain, that *whatever you ask of the Father in My name*, He may give to you" (John 15:16).

Yet another critical principle of warfare is that of *objective*, which is defined this way: "Every military operation must be directed toward a clearly defined, decisive, and attainable objective." The reason so many Christians fail in spiritual warfare is that we've ignored the right of the Lord Jesus Christ to have supreme authority and rulership in our life. *His* objectives for us—to conquer ungodliness, to be holy even as He is holy—are not *our* objectives. Instead our desire so often is to be our own commander (until, of course, we eventually find ourselves hopelessly trapped).

Imagine yourself with Joshua just before the battle of Jericho:

> He lifted up his eyes and looked, and behold, a man was standing opposite him with his sword drawn in his hand, and Joshua went to him and said to him, "Are you for us or for our adversaries?"
>
> And he said, "No, rather I indeed come now as captain of the host of the LORD."
>
> And Joshua fell on his face to the earth, and bowed down, and said to him, "What has my lord to say to his servant?"
>
> And the captain of the LORD's host said to Joshua, "Remove your sandals from your feet, for the place where you are standing is holy." And Joshua did so. (Joshua 5:13-15)

Remember, beloved believer: There is only one Captain of the host. So follow *Him*.

Intelligence is another key principle in warfare. So often in history one side in a conflict is victorious because of crucial information collected about the other side's leadership and decision-makers. They're able to anticipate what course of action their enemy will take in battle. How well this is illustrated in another good World War II movie, *Midway*, which shows how God supernaturally intervened to turn the tide of battle in the Pacific. (I told you I liked war movies!)

In the Bible God has given you a profile of your enemy: He's the liar and the father of lies (John 8:44). Your enemy is the deceiver of the world and the accuser of the brethren, accusing them night and day (Revelation 12:9-10). That's what your enemy is like—so don't listen to him! He's a Tokyo Rose of the worst sort.

Are you perhaps engaged in warfare with the enemy of your soul and finding yourself losing the battle? O dear child of God, you don't have to lose the war! You can be set free from your enemy's prison. Of course he would like to torture you until you lose all hope, turn your back on your country, deny your King, and become a traitor. But remember that "greater is He who is in you, than he who is in the world" (1 John 4:4). If the Son shall set you free, you shall be free indeed (John 8:36).

Remember, beloved believer: The outcome of the war is already determined. Jesus is victor, and all who align themselves with Him will be more than conquerors. And the promises of God are the concentration and mass of force that you need to unload on the enemy. Determine to prove these promises true. Make it your passion! If you do, you'll find yourself winning each and every battle. God would never send you into a battle you can't win—He's not that kind of foolish commander. (Look at Psalm 91.)

When you're hit with disappointment, you *can* hold your line of defense by being strong in the Lord—as we'll carefully and confidently explore in the pages to come.

So pause and reflect on what you have learned—and discuss it with God.

And now may I pray with you . . . *for you* . . .

I pray, Lord, that You will cup my friend's face in Your hands and give assurance that the thoughts You have for him or her are like the thoughts You shared with Your chosen nation of Israel— thoughts of good and not of evil, of welfare and not of calamity, to give a future and a hope.

Father, show my friend that no matter what forces the enemy amasses against us, we can be more than conquerors through Christ Jesus who loved us.

O Father, I ask You now to bring these truths home and to so pierce our hearts that as more than conquerors we will be able to stand against all the wiles and devices of the enemy, holding the ground of faith and not yielding.

I thank You now for what You're going to do. As we study this subject together, anoint us from on high. Give us the spirit of wisdom and revelation in the knowledge of Your Word—the same sword by which You will someday smite the enemy in eternal defeat.

Now unto You, O Father, be all praise and honor, for it belongs to You and to You alone. Amen.

In the world, you have tribulation . . .

JOHN 16:33

CHAPTER TWO

GOD'S TRAINING IN DISGUISE

Understanding Disappointment

I'M SURE you've been there, as I have: Something or someone hasn't turned out the way you expected, the way you hoped. You've been let down.

An important relationship or situation has gone wrong. What you counted on, planned for, prepared for, looked for . . . just hasn't happened. And what *has* happened is what you didn't foresee or desire.

Your marriage isn't what you envisioned. Your spouse isn't the person you dreamed about.

The child you raised hasn't become the kind of son or daughter you hoped for.

A close friend or someone you rely on isn't acting or responding as you'd like. Someone hasn't performed, hasn't come through, hasn't delivered.

Your profession, your career is headed in a direction you didn't anticipate and didn't want.

Something you've worked hard to accomplish is not progressing according to plan. Setbacks and stumbling blocks have caused a cherished goal to remain unrealized.

A frustrating complication or obstacle or hardship—something out of your control—has dropped suddenly into your life like a bombshell. You're reeling under drastically altered circumstances.

Something you once held dear is now gone. Something else you never wanted or asked for is now yours.

Or it could be just an overall letdown feeling about life's excitement, life's promise. The thrills haven't materialized. You could echo with sad agreement the words Peggy Lee made famous as she sang about watching her childhood home burn down, and about going to the circus, and later about falling in love:

> Is that all there is?
> If that's all there is, my friends,
> then let's keep dancing.
> Let's break out the booze, and have a ball,
> if that's all there is.

Or maybe what really hurts is that you've let yourself down. You feel like a failure as a parent, a spouse, a friend, an employer or employee—or even as God's child.

Your life has become a disappointment.

Disappointment—it comes whenever expectations aren't fulfilled, whenever you and I are left wanting. Hopes are unreached, desires unmet. To be disappointed is to be unsatisfied or displeased with some situation or person—or with ourselves or even with God.

Disappointment especially wounds us whenever our expectations were more than just a vague hope. In your heart you felt a confidence, a sense of rightness that something should and would happen in a certain way. Now that it hasn't, you feel thwarted, frustrated, unfulfilled, perhaps even betrayed and embittered.

Shattered. But are you really shattered, if you're God's child? Or is that just the way you feel? Your disappointment is like an overhanging cloud separating you from the warmth of the Son. A chill comes over you, and you shudder. Drawing your arms tighter around yourself doesn't help. You ache but not with physical pain. You find it hard to concentrate, hard to listen to what others are saying. All you can think of is the disappointment intruding into your world.

And then, if you get quiet and listen long enough, you'll hear His whisper—maybe not in these exact words but with the same message: "In the world, you have tribulation . . ." (John 16:33). He warned us. We will encounter trouble, He said. There will be disappointments; things will be hard. "But take courage; I have overcome the world." Christianity doesn't exempt us from pain, from disappointment, from the hardships of this life. Nor does it demand that we deny or hide our pain or our disappointments. But it does give us One who promises a purpose, an end, and a benefit in it all.

Because we are His and He is ours, we can take courage. We *must* take courage.

"But *how*?" you ask. That, beloved, is what this book is all about—to help you with the *how* . . . and to give you a glimpse into the *why* . . . and to make you aware of the awful pit of despair you can fall into if you do not handle life's disappointments God's way.

THE BEST STRATEGY

Remember again with me, won't you, our lesson in battle strategy: The best way to win is to respond rightly to the enemy's first penetrating attack. It's critical that in the battlefield of your mind you know how to handle disappointments before you find yourself slipping or even spiraling downward into the Deadly D's. If you fail to handle a disappointment biblically and quickly, you open yourself up to the enemy, making yourself a bigger target. You allow the enemy to infiltrate your mind and begin building a stronghold inside you brick by brick, and *he will snare you from within.*

As I write this I think of the many women I've held in my arms who, out of disappointment with their husbands, began to fantasize about what it would be like to be free, to be married to someone else—until eventually they found themselves in the bitter guilt of an affair. The enemy pierced their line of defense and moved in with his armored division.

While you can't prevent the enemy from directing fiery arrows of wrong thoughts toward your mind, every child of God has adequate armor to keep him from making a penetration.

DISAPPOINTMENT = HIS APPOINTMENT

So what do you do?

Your first response, my friend, must be an act of pure obedience. You must believe God no matter how you feel or what you think—no matter your circumstances. Tighten that belt of truth. Recognize and acknowledge that every disappointment is God's appointment. In your thinking, in that all-important mental response to the disappointment you now encounter, determine by faith that you will simply change the "D" of disappointment to an "H," then add a space—and you'll eventually see that this really is *His appointment.*

Adding that space is important. At the moment your disappointment may be overwhelming, shattering. The pain can be so overpowering that you cannot imagine how anything good could ever come out of it, for there's nothing good in it. God doesn't say the situation is good, but He does promise that because He's your God and you're His child, He will bring good from it.

This is where that gut-level faith comes in, beloved. Faith is the substance of things hoped for, the evidence of things not seen. It takes time to see what God's appointment really is, to begin glimpsing and under-standing His good plan and purpose behind a particular disappointment He has allowed. But that time will come. It *has* to, for God cannot lie.

This time gap is represented by that added space. Yet right now, at this moment—before we have any idea of God's reasons—we are to respond *by faith*. We must look beyond our current disappointment to His appointment. With our shield of faith we can then prevent the enemy's penetration. This is our defensive weapon.

Whatever the disappointment, it is God's appointment—and that assures us it's His gift, bestowed upon us in the rich outpouring of His grace. Strange as it may seem, this disappointment is something God allowed in our lives after filtering it through His sovereign fingers of love. It's something He has deemed necessary and of long-range value in bringing you, His beloved child, toward His personal goal for you—Christlikeness and fruitfulness.

That's why God had James pen the following words. Read them carefully, won't you, with a fresh, childlike faith—the kind you had as a new Christian:

> Consider it all joy, my brethren, when you encounter various trials, knowing that the testing of your faith produces endurance. And let endurance have its perfect result, that you may be perfect and complete, lacking in nothing. (James 1:2-4)

Every disappointment is a trial of your faith . . . a test that proves the genuineness of your relationship with your God and His Word. Over the years I've discovered in many disappointments that His appointment was for me to learn submission to His good and perfect will—in my not becoming bitter or angry or rebellious or fearful.

Have you ever memorized James 1:2-4? If you haven't, may I suggest that now is the time, because God will use this passage to help you live through many a disappointment.

This Scripture brings to mind my dear friends Charley and Ginger Calhoun, who teach our ministry's Bible studies in Columbus, Georgia. Charley is a prominent and respected ophthalmologist, highly esteemed by his fellow physicians. While he was teaching through the book of James, he began experiencing great pain in his back. He went to one of his colleagues to have it checked out. After much consultation, Charley agreed to have exploratory surgery. Several doctors were present when their brother "went under the knife." A tumor was found. Charley—still in his forties—had cancer.

My dear Ginger was shaken to the core, but not Charley. He told her, "God says we're to count it all joy when we encounter various trials. We *will* count it all joy." So, with tears and trembling, that's exactly what Ginger did.

Charley underwent chemotherapy and was told he would be sterile because of it. He and Ginger wanted another child, but they chose to give thanks instead. The disappointment was great, but so was their faith. Their faith was on display, and many were touched by it.

Then Ginger became pregnant. Many in the medical community advised her to have an abortion since the baby "couldn't possibly be normal" because of Charley's chemotherapy. But they chose to believe God and not listen to man.

That was years ago. Their daughter Charity—born to this so-called sterile man—is a beautiful young lady who loves Jesus.

You change the "D" to an "H" in faith, clinging to His promises. That's why I want you to memorize James 1:2-4. Simply read it aloud three times a day, each time reading it three times consecutively—and it will soon be inscribed on your heart.

Where did this concept of changing the D to an H come from? I first heard it from a sweet little woman in a nursing home who in a trembling voice read to me the following poem. Wouldn't she be thrilled to know how God has used her obedience in sharing it with me so that it's become a ministry both to me and to you! Listen, my friend:

> "Disappointment—His Appointment";
>   change one letter, then I see
> that the thwarting of my purpose
>   is God's better choice for me.
> His appointment must be blessing
>   though it may come in disguise;

for the end, from the beginning,
    open to His vision lies.
"Disappointment—His Appointment."
    Whose? The Lord who loves me best,
understands and knows me fully,
    who my faith and love would test.
For like loving earthly parents
    He rejoices when He knows
that His child accepts unquestioned
    all that from His wisdom flows.
"Disappointment—His Appointment";
    no good things will He withhold.
From denials oft we gather
    treasures of His love untold.
Well He knows each broken purpose
    leads to a fuller, deeper trust,
and the end of all His dealings
    proves our God is wise and just.
"Disappointment—His Appointment";
    Lord I take it then as such,
like clay in the hands of the potter
    yielding wholly to His touch.
My life's plan is all His molding;
    not one single choice be mine.
Let me answer unrepining,
    "Father, not my will, but Thine."

How biblical! Whoever the precious saint was who penned this poem, he or she must certainly have gained understanding from Paul's example in Philippians as he related his response to disappointing circumstances. Paul was in jail, and some believers were gloating about it. As a matter of fact, some even preached the gospel with the motive of making life harder on Paul in prison.

And what was Paul's response? Listen to Philippians 1:12-14.

> Now I want you to know, brethren, that my circumstances have
> turned out for the greater progress of the gospel, so that my
> imprisonment in the cause of Christ has become well known
> throughout the whole praetorian guard and to everyone else, and
> that most of the brethren, trusting in the Lord because of my
> imprisonment, have far more courage to speak the word of God
> without fear.

THE PROOF AND THE PROCESS

But what about us—you and me? What does it mean—practically—to
change disappointment to His appointment? If you and I are really doing
this, what will be the proof and the process in our lives?

Return again to Paul in prison in Philippians 2, where we see him
demonstrating our first essential response. In verse 17 he wrote,

> But even if I am being poured out as a drink offering upon the
> sacrifice and service of your faith, *I rejoice* and share my joy with
> you all.

No matter what happens, beloved, no matter how disappointing it is,
you must first, in an act of the will, *rejoice and pray and give thanks*. This
is what your heavenly Father wants. It is *God's will* that we react this way.

Are you scowling? Would you like to scream at me and say I don't understand because I haven't been where you are? Or maybe you want to
throw this book across the room.

I understand. But give me time, beloved—give me a chance to show
you the whole picture. Read until you run out of pages, out of book—and
then let me know.

In the meantime, let me give you some verses before we move on. These aren't verses I'm trying to toss in your face; rather, they're like offering an aspirin to help you relieve the ache.

In 1 Thessalonians 5:16-18, God tells us,

> Rejoice always; pray without ceasing; in everything give thanks; for this is God's will for you in Christ Jesus.

And then in Ephesians 5:18-20, He commands,

> Do not get drunk with wine, for that is dissipation, but be filled with the Spirit, speaking to one another in psalms and hymns and spiritual songs, singing and making melody with your heart to the Lord; *always giving thanks for all things* in the name of our Lord Jesus Christ to God, even the Father.

In Romans 5:3-5, we read,

> Not only this, but *we also exult in our tribulations*, knowing that tribulation brings about perseverance; and perseverance, proven character; and proven character, hope; *and hope does not disappoint*, because the love of God has been poured out within our hearts through the Holy Spirit who was given to us.

If such a response of joy and thanksgiving is a struggle for you at this time, look up these Scriptures on your own, read them in their context, and meditate on them. Then by faith live accordingly, even if you feel it won't do any good in your case. I promise that if you walk by their precepts, you'll experience incredible victory.

Just watch what God does when you truly trust Him and walk by faith rather than by sight or by feelings. You'll experience the heritage of God's people that David sang about: "In Thee our fathers trusted; they trusted, and Thou didst deliver them. To Thee they cried out, and were delivered; in Thee they trusted, *and were not disappointed*" (Psalm 22:4-5).

Knowing absolutely that *by faith* you became God's child, if you'll continue in the truth of Colossians 2:6—"As you therefore have received Christ Jesus the Lord, *so walk in Him*"—then the dark disappointment will fade away in the light of your rising faith. As Paul reminded the Corinthians, "we walk by faith, not by sight" (2 Corinthians 5:7). Even in your darkest moments, you yourself will be the answer to this question in Scripture—

> Who is among you that fears the LORD,
> That obeys the voice of His servant,
> That walks in darkness and has no light?
> Let him trust in the name of the LORD and rely on his God.
>
> (Isaiah 50:10)

You *will* trust Him. You *will* rely on your God.

WATCH GOD

If this is hard—if it seems impossible—then, my friend, let me suggest that you begin reading the Bible, starting in Genesis, and *watch God*. Pore over the pages of holy inscription and watch everything God does. Look at who and what He is sovereign over, what He rules over. Try marking a little triangle in the margin of the page whenever you see Him at work in His sovereignty. Look at what God allows to come to pass and how long it takes. (Remember the little space that we add between "His" and "appointment.") Sometimes God promises something and it takes hundred of years to happen. But it will happen if He said it, because God cannot lie. He watches over His Word to perform it.

But in my life, you may be saying, *I can't wait a couple of hundred years for these things.*

I know, and it won't necessarily be a long time. Rather it will be in God's timing, and God always moves and acts on His schedule, not ours. Just as God promised Israel, He will bring about His perfect plan for your welfare to give you a future and a hope.

Stop and consider some of the things you've wanted God to make happen immediately. What would you have missed if He had? If those disappointments had been bypassed, how much the poorer would you be for it?

As a new Christian I suffered great disappointment when a certain man wouldn't marry me because I'd been divorced before I was saved. I thought my heart would break. Little did I know what God was protecting me from. I wouldn't find out for years (and you won't find out until later in the book), but let me tell you, I would have been the poorer and the sadder if God had given me what I wanted when I wanted it.

I cannot tell you how many people have talked or written to me in the midst of their trials and said, "I wouldn't trade this for anything." Where normally there would be defeat, they can attest to victory. They're walking through fire, but their focus isn't on the flames; it's on the One who walks with them in the midst of the fire, as Shadrach and Meshach and Abednego experienced in the fiery furnace. They aren't thinking about what damage this will do—and they aren't coming out smelling like smoke! Instead they hear His promise: "I will never leave you nor forsake you, so that you can boldly say, 'The Lord is my helper, I will not fear.'"

I wouldn't trade this for anything. Can you and I always say that about our disappointments?

DO YOU REALLY KNOW GOD?

It falls back on this: *What do you really know about God?* Everything falls back on that—our trust, our faith, our obedience. And how do we get to know God so that *we know that we know?*

Only through His Word.

I have a set of tapes of the Bible recorded word for word. I listen while I put on my makeup in the morning—a task that's taking longer as I age! I listen when I cook and do mundane tasks or travel. And I listen when I take off that makeup at night. I make it my practice to constantly feed on the Word of God. If you aren't doing that, may I suggest you get started! Take every opportunity to plug in to the Word of God, to learn the character and the thoughts of God, and to discover His ways.

Being in God's Word and knowing it *for yourself* is the key. This is confirmed to me day in and day out. Because of our Bible-teaching ministry I have the profound privilege of hearing from many Christians who find life-changing joy and victory by pursuing God in His Word. They write us letters, or as I teach at various conferences they stick notes in my hand or tuck them in my Bible or drop them in my purse.

One woman whose teenage son committed suicide pressed a note into my hand and said, "Read it when you get time." On the plane home I found it and read,

> When I heard that my son shot himself, I was sure *I* could not live either. However, God had other plans.
>
> Many people prayed and God was at work. I knew my son had received Jesus, but I had also heard that someone who took his life could not go to heaven. Although my son left no note, and there seems to be some indication that he may not have been in the house alone, I had to deal with it as though it were a definite suicide.
>
> I needed to hear from God. I needed to know His Word. Most of what I knew about the Bible I learned secondhand—from others. *Now* I had to know for myself. . . .

With that, this dear woman went on to tell how she *did* hear from God as she learned to study His Word inductively for herself. Her letter closed with these words: "*I have peace.* . . . To God be the glory!"

Another woman who went through some of our study series wrote,

> As I started through Galatians and read and re-read God's Word and concentrated on what it said, I got excited. It seemed like God was actually talking to me and wanted me, of all people, to understand. I learned that reading God's Word and studying it were two different things.
>
> I had recently left a church where control, secrecy, and the belief that only a few leaders could know God's will was the rule, and I felt such guilt about letting God down. I was confused—thinking that

what was being done by the leaders was wrong from what I read in the Bible, but also feeling that since I wasn't a pastor or past missionary I wasn't on a high enough level to really know God.

Even though my study of Galatians went very slowly I began to see light and get very excited. I suddenly felt truly ALIVE. God could love me even if I didn't live up to all expectations. It felt like a huge weight had been lifted from me. I no longer felt that I had to make things right for everyone.

Then I started studying through Ephesians. What a rich book! I had read Ephesians a couple times before and gone to a women's retreat based on Ephesians, but I had missed *so* much.

Through this study I was able to release my fear of my parents and finally be honest with them about my hurts and feelings about abuse that happened almost 30 years ago. God miraculously blocked my fears, and I was able to tell them that I wanted our relationship to be one that would please God. Their reaction was another miracle for me. . . .

And another wrote,

I . . . find myself amazed, overwhelmed, and completely in love with God's Word; thirsting more than ever to know what He wants me to know, to hide it in my heart and to fill my conversations with the quotes of His truth.

Does your own excitement and sense of discovery in God's Word match what you see expressed by these dear brothers and sisters in the Lord?

"I can walk in His new life," said another letter-writer who started spending ten minutes each morning in Bible reading then dived into an in-depth Bible study group. "I am beginning to believe more and more each day that there are no coincidences—everything is in God's providence. And the more I relinquish control of my life and give it *all* to God—the trivial and the real—the more He blesses me with His wisdom and love."

I will never forget when this note was pressed into my hand by a woman who whispered, "Thank you":

> In the last seven years I have lost ten people very close to me. One of those was our youngest son. He was murdered in 1992 by two runaway teenagers. . . .

Now, after studying 2 Peter and Philippians, she could write,

> I thank God for what those two studies have done in my life. I didn't know if I could ever have joy again. Praise God I can, and I have.

DO YOU REALLY KNOW THE TRUTH?

These are people who are after *truth*. They're doing what we're counseled to do in Proverbs 23:23—"Buy truth, and do not sell it; get wisdom and instruction and understanding."

To get the truth we first have to *know where truth is found*. And it is found unadulterated in only one place: the Word of God, the Holy Bible, which says, "The sum of Thy word is truth, and every one of Thy righteous ordinances is everlasting" (Psalm 119:160).

Second, we must make it our goal to *understand* truth, something much more than just knowing where to find it. Read through Proverbs someday and mark every reference to *wisdom* and to the *wise*. Wisdom is the *application* of truth, and Solomon, the wisest man who ever lived, showed us that it's to be desired above all else.

Third, we must *embrace the truth*—allowing it to sanctify us, setting us apart so we'll live with a different mind-set, so we'll not follow the dictates of the world but will follow the precepts of God.

Do you remember how, just before Jesus was arrested in the Garden of Gethsemane, He prayed on our behalf: "I do not ask Thee to take them out of the world, but to keep them from the evil one. They are not of the world, even as I am not of the world. *Sanctify them in the truth; Thy word is truth"* (John 17:15-17)?

From this foundation in your life will come *walking in truth* (3 John 3) and *speaking the truth in love* (Ephesians 4:15). But these can happen only as we know and understand and embrace the truth.

O beloved, I urge you: Go deeper and deeper into His Word. You cannot exhaust it. It cannot be comprehended in its fullness in all the days of our lives. So number your days; discipline yourself to be a man of the Word, a woman of the Word. Study it, learn it, know it, believe it, and obey it. Then I guarantee that when the test or the trial or the temptation comes, you will be the overcomer: "This is the victory that has overcome the world—our faith" (1 John 5:4).

Reason with me a moment: If you tithed the hours of each day, you would owe God two hours and twenty-four minutes *a day*. How much time *are* you giving to knowing Him and to having fellowship with Him? How much time are you spending in His Word, the Word that is the very bread by which we live?

O beloved, beloved—where are the men and women who will be serious about knowing their God and who will spend as much time learning His Word as they would learning what they have to know for their profession or job?

Won't you press on with me to know the Lord?

Not long ago I met an excited young single mother who was dancing on one foot and then the other, dying to tell me what was happening as she learned to study the Bible inductively. As a result of getting into the Bible herself, she made the decision to read to her two preschool children from the Word of God rather than from the children's Bible storybook she had been using. Now, each night as she tucks them into bed, she gets in bed with them and reads aloud to them from the Bible. She tells them to listen for a certain key word that will be repeated as she reads; when they hear that word, they're to stop her, and she will mark it in her Bible.

They get so excited as they listen intently. And then they say, "Mommy, that's a key word. Mark it!" They peer over her arm to watch her mark their discovery.

She has reminded them that this is Mommy's Bible and they're not to mark in it themselves. "You have your own Bible to color," she told them, "but don't touch mine." She feared her precious marked Bible might be ruined by eager little hands.

Then one night it happened. As she stepped from the shower, there was her five-year-old daughter with her mother's forbidden Bible open on the bathroom floor.

As the mother rushed toward her to chasten her, her words of frustration came to a halt when her daughter's delighted little face turned upward, and she said with a smile, "Mommy, Mommy, look! Jesus is all over the Bible. Look at all the crosses!" Her mother had been marking references to Jesus with a red cross.

Yes, it's true: Jesus—who said, "I am . . . *the truth*" (John 14:6)—is everywhere in the Bible. He is the truth, and He is the Word. To know and embrace and live by His Word is to know and embrace and live by Him; it is to build that solid, unshakable structure that will keep you from collapsing in the rubble of disappointment's earthquakes. Not that "quakes" won't come, but you'll be able to structurally handle them because you'll see they are God's appointment. The things that cannot be shaken will stand!

"I'M ON A JOURNEY . . ."

I wouldn't trade this for anything. Harry Beck was someone who could say that, in what many of us would judge to be his or anyone's greatest disappointment and greatest test.

Harry had studied the Bible inductively. In our ministry we had the privilege of getting Harry into the Word this way. Harry's wife, Madera, reminded me of that at a recent women's conference. Harry knew truth for himself.

In November 1994 this dear brother was told by a doctor that he had amyotrophic lateral sclerosis (ALS)—commonly known as Lou Gehrig's disease. ALS is a progressive and incurable disease that deteriorates the body's nerve cells but does not affect mental awareness. Eventually it paralyzes the whole body, bringing death as it invades the muscles that control breathing. As the disease advances, the patient becomes dependent upon others for literally every aspect of life.

On New Year's Eve, 1995—a Sunday—the Becks heard this question asked in the morning worship service at their church: "What did you trust the Lord for in 1995, and what will you be trusting Him for in the new year?" On their way home, Madera told her husband, "Babe, I sensed that you'd like to have answered those questions, if you could talk."

That afternoon Harry signaled to her to sit down and write down his thoughts. He spoke slowly, one sluggish word at a time, as Madera recorded them:

> As we count down the final hours of 1995 I can truly say that this has been the best year of my life.
>
> When I was diagnosed in November of '94 and as we walked out of Dr. Ray's office, I told my wife that we had been learning to live one day at a time, and that is the way we are going to live this. Then as we were in the car on our way home, Madera asked me what I was feeling on the inside, and I said, "Most people will think I'm crazy, and you're going to think I'm crazy, too, but I feel like I'm on a journey. I don't know where I'm going, but I'm so excited."
>
> I know that this was the Holy Spirit speaking to me and through me.
>
> Three days after the diagnosis, I asked Bill Crawford to go to Southern Bell and tell my co-workers of the diagnosis. I asked him to be sure to tell them two things:
>
> (1) I know this is for my good; I just want God to be glorified. And . . .
>
> (2) this is not a curse; this is a blessing.
>
> Again this was the Holy Spirit speaking not only through me but

to me. At that time I had no idea of the blessings He had in store for me.

As I look back over '95 and the last two months of '94, I would never have dreamed that God would bless me and my family the way He has through family members, friends, the body of believers here at the Fellowship, and people I don't even know.

God has, in love, placed me in a position to be totally dependent on Him. He has taught me so much this year. I have learned to love and to be loved. I've learned patience, like giving my needs to Him and trusting His timing and His methods.

Bottom line: I have learned to trust Him, try Him, and prove Him. . . .

One day in the following April, Harry's neurologist said to him, "As your professional, I need to know: When breathing becomes difficult, do you want to go on a ventilator?"

Harry answered by way of his alphabet board: "Dr. Ray, no ventilator. I'll breathe as long as God wants me to breathe, and when I'm not breathing anymore, God is calling me home."

Just over a hundred days later, God called Harry home. He was fifty-three.

At a women's conference a few months after that, Madera—a beautiful Christian and a faithful wife who had no regrets—tearfully placed a note in my hand that included the following:

My dear Kay,

Although I cannot explain the difficult diseases like ALS which strike at us, I do *know* and *trust* and *rest* in the sovereignty of a God who is too loving and kind to be cruel and too all-knowing and wise to make a mistake.

Madera went on to tell how God spoke to her through the Word of God we had taught that weekend. It was a series of messages on the fact that many times God puts us on "display" in arenas of difficulty and trial.

It's in these arenas that we're "accounted as sheep for the slaughter," so that others might see the sufficiency of our God and of His Word, which makes us more than conquerors through Him who loves us.

Included with Madera's note was a recent wire-service article carried by her local newspaper. It told of a forty-seven-year-old victim of ALS in a different part of the country. This man, the article stated, "knows exactly how he will spend his final hours: He'll party with friends, spend time with his girlfriend, and eat some of his favorite foods. The next morning, he'll take a deadly mixture of drugs."

Describing the man as a spokesman for the right-to-die movement, the article quoted him as saying, "I'll do the things I love most in the world—food and sex. Then I'll inject myself with a compound . . . and I'll go to sleep. Then the fun begins. It's the greatest adventure I'll ever have."

Harry Beck's nephew saw that article and responded to it with a tactful letter published by the same newspaper under the headline, "Remembering a Hero":

> My uncle, Harry Beck, received the same diagnosis in November 1994, but he dealt with it differently. In January 1996, Harry had lost the use of his arms, he could no longer eat many of the foods he loved, and he communicated with grunts that only his wife of 30 years could interpret.
>
> Yet in a two-page letter that took him hours to dictate, he said, "I look forward to 1996 with great anticipation." Harry refused to call his disease a curse; rather, he said it was a blessing. You see, Harry realized that God is sovereign and that all things are in His control. Harry wanted to glorify God in everything, even if it meant denying self, and he did. He touched so many through his testimony.

What a contrast between Harry Beck and the right-to-die spokesman described in the newspaper article! Harry based his life on truth he discovered for himself and then woke up in the presence of God Himself. The other man—if the newspaper story was accurate—based his life on a lie, *not* knowing that he would wake up in a place of torment called Hades.

Harry not only heard that Jesus was the way, the truth, and the life, but he also knew the exact truth for himself. Thus Harry knew how to live *and* how to die—and he did both valiantly. The other man believed a lie. He was deceived by the father of lies, the devil, a murderer in whom there is no truth. Thus he will experience the second death without ever having really lived. Although this man ate, drank, and was merry, he played the fool and did not know his soul was required of him the moment he left this life.

All men die, but not all live. True life is lived—and lived to the fullest—when we partake of the Bread of Life, the incarnate Word, the Lord Jesus Christ, first at salvation and then daily in the God-breathed Word, the Bible.

HOW GOD USES OUR DISAPPOINTMENTS

How is a joyful response like Harry Beck's possible in circumstances we don't like?

It is possible because of *who God is*—the sovereign Ruler of all the universe. And because He is what He is, He is able to cause "all things to work together for good to those who love God, to those who are called according to His purpose" (Romans 8:28).

It is possible because we can know and believe that disappointments are God's training in disguise.

Yes I know, beloved, that there are times when to "consider it all joy" sounds a little insane and masochistic. How can you count it all joy when you're overwhelmed with pain and imprisoned by disappointment? When the next scene that you thought would be a comedy turns out to be a tragedy?

It is possible, my friend, because it's not the final act of the play. It's possible because if God commands anything of us, He also provides what we need in order to obey.

It's possible because if this trial were not for your benefit and His glory, He would never have allowed it to seep through His fingers of love into your life.

44

The disappointment has come, precious child of God, not because God desires to hurt you or make you miserable or to demoralize you or ruin your life or keep you from ever knowing happiness. Rather, it comes because He wants you to be perfect and complete in every aspect, lacking nothing. When you see your Father face to face, He doesn't want you to be ashamed or sorry.

Hebrews 12:6-7 tells us,

> Those whom the Lord loves He disciplines, and He scourges every son whom He receives. It is for discipline that you endure; God deals with you as with sons; for what son is there whom his father does not discipline?

If we learned this verse in the King James Version, we have a tendency to view the Lord in this passage as a father chastening or spanking his son. That idea is reinforced in the word *scourges*. Yet the predominant idea is *discipline*. The Greek word for discipline here is *paideuo*, and it means "to train, to educate, to instruct, to teach." Those whom the Lord loves He trains, educates, instructs, teaches. He's grooming you for eternity, for the day you'll rule and reign with Him in the kingdom.

God *will* use the disappointments of life to teach and train you and to make you more like Jesus Christ. God will use them to do something awesome: to reproduce Himself in you. And honestly, nothing else will really matter; everything else will be valueless when the temporalness of this life is ended and eternity takes over.

It's not the easy times that make you more like Jesus but the hard times. So don't be surprised that God permits crushing disappointments in your life; instead, keep on rejoicing. As Peter instructed us,

> Beloved, do not be surprised at the fiery ordeal among you, which comes upon you for your testing, as though some strange thing were happening to you; but to the degree that you share the sufferings of Christ, *keep on rejoicing*; so that also at the revelation of His glory, you may rejoice with exultation. (1 Peter 4:12)

So let me stop and ask you: Is there a situation in your life in which you haven't yet changed the "D" of disappointment into an "H"? If so, I want to urge you to pause right now and do so, putting your feelings and your desire and commitment into a prayer to your heavenly Father. Say to Him, "I don't understand it all, Father, but I will believe that this is *Your* appointment. Your Word says that You are sovereign, and You must have a purpose in this. Therefore I choose to believe it. *I rest in You.*"

LIVING EPISTLES

As you rest in Him, obedient friend, let me share one last insight with you that should be a great encouragement.

God may not let you see how at the moment, but *He will use your trusting submissiveness to minister to others.* As you so well know, most of the world around you doesn't read the Bible. So what does God do? God shows the world pictures of Himself and of the sufficiency of His grace *through your life.* He gives the world a living epistle—*you.* And oftentimes He'll place you, His living epistle, in the same kind of fire, the same kind of disappointments and trials that so many others experience. He'll put you with them in the same hospital, or He'll allow you to suffer rejection or allow you to live with a rebel or to experience a financial blow. In any of a variety of disappointments, He lets you hurt as others hurt, knowing that the way in which you handle this hurt will be an undeniable testimony that there's something awesomely different about you.

This is where Romans 8:36-39 comes in: We're put to death all day long; we're considered as sheep for the slaughter. Yet in all these things we overwhelmingly conquer, for we're "convinced that neither death, nor life, nor angels, nor principalities, nor things present, nor things to come, nor powers, nor height, nor depth, nor any other created thing, shall be able to separate us from the love of God which is in Christ Jesus our Lord."

As I bring this chapter to a close, I think of the story of the Christian huddled in a cold prison cell who had only one small blanket separating him from death by exposure. He was awakened from the twilight of sleep when the cell door clanked open. Another human being, beaten and bruised, was pushed into his cell and fell in a heap on the bitterly cold cement floor then curled up with his arms between his legs.

He lay there, sobbing and shaking. He had obviously been through torture.

He'll be dead by morning, the Christian thought to himself. *He has no blanket.*

Then the still small voice of the One for whom the Christian had suffered imprisonment said, "Give him your blanket."

"Lord," he replied, "if I give him my blanket, I will die."

"I know," God answered. "But if you don't give him your blanket, *he* will die and spend eternity separated from Me. If you die, you'll be at home with Me tonight."

In obedience, the Christian rose to his feet, took those few steps across his cell, and handed the man his blanket.

The other man looked at him in disbelief. He had just been beaten almost to death; now a perfect stranger was handing him his only blanket.

The Christian told him why.

And that night God called him home, where I am sure the Christian greeted his Father unashamed.

How do we know of this incident? The man who received the blanket later told the story when he gave his testimony for the Lord. There was no Bible in that cell, but there was a living epistle. The man heard the Christian's words, saw his works, and believed.

Selah . . . pause and think on that, precious one.

Therefore, strengthen the hands that are weak
and the knees that are feeble,
and make straight paths for your feet.

Hebrews 12:12-13

CHAPTER THREE

PRESENT FAILURES, PAST REGRETS

Two Dangerous Disappointments

WHETHER YOU'RE IN CURRENT DANGER of descending into the Deadly D's or have been partway (or all the way) down that spiral before or some loved one or dear friend is in danger of it—you must learn well, beloved, how to handle disappointments. You need to know how to help both yourself and others.

Let's look now at two especially perilous forms of disappointment so we won't be ensnared by them and will instead guard against them.

DEALING WITH FAILURE

When I say that your every disappointment can become *His* appointment to make you more like Jesus, do you wonder, *Even if I fail? . . . Even if I sin?*

Yes, beloved, even if you sin, even if you fail. And though you can't get away with using this as an excuse to sin or fail, if you're truly His child, you can know that when you do sin God will teach you a lesson through it and use it to change you more into His likeness.

Sin and failure hurt. And when something keeps hurting long enough, we usually learn to back off—and that works together for our good.

The latest edition to our middle son's family is a rambunctious beagle puppy his boys wanted after an older dog died. They're putting up an invisible fence to keep the puppy close to home. A collar the dog wears is activated whenever he attempts to cross the invisible line. It might give him only a light charge or one that bounces him back a foot or so—whatever it takes to keep him from going "out of bounds." That's the purpose of the fence: to give that eager little beagle freedom to roam within safe boundaries, for his ultimate good.

To cross God's line, to transgress His boundaries, is sin. And whatever it takes—whatever disappointment is necessary—to convince us to stay on our side of the line will be for our good.

But if you're like me, it isn't sin that does me in, because I really try to walk in obedience to God. Rather it's *failure* that drags me down.

Can you relate, or are you more relaxed with yourself than I am? Either way, when it comes to dealing with failure, know this: You're not alone.

You may *feel* alone. You may even feel like the biggest of failures, beyond comparing with anyone else. But to one degree or another, we all fail. I have—many times. Often I could kick myself around the block several times then, after I'm rested, start around again. I hate to fail. And in a sense, I think even my hating it as much as I do is a failure on my part.

Do you ever look at all those people around you with envy, wishing you could change places with them because their circumstances, their personalities, their whatevers look so much better than yours? Do you realize, beloved, that at one time or another every one of those people has failed? And though they may not tell you, at this very moment they're probably dealing with a feeling of failure to one degree or another in one or more areas of their lives.

If we're honest we all admit to dealing with tendencies toward defeat, depression, and even the despair that failure can bring when it isn't dealt with in a biblical way.

WHAT IS FAILURE?

To fail means:

You didn't measure up.

You didn't achieve your goal.

You didn't hit the standard you or someone else had set.

You didn't accomplish what you thought you should accomplish, what you wanted to achieve.

But why? *Why* do we fail? And why in some cases do we repeatedly fail in the same situations?

Sometimes we fail when we try to do something we aren't capable of doing, something we aren't gifted in or talented in. Therefore it's important, as Romans 12:3 tells us, to "not think more highly" of ourselves than we should. We need to take an honest and objective look at ourselves and recognize our limitations.

We also fail when we try to do something "our way," when we don't learn and live by God's precepts, His commandments—or when we think we're smarter than God or when, at least for *this* time or in *this* situation, we think we don't need to involve Him.

I think we should be shocked to see how many are failing in relationships and responsibilities in the home and at church and at work simply because they aren't studying God's textbook for life so they don't know God or His ways. They fail to do God's will because the will of God is discerned by knowing the Word of God.

People also fail because they don't put themselves on the altar and tell God He can direct their lives in any way He desires. The steps of a righteous man are ordered by the Lord.

We also fail when we walk in presumption. Like the children of Israel in Numbers 14:39-45, some of us think all we have to do is to admit our mistake, and then our situation and the resulting consequences will disappear as if our mistake never happened. But God is not mocked; for whatever a man sows, this he will also reap (Galatians 6:7).

It's also presumption (and a ticket to failure) when we try to hide our disobedience. If we choose to cheat, we'll eventually get caught. The Bible warns us, "Be sure your sin will find you out" (Numbers 32:23).

All this is failure, and in one form or another it happens to all of us. So the question isn't *whether* we will fail or have failed but how we handle it when we do.

Why can I say this? Because we're born into a state of failure. We all have sinned and fallen short of the glory of God (Romans 3:23). The word for *sin* in this verse means to miss the mark—in essence, to fail to be all we should be. Man was made in the image of God, but man has failed to manifest that image to the world. We fall short of Godlikeness—the godliness we were created to possess and display.

In a sense, this is where life begins—in that state of failure. David wrote, "In sin my mother conceived me" (Psalm 51:5). Consequently we're all slated for failure apart from God.

FROM STUMBLING TO STANDING

But—good news! Failure doesn't have to be the end of the story—not with God. That's why the Father, in the fullness of time, sent us His Son . . . the Savior we all so desperately need.

Christianity is God's means of bringing us out of failure, but it's a process. And that, beloved, is what we forget! It's what so many of us fail to remember in our relationships with others and in our understanding of where we are in the process of sanctification.

By sanctification, I mean knowing, believing, and embracing what God says so that we live our lives and order our actions and thoughts according to His precepts—and thus experience success rather than defeat.

Remember, the world's definition of success is far different from God's—which is only logical, because the world doesn't know God or fear

Him or trust Him. So you must not measure yourself or your success by the world's standard. To do so would be foolish. You are *in* the world but not *of* the world.

What the world considers "failure" may not be failure at all. If you didn't meet your goals today (I can see I'm not going to meet mine!), it doesn't necessarily mean you failed. But if you violate one of God's principles or precepts (which the world could care less about), that *would* be real failure—and should be handled immediately by repentance and confession.

I recently ate lunch with a group of men attending our ministry's men's conference. As we sat and talked, one of them told me what a difference the Bible studies are making in the men's lives and in his own. He wanted to be a man of God but had been constantly failing in his thought life until our study on spiritual warfare brought him out of failure and into victory. Then he told of another man he had taught who, with a laugh of sweet relief, said, "You know, before when I'd drive home from work my thoughts were either on booze or women. Now all I can think about is what I'm learning in 2 Timothy."

Another man wrote me this in a letter:

> I was saved several years ago but was plagued by my besetting sin of alcohol and drugs. I would be substance-free for months at a time but would compromise and "party" when it was convenient (wife out of town or when I was on a camping trip with my friends). I loved the Lord dearly, and it would destroy me when I willingly and knowingly would sin against His love. Also I would lose my joy when I sinned. . . . *[I was thankful to hear that! He should lose his joy when he sins.]*

What could pull a man out of such failure? In this case, he first listened with an open mind and heart to some straightforward teaching (on our ministry's radio program) about sin and righteousness. His letter went on:

> It all came together when you taught the message several weeks ago about declaring war on my sin, completely destroying the enemy and

never compromising (Deuteronomy 3:6). You taught me that God wants us to crucify the old man and become blameless, and that we must deal thoroughly with our sins. . . . *[Actually I taught that "the old man is crucified—so now live like it." But at least he came close, and it worked! God knows our hearts.]*

After learning and applying God's truth, this man could now report to me in his letter how much he had been strengthened.

God and obedience to His precepts are what take us from failure to success by humbling us to the point where we know the only way to genuinely succeed—to be blameless—is *through Him.*

Listen to Jude 24: "Now to Him who is able *to keep you from stumbling,* and to make you stand in the presence of His glory blameless with great joy. . . ." Jesus is the One who rescues us from eternal death and destruction, brings us into eternal life, and then protects us—keeps us from stumbling. He *is able* to do this! He is able to bring and keep us out of sin, out of failure, to be what God intends us to be: blameless and joyful.

This is where success and maturity in life begin—with our salvation and the gift of the indwelling Holy Spirit. The Lord will never leave us nor forsake us. You can *believe* it—because it's what God says in Hebrews 13:5, and God does not lie.

So how do we go from stumbling to standing? The answers will vary according to where and how we fail, but the source will always remain the same: God and His precepts of life. That's why *you must be in the Word of God on a consistent basis.*

And that will take discipline on your part. You have to *determine* to take advantage of what God has made available to help you get into the Word in a knowledgeable and practical, life-changing way—a way that will help you first to really know and understand truth so you can succeed in your relationships with God and with man, a way that will help you succeed in the ministry for which the Lord has gifted you.

The Wrong Response to Failure

So what must you do when you fail as a child of God?

The first thing you must *not* do is to think there's no hope, no help, no way out. That would be to deny the power of the One who rescued you from the greatest of all failures or to deny the fact that God is *for* you. Remember: "If God is for us, who is against us? He who did not spare His own Son, but delivered Him up for us all, how will He not also with Him freely give us all things?" (Romans 8:31-32).

God is always there for you. To not believe this is to insult Him. To not believe it is to say, in essence, that God doesn't mean what He says and doesn't watch over His Word to perform it—which is a blatant lie!

If you say there's no hope, you're listening to the father of lies (John 8:44). You've encountered the thief who comes to steal, kill, and destroy (John 10:10)—the one who's determined to keep you a failure, to defeat you on every front he can. The only way you'll bring him down, the only way you'll extinguish those fiery arrows that will impale you on the stake of continuous defeat until you're consumed in its flames of destruction is through the Word. His Word is truth, and it alone can sanctify you—set you apart for victory.

You may think there's no recovery from your failure. But my friend, if you have God, you have a future—and it's not a dismal one.

Before Peter ever failed and denied his Lord, Jesus told him He had prayed for him that his faith might not fail; then the Lord told Peter that *once he turned again* he was to strengthen his brethren. From the very beginning there was hope for Peter in his failure, and there's always hope for us. *There is hope*, beloved.

So do not give in to despair—God is *your* Redeemer. He buys back, buys out, rescues, sets free, protects. He's the God of another chance to all who genuinely have a change of mind and throw themselves into His outstretched arms and bury their heads in His all-sufficient breast. When you do that, you'll feel His heart beat for you.

THE RIGHT RESPONSE TO FAILURE

So what do you do when you fail as a Christian? Let me give you precepts from God's Word that give understanding for any particular failure you may have experienced.

First, remember what Jeremiah wrote of Israel after her greatest failure and judgment—a judgment that led to the destruction of her temple and her holy city:

> Remember my affliction and my wandering,
> the wormwood and bitterness.
> Surely my soul remembers
> And is bowed down within me.
> This I recall to mind,
> Therefore I have hope.
> The LORD's lovingkindnesses indeed never cease,
> For His compassions never fail.
> They are new every morning;
> Great is Thy faithfulness.
> "The LORD is my portion," says my soul,
> "Therefore I have hope in Him."
>
> (Lamentations 3:19-24)

There is hope because God is God. Even in our most bitter afflictions we can call to mind the Lord's unceasing lovingkindnesses and His mercies that are new every morning. The Lord is our portion, and therefore we are never without hope.

Second, recognize that God had a reason for not restraining you from failure. It was either because you *deserved* to fail since you didn't choose to obey Him in this area, or it was because He wanted to teach you something, to cleanse you, to make you more like Him. This is part of the discipline, the training we spoke of earlier.

God disciplines those He loves. Don't forget that. It isn't vengeance; it's *love*. "It is for discipline that you endure; God deals with you as with sons; for what son is there whom his father does not discipline?" (Hebrews 12:7).

If you don't know the reason for your failure, run to God. Ask Him why. Seek His counsel. You lack wisdom, so "ask of God, who gives to all men generously and without reproach" (James 1:5).

Third, if God shows you that you failed because you sinned, do as David did in Psalm 51. Throw yourself upon God's mercy, upon God's grace. Cry out these words with David:

> Be gracious to me, O God,
>   according to Thy lovingkindness;
> According to the greatness of Thy compassion
>   blot out my transgressions.
>
> (51:1)

Make this your prayer:

> Create in me a clean heart, O God,
>   And renew a steadfast spirit within me. . . .
> Restore to me the joy of Thy salvation,
>   And sustain me with a willing spirit.
>
> (51:10,12)

If you have sinned, then confess it. Confess your disobedience, your failure to trust and obey. Name your sin for what it is. Call it nothing less. Don't sugarcoat it or gloss over it. Call it by name. *Lord, this is how I failed you. I lied; I . . . whatever* (just make sure you say the "whatever"). Be honest; be blunt. Say it aloud. Tell God you want to succeed, not fail, and that you know only He can do that for you. Tell Him you're willing to do whatever is necessary if He will simply show you what to do by laying it upon your heart, putting it in your mind.

Then check it out. Make sure that whatever you're hearing in your mind or feeling in your heart is in accord with the consistent teaching of the Bible. Remember, if what you're feeling and hearing is of God, it will be in keeping with His character and with His Word. If you're wrong but your heart wants to do right, God will make it known; He "will reveal that also to you" (Philippians 3:15).

Once you have that assurance, do whatever God leads you to do. Make it right with God—and with man, if necessary. Clear the air. Observe and listen and do according to all He tells you. Don't turn to the right or to the left. Then you will have *success* (Joshua 1:7-9). God intends for you to succeed rather than to fail.

Did you hear that, beloved, with the hearing of your heart? Let me say it again: *It is God's intention that you succeed rather than fail.*

And what will that success mean? You'll become a man, a woman, a teenager "for renown, for praise, and for glory" unto God, because you are clinging to Him as you should (Jeremiah 13:11).

So endure this discipline by keeping your heavenly Father's good purpose in mind:

> All discipline for the moment seems not to be joyful, but sorrowful; yet to those who have been trained by it, afterwards it yields the peaceful fruit of righteousness. *Therefore*, strengthen the hands that are weak and the knees that are feeble, and make straight paths for your feet. (Hebrews 12:11-13)

Lift up the hands that hang down in defeat, and set your feet on straight paths (commit to walking righteously!).

Throw yourself upon God. And know that there is still a future for you (if there weren't, He would already have taken you home by now!). Yours can even be the same future of ministry that David envisioned:

> Then I will teach transgressors Thy ways,
> And sinners will be converted to Thee.
>
> (Psalm 51:13)

Fourth, remember this:

> The sacrifices of God are a broken spirit;
> > A broken and a contrite heart, O God,
> Thou wilt not despise.

(Psalm 51:17)

Your sincere brokenness in this hour of failure is pleasing and acceptable unto God. God does not despise brokenness, because it's *right* that you are broken.

To fail is to be humbled. Failure makes us aware of our own impotence, our imperfections, our shortcomings. Failure brings us low. If we respond properly by humbling ourselves before our heavenly Father, then according to James 4:10 we'll find Him exalting us. And when God exalts us after we experience the humiliation and defeat of failing, then it's a safe exaltation rather than a source of pride that eventually leads only to greater defeat and failure.

Remember the character of God! Remember His promises and cling to them and to Him. Let me quote more from Jeremiah 13:11. God said, " 'For as the waistband clings to the waist of a man, so I made the whole household of Israel and the whole household of Judah *cling to Me*,' declares the LORD, 'that they might be for Me a people, for renown, for praise, and for glory.'" The secret to recovering from failure, beloved, is to continue to cling to your God and not let go.

Fifth, like the apostle Paul, who realized he had not yet attained his goal (he hadn't hit that measure of perfection), you need to say with him,

> Forgetting what lies behind and reaching forward to what lies ahead, I press on toward the goal for the prize of the upward call of God in Christ Jesus. (Philippians 3:13-14)

Those who keep looking back at their failures will never win the race set before them. We can evaluate where and how we failed for the purpose of learning and growing, but the past is never, ever to be our focus. If it is, it will cripple our future.

So pull out of spiritual defeat or depression as a survivor, forgetting what lies behind and pressing on to what lies before you.

If you'll take God at His Word (and it's printed out in black and white in your Bible), your failure will become a steppingstone to greater Christlikeness and intimacy with God. Failure will become a means to an end rather than "The End."

Failure can be either a stumbling block that flattens you or a steppingstone to a life of success built upon the immovable Cornerstone. It's all a matter of whom you choose to believe.

God wants every one of His children to switch from walking by feelings to walking by faith—faith that's based in the truth of His Word. And how well He teaches us this through our disappointments, including our failures past and present.

When you pause and take a good look at whatever defeats you've known in your Christian life, isn't it true that most or all of them came because you walked by feelings rather than faith? You allowed emotions to control you rather than the Holy Spirit of God. You allowed your own human attitude to dictate your actions rather than the Word of God. How tragic it is when our reasoning is skewed by our emotions and wrong perspectives! That's where our minds must be renewed (Romans 12:2, Ephesians 4:23).

Do you realize how much depends on your perspective? Ask yourself, What's my goal? What's my ambition? Is it my happiness or my holiness? Is it a temporal happiness that can last only a life span, about threescore years and ten? Or is it my holiness that will have eternal ramifications and will determine what it's like when I see Him?

FACING—AND FORGETTING—THE PAST

Now let's look at a second particularly dangerous kind of disappointment: our regrets over the past.

Something I constantly have to remind myself of (and I wish it weren't so! I wonder sometimes if I'll ever learn, and I know my co-laborers wonder that also) is that *whatever happens, happens*. Once it's done, there's no changing it. No matter how hard I try, I cannot erase the past. No matter how much I might wish, stew, worry, or weep, no matter how long I kick myself around the block, I cannot undo what's been done. If it were possible, I would undo it. But I can't. I know that, you know that, and God knows that.

Whatever happened, happened. We can't remake our pasts. *But with God we can handle the past*. With God, whatever has happened in the past need not destroy us.

Of course we'll face and many times reap the consequences of the past. But for the child of God there is hope. God is God, the God of all hope. No matter what has happened in our backgrounds, with God there is grace, peace, and hope if we'll run to Him and bring every past disappointment captive to faith in His Word.

Where there is hope there can never be despair. (You may want to pause and think about that one!) And since He's the God of all hope, the reality that our pasts cannot be changed need not demoralize and destroy us.

Let me give you a true-life illustration in a letter written to me from a dear woman:

> My mother died suddenly last summer, and as a result, so much I
> had buried for years started coming up—fear, pain, guilt, believing I
> should have never been born and that I had no right to subject
> people to being around me. I was struggling to deal with all of this
> and lost sight of God. There was a wall up and I didn't know how
> to get past it.

Then this woman sat under our ministry's teaching. She began listening to God's perspective. "And that wall came tumbling down," she was now able to write.

> This just showed me how much He cares. . . . I still have a lot of
> things to work through, but at least God is here now.

God doesn't want you to have any regrets on the day when at last you
see Him. So don't live with the "what if's." Don't be obsessed with them.
Don't dwell on them. God's sovereignty is ruling (and has always ruled)
over the contingencies of this life. In the sovereignty of God, those what-
if's didn't happen. Conjecture is foolish, a time-waster. Not only that, but
conjecture will also drive you down into discouragement and dejection,
speeding up the downward spiral into the Deadly D's.

Here again we have the opportunity to see and understand the redemptive power of our sovereign God—because even the negative consequences we face from our pasts are part of the "all things" God uses to
work together for our good. The consequences themselves may not be
good, but what they work together for *is* good. We must keep God's goal
for us in mind, and that goal is Christlikeness.

But is all this true even if those past mistakes happened before you were
a child of God?

How delighted I am to say Yes! *All things* work together for good—even
the things in your pre-Christian past. Although you may not know the
Scriptures well enough yet to realize it, at the time you made those mistakes
God had already chosen and rescued you to be His own. The Scriptures
clearly teach that your redemption was planned *before the foundation of the
world*. It says that those whom God *fore*knew He *pre*destined. In His omniscience He knew you would be saved. He foreknew and planned your salvation, and He sovereignly governs all of your life before and after
salvation.

If you're looking at your past, then you need to look back even further.
Look to the eternity before time:

> Just as He chose us in Him before the foundation of the world, that
> we should be holy and blameless before Him. In love He predestined
> us to adoption as sons through Jesus Christ to Himself, according to
> the kind intention of His will. (Ephesians 1:4-5)

We've got to remember that all this is *according to the kind intention of His will.* This is just as true of the events and circumstances He allowed in our pasts as it is of those which He allows in the present.

I love this whole, awesomely marvelous first chapter of Ephesians, including what we see about God in verse 11 in this same chapter, which says that "we have obtained an inheritance, having been predestined according to His purpose *who works all things after the counsel of His will.*"

Here's God, who sees our disruptive pasts and those foolish decisions we've made—yet He allowed us the liberty within His sovereignty to make them. According to His kind intention and according to His purpose (which is worked out after the counsel of His will), He will work all these things for our good.

That, beloved, is why those past circumstances were allowed to seep through His fingers, for in His omniscience God knew its end result would be for our good and His glory.

How well Paul realized this! Paul knew he was the foremost of sinners (1 Timothy 1:15). As far as Christianity goes, his past record was shameful: "I was formerly a blasphemer and a persecutor and a violent aggressor" (1:13). But Paul also knew something bigger than his past, bigger than his sin. He knew "the grace of our Lord was more than abundant, with the faith and love which are found in Christ Jesus" (1:14).

Paul could rest in God's perfect timing for all this. Paul knew, according to Galatians 1:15-16, that God saved him *at the time that pleased Him* . . . "when He . . . was pleased to reveal His Son in me."

I'm sure that at some time or another in your life you've missed an opportunity to be what you should have been. (I know I have—more times than I want to remember.) When the opportunity came, you chose what you wanted at that moment, and yet later you were sorry you responded as you did. Now you regret it. You grieve because you failed. In your mind you go over and over what could have been different if you had responded as you should have responded.

But take a few minutes now to think about these negatives from your past that linger in your thoughts and concerns. What positive changes have they brought about in your own character and in your relationship with God and with others?

WILL I BELIEVE HIM OR NOT?

For years (and here I'll repeat what I've told elsewhere in print) I lived with what-if's regarding our oldest son, Tom, before he came to know the Lord. What if I had only done this as his mother? What if I had only done that?

This was my "hidden" heartache. Tommy was a "beloved adversary" who tried to discredit my name, my God, and His calling upon my life.

My husband and I cried out to God for him. Again and again I beseeched God on behalf of my firstborn. The only time in my life I ever journaled was when he was about to break my heart.

I bent over backward trying to please this young man I love so much. I did all I could to turn him around. But nothing worked. On top of it all I had to deal with envy as I watched other mothers whose sons loved the Lord. At other times I relived my own failures over and over until I was exhausted. Then I'd run back and cling to His promise in Romans 8:28-30.

One day the Lord just spoke to me—not audibly, but in quietness to my heart. He said, "Are you going to live by the things you've taught or not?" And I heard Him say, "Be still, and know that I am God."

To be still means to cease striving, to let go, to relax.

So I shut up and quit trying to straighten Tommy out. I just started listening and loving him unconditionally and persevering in prayer. As a matter of fact, I think my prayers became more fervent, because I was shut up to everything but God. What intimacy this brings—what dependence!

God had me right where He wanted me—right where I needed to be.

Then the day came (four years ago) when Jesus set our thirty-eight-year-old son free from a lifetime of immorality and gave him a passionate love for God the Father, for God's Word, and for God's people—and, hallelujah, for his mama! My joy knew no bounds. I stood in awe (as others did) at the miracle of it all, for God had truly transformed our son.

O beloved, wouldn't it make a difference if we could see that each one of our hurts from the past represents an opportunity to take God at His Word? "Be it done to you according to your faith," Jesus said in Matthew 9:29. If we have faith and do not doubt, He said that we can tell this mountain (this obstacle of regrets, this hill of what-if's) to be taken up and cast into the sea, and it will happen (Matthew 21:21).

Even faith that's only the size of a mustard seed can accomplish this (Matthew 17:20). Do you think you might be able to rummage up even a mustard seed's worth? It's such an incredibly tiny seed.

So, my friend, what does it boil down to? Simply this: Are we going to believe God or not?

It's like the time Jesus saw the sick man at the pool of Bethesda and asked him, "Wilt thou be made whole?" (John 5:6, KJV). It's our choice, our decision, by faith: Will we be made whole? Will we believe Him?

Will we operate only by our feelings and emotions?

Or will we walk in precious freedom, by living according to what God tells us?

Receive with meekness the implanted word, which is able to save your souls.
But be doers of the word, and not hearers only, deceiving yourselves.

JAMES 1:21-22 (NKJV)

CHAPTER FOUR

FACING THE STRESS

God's Provision in Our Pressure

WE'RE A SWARM of stressed-out people living in a stressed-out world, aren't we?

Stress is everywhere.

And it tells. It tells in our bodies. It tells in our relationships, including our relationship with God. It's hard to find time for intimacy, because intimacy takes time.

Time is a commodity you wish you could buy, and if you could you would use it simply to buy peace, quiet, leisure—to do some things you long to do and not have to do them in such a rush. Just having time to think and to have the right atmosphere for thinking . . . that would be nice, wouldn't it?

There'll always be tension to life. Yet it needs to be a healthy, creative tension, not life-sapping stress. Few of us can truly cope well with unrelenting stress. It's destructive. Our society bears witness to that. It's more than people can take. Marriages and families and personal lives are falling apart as stressed-out people run away, withdraw, explode, crash, burn out—and eventually find themselves so very much alone. Or they end up in the wrong setting with the wrong people because they've neglected the natural, normal God-ordained relationships of life. So much of this occurs because our values are skewed by the philosophies and pressures of the high-stress society and age in which we live.

I believe a major cause for this stress is that we *react* rather than act. We're moving so quickly that we don't stop and consider our future: What will it demand of us? What will it cost? Are we willing to pay the price?

We simply *move*—reacting to the immediate.

I know this is an area I really battle in. I want to do everything. There's so much I like to do that many times I respond in the flesh rather than being led by the Spirit. I have so many ideas, and I love the excitement and the challenge of the new venture of the moment, the potential of "the project." So I react in the moment—I say yes to this and to that, forgetting that my time is already allotted to other things. I get in a react mode instead of taking time to think it all through.

This can also happen when we encounter life's disappointments. So many times when we face unmet expectations big and small we react rather than purposely "act" by appropriating what God has provided for the present situation. We react in a response of the flesh instead of acting under the Holy Spirit's control.

You see, God knows what each one of us is dealing with. He knows our pressures. He knows our conflicts. And He has made provision for each and every one of them. That provision is Himself in the person of the Holy Spirit, indwelling us and empowering us to *respond rightly*.

This liberating response is wrapped up in a single word, and if you grasp the meaning of it and put it into action in your life through the Lord's grace and power, I can promise that you'll know how to walk with the Spirit in complete control and that not one single stressful situation or circumstance in your life will be beyond your ability to handle.

The word is *meekness*. Meekness is the key to *acting* rather than *reacting* when disappointments come. I'll soon give you a more extensive definition, but at this point let me say that *meekness* carries the idea of humility and submission and of bringing yourself low.

My dear friend June Hunt wrote a song about this when life's irritations had really gotten to her. Here's the chorus (and I wish she could sing it for you, because it has a catchy tune):

> Lord, teach me to act rather than react
> with the Spirit in control of me.
> Oh teach me to help rather than hinder
> with the Lord being Lord of me.
> Oh teach me to trust rather than mistrust
> with the Spirit inside my soul.
> Oh teach me to act rather than react—
> I give You complete control.

God will answer this prayer, beloved. He will indeed teach us to act rather than react. And this is how: Since meekness is the key to this right response, God is at work to build meekness into our innermost beings. And the way He works meekness into our characters is through disappointments and trials.

We see this happening in Deuteronomy 8:2-3. Look at what God allowed His chosen and beloved people to go through—and *why*:

> And you shall remember all the way which the LORD your God has
> led you in the wilderness these forty years, that He might *humble*
> you, testing you, to know what was in your heart, whether you
> would keep His commandments or not. And *He humbled you* and
> let you be hungry, and fed you with manna which you did not know,
> nor did your fathers know, that He might make you understand that
> man does not live by bread alone, but man lives by everything that
> proceeds out of the mouth of the LORD.

Remember how the children of Israel wandered in the wilderness for forty years after coming out of Egypt? When you're wandering in a desert you aren't planting crops and reaping harvests, so you get hungry.

It was God's obligation—as their God and their Redeemer—to provide for all their needs (just as it's His responsibility to provide all your needs and mine). One of God's names is *Jehovah* (which is actually YHWH, *Yehovaha) Jireh*, which means "The Lord Will Provide." In providing for the children of Israel in the wilderness, God told them to gather manna every morning. The first morning when they went out and found this stuff covering the ground and looking like hoary frost, they said "What is it?" It was manna. The word *manna* comes from that Hebrew expression for "What is it?"

God said He didn't want them keeping any manna overnight; He told them they had to gather it each and every morning. Only on the day before the Sabbath could they gather enough for two days and have the manna keep that long.

But some enterprising people thought, *What's the sense in that? I'll gather enough today for tomorrow too, and in the morning I can sleep in.* So even on a weekday they gathered extra and stored it away. Then after waking up late and going to their storage pots to bring out a leisurely manna breakfast, they found it crawling with worms.

What was God doing? He was feeding them, but He was doing something much more. He was teaching them a lesson on meekness.

"That He might *humble* you," Deuteronomy 8:2 says. "And He *humbled* you," the next verse affirms. The Hebrew word translated *humble* here is from a root word meaning to afflict, to oppress. This humility, this meekness that God was forging in their lives would be the outcome of affliction, of being oppressed, of humiliation.

God was letting them be hungry, giving them a little affliction and difficulty. Why? It was a testing, the passage says, "to know what was in your heart, whether you would keep His commandments or not." He wanted certain attributes to be tested and proven in their character. He wanted them to grow in faith. He wanted to teach them a principle about *life*: that we don't live by bread alone (and I like the King James Version here) "but *by every word* that proceedeth out of the mouth of the LORD." Life is much more than food and clothing and shelter. Real life is in the spiritual dimension, in the kingdom of God, in full dependence on God and on the bread of His Word.

It takes *meekness* on our part to understand this, and it takes affliction to bring about the meekness.

Meekness is born in stress, in trials, in affliction, in conflict . . . in difficulties. Meekness is born in situations that humble you. This meekness that God so highly values in your life will show itself—prove itself—in oppression and pressure and disappointment. It was true for God's people Israel, and it's true for you and me.

IT IS GOOD TO BE AFFLICTED

Let me ask you: When do you run to God the most? When do you most often make tracks for the throne of grace, crying "Abba Father!"? When do you pray the most? It's when you're hurting the most, isn't it? When you're disappointed, afflicted, stressed, pressured, you fall back in dependence upon the Lord instead of upon yourself.

God works in affliction, and those times when we're afflicted are the times when we're open to see it. Go to Psalm 119 to see the heart of someone who truly understands this as he goes through severe trial. "I know, O LORD, that Thy judgments are righteous, and that *in faithfulness Thou hast afflicted me*" (verse 75). "Before I was afflicted I went astray, but *now I keep Thy word*" (verse 67). And verse 71—"*It is good for me that I was afflicted*, that I may learn Thy statutes."

In God's wise care, it is *good* for us that we are afflicted.

I recall a time when Jack and I saw something negative in our youngest son's life, and we confronted him about it. I knew it would be hard, and it was. It brought some conflict, and in that conflict I had to hold on to what I knew was my husband's stand and what I knew about the faithfulness of God.

I handled it and got my peace by running into the arms of my heavenly Father and crying, "Father, You know. You understand. You're the God of all flesh, and there's nothing too hard for You. You know we're doing this for our son's good, and Lord, I just ask You to vindicate Jack."

Then our son left to go back to college. As he walked out the door I thought, *What if he drives too fast and has an accident?* I knew better than to run out and call after him, "Now David, don't drive too fast!" But the remembrance of one of our dear friends who was only thirty-one and had just been killed in a car wreck was too much for me. I ran out to remind David about Beth, hoping this would calm him down and make him drive more carefully. But he had already driven away.

So I rushed back to the Lord in my "motherly" affliction.

Three days later he called us from college and said, "You and Dad are right, and I was wrong. Will you forgive me?" I tell you, I was so proud of him! I knew he would come through. But in those three days I sure prayed and talked to the Father a lot more than ever for David and for that whole situation. I claimed and clung to every promise I knew. I had to embrace all that I knew from God's Word.

Sometimes you think you won't survive, but eventually you see "it was good for me that I was afflicted, that I might learn His statutes."

Are you going through a difficult situation, a trial? Does it feel like more than you can bear? It is not. The situation, whatever its shape or form, is designed to *make* you, not to destroy you. It has been permitted by God to mold you into the image of His Son rather than disfigure you for life. God doesn't test us to see if we'll fail but to show us how strong we are. He does it for the sake of proving us, and He wants us to score a hundred on the exam!

Strange as it may seem, meekness is the key to understanding and believing and experiencing this God-given strength. And what is so wonderful—full of wonder—is that if I'm truly a Christian then the Holy Spirit produces that meekness inside me.

In our ministry we've met people whose lives seem to be absolute wrecks. The traumas and trials they've endured have been horrendous, almost incomprehensible. Yet as the months or years go by while they're living in the Word of God we see them come out of the furnace of affliction, and they're beautiful!

Remember, my friend: Whatever this trial, whatever this difficulty, it is *not* more than you can bear. Why is that true? How do I know? Because God has promised this, and God cannot lie. One of the first four Scripture verses I memorized as a new child of God was 1 Corinthians 10:13, and it became *my* scripture for facing trials: "No temptation has overtaken you but such as is common to man; and God is faithful, *who will not allow you to be tempted beyond what you are able*, but with the temptation will provide the way of escape also, that you may be able to endure it."

The Greek words translated here as "temptation" and "tempted" have the broader meaning of a trial or testing. "No temptation, no trial, no testing"—how awesome that these will never be more than I can bear! If they were, God would not permit them.

And there's a way of escape—God's way. No difficulty or trial or temptation will ever come my way that God cannot deliver me out of.

Think about this, beloved, for that verse is as sure as God.

I also saw that none of my trials—*none*—was really unique to me. They were all "common to man," and common to the Son of Man, Jesus, who was tempted and tried and tested "in all points . . . like as we are, yet without sin" (Hebrews 4:15, KJV). Since He was without sin, *we* can be without sin, because we have Him within us to handle the trial. He is our sustainer in our every difficulty—because whatever *He* went through, He can take *us* through.

He understands.

Our God is faithful—our faithful, sovereign God will not permit us to be tried or tested or tempted beyond what we can bear. But along *with* that trial or test or temptation He will also make a way of escape. And His way of escape is *not* to lift us by the scruff of the neck, as we would pick up a kitten, and move us out. No, the way of escape is that He will be *in* us and with us; therefore, His grace will be sufficient for anything that comes our way.

No matter what happens to us, God has totally and completely and absolutely equipped and prepared us for it.

So I'm not to fight these afflictions I encounter, the trials and disappointments, these oppressions, these humbling situations. God is in perfect control of them, and in His perfect design He's permitted them to teach me to act rather than react. He has me in training.

How practical this is, not just in the big and hard situations but also in the little foxy ones that seek to rob the vines and keep us from walking in the fruit of the Spirit.

Let me ask you to put this book down, my friend, and think about what you've just read. Meditate on it. Talk to God about it. Allow it to soak deep within you, like a gentle rain upon the soil; don't let it just run off the surface of your soul like a short, driving downpour.

OUR PERFECT TEACHER OF MEEKNESS

When it comes to learning about meekness, we have the perfect Teacher.

In Matthew 11:28-30, Jesus said, "Come *to Me*, all who are weary and heavy-laden." Doesn't pressure make you weary? Doesn't it make you heavy-laden?

But Jesus promised, "I will give you rest" and again, "you shall find rest for your souls." Jesus offered rest—a key word in these verses—then He added, "Take my yoke upon you, and *learn of me; for I am meek* and lowly in heart" (KJV). We're invited and commanded to learn meekness from Jesus Himself. Jesus wants us to be meek with *His meekness*.

When we learn from Jesus to act rather than react, we'll have rest. We won't want to straighten out all our own circumstances or the rest of the world. What a relief for strong-willed people like me! We'll let God do it. We'll let God be God, and we'll remember that we are only man and we're not in charge of the universe. When we learn this, the stress of this life will not undo us, overwhelm and overpower us. We'll live in the practical knowledge that God is in control, and in His grace and strength we can control our responses to every disappointment and stress.

The minute we act rather than react, the situation is no longer controlling us. We know God is in control of it, and the Holy Spirit is in control of our responses. As we follow Him, as we yield to His yoke, as we yield to the Spirit's sweet control, we become meek even as Jesus is meek. Isn't that encouraging?

You and I are here on this earth for one purpose, beloved: to be the light of Jesus Christ in the midst of a crooked and perverse generation. To do that, we have to walk just as He walked. And how did He walk? In meekness. Jesus lived in total, complete, absolute submission to the will of God. How clearly this is summarized in Jesus' words in John 5. You might want to stop and read that chapter, marking everything that indicates what the Son did in respect to the Father.

When you read the gospels you never read of Jesus murmuring, complaining, disputing, resisting—even when He faced the cross. The Old Testament prophets bore witness to this: "He was oppressed and He was afflicted, yet He did not open His mouth; like a lamb that is led to slaughter, and like a sheep that is silent before its shearers, so He did not open His mouth" (Isaiah 53:7).

You know, when you take hold of a sheep to shear its wool or to slit its throat, it doesn't utter a sound. But go after a hog, and it squeals to high heaven. Which are *you* more like in times of affliction—a squealing pig or a silent lamb?

Jesus, the Lamb of God, was the perfect model of meekness before His Father. He said, "I always do the things that are pleasing to Him" (John 8:29). Jesus wasn't looking out for Himself, doing His own thing, pressing His own cause, pushing His own opinions.

Did you notice in the gospel of John how strongly we see this portrait of Jesus in full and meek dependence upon His Father in all He said and did? "The Son can do *nothing* of Himself," He said, "unless it is something He sees the Father doing; for whatever the Father does, these things the Son also does in like manner" (5:19).

Jesus said, "I do nothing on My own initiative, but I speak these things as the Father taught Me" (8:28).

He said, "I speak the things which I have seen with My Father" (8:38).

"For I did not speak on My own initiative," Jesus said, "but the Father Himself who sent Me has given Me commandment, what to say, and what to speak" (12:49).

"I speak just as the Father has told Me" (12:50).

"Do you not believe that I am in the Father, and the Father is in Me? The words that I say to you I do not speak on My own initiative, but the Father abiding in Me does His works" (14:10).

"I love the Father, and as the Father gave Me commandment, even so I do" (14:31).

Jesus, the One who was in the beginning with the Father, the One by whom all things were made, was meek before God His Father and also before man whom He Himself created!

We see this awesome truth throughout His life on earth, even as He was rejected, even when He was actually accused of being Beelzebub, His archenemy and the one whose head He came to bruise, the one He came to defeat and destroy. All through His life, Jesus—God in the flesh—moved in meekness.

As you walk through the gospels, you never get the sense that Jesus was stressed or irritated by daily circumstances, that He was pushed or driven or harried by whatever obstacles and difficulties and resistance He encountered.

That doesn't mean we don't see Him responding with strong emotion. He wept with passion after Lazarus died, though He knew He could and would raise Lazarus from the dead.

And behold Him in the Garden of Gethsemane. Here He was under greater pressure than any of us will ever know, to the point that "being in agony He was praying very fervently; and His sweat became like drops of blood, falling down upon the ground" (Luke 22:44). When our human bodies become stressed our blood pressure rises; our bodies are designed for us to faint before the pressure gets so high that it breaks our capillaries and causes a stroke. That's why people faint under stressful situations. But Jesus didn't faint. Instead He bore the pressure to such a degree that blood seeped from His capillaries, manifesting itself in His sweat. Luke, the careful doctor, was the only one of the four gospel writers who told us this. He also made a point of telling us that Jesus' blood didn't stay on His brow like the beads of sweat we typically see. Instead the blood in His sweat made it heavy enough to drip from His head, "falling down upon the ground."

Such was His agony. Yet in all this extremity of suffering, we don't see Him departing from meekness before God and man or being anything other than totally submissive to His Father's will.

Jesus knew the conflict within Him. But what was His desire? Three times He cried it out: "Not My will but Thine be done." Three times He went back to the Father, and three times He prayed, "If it be possible, *take this cup from Me*." But then His further prayer was always the essence of meekness: "Not My will but Thine be done."

As Jesus arose from praying the third time, once again He found His disciples asleep. This time His captors had come, led by the traitor Judas. Peter launched an attack, reacting with a sword. But Jesus commanded him to put it away and spoke of what He had committed Himself to moments earlier in prayer: "The cup which the Father has given Me, shall I not drink it?" (John 18:11).

Jesus is truly our perfect Teacher of meekness, even modeling for us how to *learn* it: "Although He was a Son, *He learned obedience from the things which He suffered*" (Hebrews 5:8). In whatever things *we* are suffering—are we learning obedience?

For Daily Salvation

In several ways God makes it clear to us in the Scriptures that we're to acquire and master this meekness.

We read in Colossians 3:12 that meekness is something we're to *put on*. We're to get dressed in it. We're to do this because we're "the elect of God, holy and beloved" (KJV). We're to wrap ourselves in meekness, along with "a heart of compassion, kindness, humility . . . and patience."

Meekness is also something we're to *pursue*. After warning Timothy about the many evils that have the love of money as their root, Paul told him, "O man of God, flee these things; and *follow after* righteousness, godliness, faith, love, patience, *meekness*" (1 Timothy 6:11, KJV). This is not something you're to pray for—rather, it's what you're to walk in. It is already there, because meekness (sometimes translated "gentleness") is part of the ninefold fruit of the Spirit of God, the Spirit who is in you if you are in Christ.

Meekness is also how we're commanded to *walk*, the way we're to habitually live as saints of God—"I therefore, the prisoner of the Lord, beseech you that ye *walk* worthy of the vocation wherewith ye are called, *with all* lowliness and *meekness*" (Ephesians 4:1-2, KJV).

And finally, meekness is the *way we're to receive God's Word*. "Receive with *meekness* the engrafted word [or "implanted word," NASB], which is able to save your souls" (James 1:21, KJV).

The Word falls on hearts that are hard ground, where Satan has his way. The Word falls on shallow hearts that are rocky ground, where there is no perseverance. The Word falls into hearts full of thorns, hearts that are occupied with the worries of the world and the deceitfulness of riches.

But the Word also falls on hearts that are *good ground*, hearts that receive the implanted seed with meekness and then respond properly.

Which of those pictures describes your heart, beloved?

It's critical that you receive the Word meekly, because this Word "is able to save your soul." I don't think this verse refers to our salvation from hell, because James was addressing these words to "my beloved brethren" (verse 19), those who were already his brothers and sisters in Christ. But James was concerned about the way they were living. He was concerned that they might "stray from the truth" (5:19). So he reminded them that God's Word has the power to save their souls—to bring freedom and deliverance to their inner being in day-by-day situations, hour by hour, moment by moment. God's Word saves my thinking. It saves my emotions. It's a day-by-day salvation, an ongoing walk of daily sanctification.

Then James gave us another clue about what this meekness means in regard to God's Word. He said, "But prove yourselves doers of the word, and not merely hearers who delude themselves" (1:22). The good soil of a meek heart is a ready obedience that *acts* on what it hears and receives. Those who please the Father are doers of the Word, not just hearers.

THE BLESSINGS OF MEEKNESS

What blessings will we see in our lives as we learn to live in meekness, as we put it on and pursue it and walk in it and receive God's Word with it? What makes meekness so worthwhile to know about and to live out?

First of all, meekness in your life will bring guidance and direction from God. "Good and upright is the LORD: therefore will he teach sinners in the way. *The meek will he guide in judgment: and the meek will he teach his way*" (Psalm 25:8-9, KJV). If you're willing to submit to God, to put yourself in neutral as far as your own will is concerned and say, "God, not my will but Thine be done"—then God will lead you in the way.

But if you're stubborn, if you're like the wild horse that has to be reigned in, if you're always bucking and pounding and rebelling at everything, always wanting to go your own way—God cannot lead you.

When is the last time you came before God in meekness and asked, "God, what do You want me to do?"

Meekness in your life will also bring increased joy as well as the peace and confidence that go with it. "The meek also shall increase their joy in the LORD" (Isaiah 29:19, KJV). Meekness brings a joyful satisfaction with God and a sense of fulfillment from God for what He has done and is doing and will do. There's an equilibrium of spirit about us, a calmness. We don't fluctuate between being high and being depressed. We're neither overly elated nor cast down. We can face everything that comes our way with the assurance that it's been permitted for our good and for His glory. That's why Jesus promised rest as He invited us to come and learn meekness from Him.

There have been times when I've reacted instead of acted—and been ashamed afterward. There have been times when I've wept before God: "God, I'm so sorry. I totally and completely and absolutely failed You." But there have been other times when meekness was allowed to be demonstrated, when in the midst of affliction or oppression I responded in meekness. And the sense of peace in my heart between God and me was so wonderful that I never want to miss it again.

Maybe you don't have that peace now in your relationship with Jesus Christ. Maybe you're fighting God about something. You're trying to take control. You're trying to manipulate. You're trying to maneuver. You're trying to adjust your circumstances to the way you think they ought to be instead of allowing that trial to accomplish what God wants it to accomplish in your life. If this is your situation, beloved, confess it now to Him in meekness and enjoy the return of peace.

Meekness brings a deep and delightful peace, an overflowing peace: "But the meek . . . shall delight themselves *in the abundance of peace*" (Psalm 37:11, KJV).

Meekness brings an astonishing inheritance from God. Jesus said, "Blessed are the meek: for they shall inherit the earth" (Matthew 5:5, KJV). In Psalm 37:11 we see it as well: "But the meek shall inherit the earth" (KJV).

More and more these days we think we get what we want by asserting ourselves, promoting ourselves. But meekness isn't interested in self-promotion and assertiveness.

"How will I conquer?" you ask. "How will I win?" By bending the knee, beloved, and saying, "Lord, what pleases You pleases me."

It's the meek who gain the true inheritance.

Someday we'll come back to this earth with Jesus to rule and reign with Him. But when He comes and establishes His kingdom, I don't believe it's going to be the same for every Christian. I believe that those who have walked in meekness and obedience to Christ (and meekness is synonymous with obedience to Him) will rule and reign over more than others will.

VINDICATION FROM GOD

And in that day we will also fully see and understand that meekness brings vindication from the Lord. As the psalmist wrote, "Thou didst cause judgment to be heard from heaven; the earth feared, and was still, when *God arose to judgment, to save all the meek of the earth*" (Psalm 76:8-9, KJV). And then he added "Selah"—a reminder for us to pause and think on that.

What was God saying here? He was saying that He will arise to judgment for the sake of the meek.

Many who are greatly humiliated now will be vindicated before the throne of grace and glory. God will give crowns to those who have loved His appearing and therefore are willing to suffer now, those who have been used of God to proclaim the gospel not only with their lips but also with their lives.

God will arise to judgment, to save all the meek of the earth. For the meek, *God will make it right*. We may not recognize that judgment now, but one day God will deal in equity.

And when I know that justice will be done, it's easier to be meek. It's easier because I know that no one is getting away with anything.

That's why the meek don't have to defend themselves. God Himself is their defender. He vindicates the meek. He's on their side. He supports them. "The LORD lifteth up the meek: he casteth the wicked down to the ground" (Psalm 147:6, KJV). By walking in meekness we allow God to be our defender and the upholder of our cause. And who greater could we ask for?

Maybe you're like me: I hate it when somebody pulls something over on me. I don't want to be done in. I don't want to have anyone finagle me. I don't want anyone to cheat me. If someone wants what I've got, I want that person to come after it straight on. And when someone does something wrong, I want justice done, and I want it done right now.

The Lord does bring justice but usually not right now. However, I can know that God will make it right, that He will judge in righteousness and holiness.

So what will you do if someone cuts you down in public? Have you thought about that? What will you do if someone you love discredits you in front of people? If you're wrongly accused, will you act or react? How will you respond if members of your family turn against you and your commitment to Christ? Will you remember that God is your defender? These are circumstances to consider right now and determine that you'll respond in meekness, so that when they come, the Spirit of God will be quick to remind you of your commitment. Then you'll act rather than react, giving the Spirit full control.

Just remember, precious one: We may be despised and rejected now, but someday we'll sit with Him on His throne. Someday we'll reign with Him. And someday when every knee shall bow before Him and every tongue confess that He is Lord, all will lift their heads and see us standing there with the King of kings, and then they'll realize who had true wisdom.

The founder of Wycliffe Bible Translators, Cameron Townsend was called by God to lead a movement to translate the Scriptures for the thousands of people without a Bible in their own language. He was affectionately known as Uncle Cam by those who labored with him or who knew and respected his work.

But Uncle Cam had a thorn in his flesh that many were not aware of. His first wife did not understand and respect God's calling upon his life, and quite often she let it be known. One day in a gathering of dignitaries she hauled off and kicked her husband in the shins. But Uncle Cam did not react. He acted in meekness both then and throughout their marriage. The dear man continued to shower her with gifts. He sought to meet her needs, and he responded the way God wanted him to respond. And so his ministry was not hindered.

I personally believe the time came when God—as Uncle Cam's defender, the vindicator of the meek—finally said, "That's enough," and He called Uncle Cam's wife home. Then He led Uncle Cam into a second marriage, this time with a truly godly wife more than thirty years his junior. She became the delight of His heart and the strength of a powerful partnership.

We don't have to defend ourselves, to justify ourselves, to retaliate. We don't have to fight our own battles.

This is often a problem with people who've known great pain. *I've been sexually abused*, they say, *and I will not forgive. I've got to punish.* But vengeance belongs to God, and He Himself will come to our defense when we don't try to step into His role.

Meekness is deciding, *I'm not going to jerk a knot around someone for what he or she has done.* We leave all that to God. God's vindication may come in this life, or it may come only later; but it does come. We don't have to fight our own battles, because God will fight them for us in ultimate triumph.

How well this comes out in 2 Thessalonians 1:6-8:

> For after all it is only just for God to repay with affliction those who afflict you, and to give relief to you who are afflicted and to us as well when the Lord Jesus shall be revealed from heaven with His mighty angels in flaming fire, *dealing out retribution* to those who do not know God and to those who do not obey the gospel of our Lord Jesus.

In other words, there's a day of reckoning coming.

When we see oppression and unfairness and wicked misdeeds, we want to see justice. And God says there *will* be justice. It may not come now, but full justice will come, rolling down like waters (Amos 5:24). Nothing will remain unrequited or unpunished. God's Word says that everyone will be responsible even for those things that are whispered in secret. Everyone is accountable every moment for everything he or she says about anyone. God is a God of justice, and He will bring every hidden thing to light.

Scripture says that record books are being kept of every unsaved person's deeds:

> And I saw the dead, the great and the small, standing before the throne, and *books were opened*; and another book was opened,

which is the book of life; *and the dead were judged from the things which were written in the books, according to their deeds.* And the sea gave up the dead which were in it, and death and Hades gave up the dead which were in them; and they were judged, every one of them according to their deeds. And death and Hades were thrown into the lake of fire. This is the second death, the lake of fire. And if anyone's name was not found written in the book of life, he was thrown into the lake of fire. (Revelation 20:12-15)

Knowing this promise can change our perspective toward others who have wronged us, because we no longer see them as our enemies but as those for whom there is ultimate judgment. We want them to know the gospel, because they need to be saved. But we realize that if they refuse to come to God and receive the same forgiveness we've received, they won't get off scot-free. They will be held accountable.

At the same time, the Bible says, another book is being kept, a record of remembrance for those who fear the Lord.

Then those who feared the LORD spoke to one another, and the LORD gave attention and heard it, and a book of remembrance was written before Him for those who fear the LORD and who esteem His name. (Malachi 3:16)

For the meek—for those who fear the Lord—the memories of their trust and obedience will be eternally sweet, treasures to be shared in the presence of the Lord.

The meek will he guide in judgment:
and the meek will he teach his way.

PSALM 25:9 (KJV)

CHAPTER FIVE

TRANSFORMED
UNDER HIS CONTROL

The Gift of Meekness

BELOVED, WE HAVE so much to explore about meekness, so much that is good and practical in helping us respond righteously to life's disappointments. God's Word for us on this is a sure word, a word we can believe. And it's alive and powerful, the discerner of thoughts and intentions of the heart.

First let's review the depth and richness of this word, which describes the key to acting rather than reacting.

The Greek noun in the New Testament for "meekness" is *prautes*, and its adjective form ("meek") is *praus*. Meekness is something our culture doesn't usually respect or value, and this could be why in most modern Bible versions these Greek terms are translated as "gentle" and "gentleness"; they do appear as "meek" and "meekness" in the King James Version, which I'll quote below. But *meekness* is truly a powerful word when we understand and embrace it.

We encounter this Greek term in Matthew 11:29 where Jesus invited us to come to Him and learn from Him. There He said, "I am *meek* and lowly in heart, and ye shall find rest unto your souls" (KJV). We see it in Matthew 5:5 where Jesus said, "Blessed are the *meek*: for they shall inherit the earth" (KJV). We find it again where Matthew employed an Old Testament prophecy to describe Jesus' riding into Jerusalem triumphantly yet humbly on a donkey colt: "Behold, thy King cometh unto thee, *meek*, and sitting upon an ass" (21:5, KJV).

Paul used this same Greek term in referring to "the *meekness* and gentleness of Christ" (2 Corinthians 10:1). It's the eighth word used in defining the ninefold fruit of the Spirit in Galatians 5:22-23 (KJV)—"love, joy, peace, longsuffering, gentleness, goodness, faith, *meekness*, temperance."

It's the way we're to walk—"with all lowliness and *meekness*," as Ephesians 4:2 (KJV) says. And it's what we're to "put on" as God's elect, according to Colossians 3:12 (KJV).

Paul also used *prautes* to tell Timothy how the Lord's servant must deal with adversaries: "in *meekness* instructing those that oppose" (2 Timothy 2:25, KJV) and in reminding Titus how God's people are to always behave, showing "all *meekness* unto all men" (Titus 3:2, KJV).

James used the word to show how we're to receive God's implanted Word (1:21) and to show how someone proves he or she is genuinely wise: "Let him show by good conduct that his works are done in the *meekness* of wisdom" (3:13, NKJV).

Peter applied the term to a wife's inner beauty—"the ornament of a *meek* and quiet spirit," which is "of great price" in God's sight (1 Peter 3:4, KJV). And he advised us all to be constantly ready to answer "with *meekness* and fear" whenever we're asked about our hope (1 Peter 3:15, KJV).

In the Old Testament, the Hebrew word for meek and meekness is from the root *anaw*, and it expresses the outcome of affliction or humility, as we saw earlier. We see this term in the King James Version of Psalms where we're told that God will guide and teach the meek (25:9), that He will save them (76:9) and lift them up (147:6), and that the meek will inherit the earth (37:11). God promises to "beautify the *meek* with salvation" (149:4).

In Isaiah we're taught that "the *meek* also shall increase their joy in the LORD" (29:19, KJV). And Moses is described in Numbers 12:3 as "very *meek*"—in fact, more meek than "all the men which were upon the face of the earth" (KJV).

In ancient times this term was used in reference to domesticating animals—taming them, teaching them to come under the control of their masters, changing them to be gentle and properly behaved. This is what God is in the process of doing with us: bringing us under His control, transforming us under His power, so we'll walk under His lordship. The opposite of meekness is not strength but rather a lack of control, an untamed and unbroken wildness.

A SUPERNATURAL GIFT

What else should we know about this profound and mighty word?

First of all, meekness isn't natural. We may picture timid, quiet folks who never have an opinion, pliable people who never do anything risky or bold because they dare not rock the boat. But that isn't biblical meekness.

Meekness is something God works into us. It isn't a personality temperament but a fruit of the Holy Spirit, as I said earlier. If you're a believer, your genetic structure spiritually is all there for meekness. You only have to walk in it, participate in it. If there's absolutely no degree of meekness in your life then you aren't saved and Christ doesn't live in you, since He must manifest His presence in you in some way and at some time, and He Himself is meek.

Therefore no matter how trying the situation, you as a believer will always have the opportunity to respond powerfully in the meekness of the Spirit rather than to react in the flesh. Your flesh and the Spirit are in warfare (Galatians 5:16-17), and if you fail to act in the Spirit, then you're being controlled by the flesh. To walk in meekness is to be controlled by the Spirit, filled by the Spirit.

To be meek is to be calmly strong. Meekness is supernatural. It's an inwrought grace of the soul. And since meekness is from God rather than being a natural personality trait, then even strong, outgoing people can be meek—and that's a relief to me. Most people would not think of me as being naturally meek, and a lot of times I'm not meek, though I should be. But as someone with a strong personality I find it a great comfort that this meekness God requires is also something He supplies.

TOWARD GOD AND TOWARD MAN

Meekness must be both Godward and manward.

Toward God, meekness is first of all accepting all things without murmuring or disputing or resisting or retaliating. Meekness can do this because it sees everything as permitted by our sovereign God for His purpose of transforming us into the image of His Son.

In every situation, in any and all things, meekness is able to remember the meekness of Christ and to give thanks and to praise God.

We see this in *The Hiding Place*, when Corrie ten Boom and her sister, Betsy, are in line with other women being herded like animals into imprisonment at a Nazi concentration camp. These two Dutch sisters who helped hide Jews in their family's house had been suddenly wrenched from a home where they were sheltered by a godly father who taught them the Word of God and lived a righteous life before them.

Now these two virgins were being forced to strip and stand naked with all the other women prisoners before the leering German soldiers. Corrie could hear Betsy's soft voice behind her, talking to her very present Help in time of trouble: "Lord Jesus, You hung naked before the world on Your cross. . . ." Rather than wailing, in meekness Betsy entered the fellowship of her Lord's sufferings.

Meekness is also *humble submission to the sovereign will of God*. (I don't mean to be overbearing, but I'm giving you all these various descriptions and definitions so if they don't hit you one way, they'll hit you another. We don't want to waste or miss what God is saying, my friend, because this is part of His refining process to get rid of the dross so all the wonderful redemptive silver inside you and me and can reflect our Master's image. So please bear with me—and ask God to use the fire of these scriptures to release from within you the hidden, stubborn dross.)

Meekness says, "God, if this is what You want, then since You promised me it will work together for good, since You promised that it will make me like Christ, since You promised that by enduring this I won't be ashamed when I see You at Your coming, and since you promised that this endurance gives me a crown to lay at Your feet—then God, *if it pleases You, it pleases me.*

When I understand this, then why should I ever resist any delay or disappointment, any affliction or oppression or humiliation—when I know God will use it in my life to make me like Jesus and to prepare me for heaven? Our purpose in life is holiness, not happiness. Each of us is to be something other than an ordinary person who lives by merely reacting to circumstances and who doesn't allow God to be God in his or her life. We're to be what God intended when He first created man and before man sinned. By His command we're to be holy as He is holy. And we're able to be made like this because Christ, "the hope of glory," is in us (Colossians 1:27).

When there's true meekness toward God, then there also can be and must be true meekness toward other people.

Meekness can accept all insults and provocation without retaliation, because meekness sees even these negatives as being permitted by God to make us like His Son. You're always in trouble when you start fighting back. But meekness doesn't reciprocate. The meek are not ruled either by their circumstances or by the actions or reactions of others. They stay composed because they're ruled by God and they understand that God is the ultimate victor.

David gave us a good picture of this as he was fleeing from Jerusalem under the pressure of his son Absalom's rebellion. He encountered curses and rocks thrown his way by a man named Shimei. David's nephew and military leader, Abishai, wanted to retaliate. "Why should this dead dog curse my lord the king?" he said. "Let me go over now, and cut off his head" (2 Samuel 16:9). He was like the Queen of Hearts in *Alice in Wonderland* shouting, "Off with his head! Off with his head!"

David had the power and probably plenty of human motivation as well to order Shimei's death. He even had a legal and moral right, because God's law commanded, "You shall not curse God, nor curse a ruler of your people" (Exodus 22:28). But David determined to trust God's sovereignty and to display meekness. He gave the order: "Let him alone and let him curse, for the LORD has told him. Perhaps the LORD will look on my affliction and return good to me instead of his cursing this day" (2 Samuel 16:11-12).

David's meek response didn't soothe Shimei. In fact, as the king and his men continued on their way, "Shimei went along on the hillside parallel with him and as he went he cursed, and cast stones and threw dust at him" (16:13). More curses, more stones, and this time dust as well.

But Shimei would be held responsible for his rude and violent contempt. Years later, King Solomon dealt with Shimei because of his improper behavior toward his father, David. And when Shimei broke a travel ban that was punishable by death, his execution was ordered by Solomon with this reminder: "You know all the evil which you acknowledge in your heart, which you did to my father David; therefore the LORD shall return your evil on your own head" (1 Kings 2:44). Judgment was delayed, but judgment came nevertheless. Because David was meek, God in His proper time acted through Solomon to show Himself as David's defender and David's vindicator.

Aristotle described meekness as the mean between excessive anger and the inability to show anger at all. As I write this, I want you to know there *is* such a thing as righteous indignation; yet we're to manifest meekness as we obey Ephesians 4:26—"Be ye angry, and sin not: let not the sun go down upon your wrath" (KJV).

INSIDE AND OUT

Toward other people, meekness is always gentle and gracious, both inside and out. I remind myself of this principle when I find myself hurrying through life. As I've prayed and asked God to teach me—because I want to be what He wants me to be—He has shown me when I was reacting to life's pressures instead of being meek. I might have appeared to be enduring something just fine, but under my breath I'd be saying, "I wish these people would get their act together." I live a fast-paced life, and I want to hurry everybody else as I zoom through, or at least I want them to step aside so I can move ahead. The Lord showed me I didn't have the equilibrium of spirit that comes from meekness. I had it on the outside—the Lord had taught me that—but not on the inside.

I was in an airport restaurant with my mother and sister, and I was getting distressed with our waiter because we had to wait so long for our food. He finally brought it but then abandoned us. He just wasn't doing his job. So I made a complaint. (I honestly don't think it's best for a person to be allowed to continue in improper behavior.) But I complained *nicely*—in fact, my sister was rather impressed. So was I. But I tell you, inside there wasn't meekness. Inside I was murmuring and disputing.

Meekness knows, however, that God will use other people in this way to mold me and make me like Jesus.

I hate to tell all this on myself, because my heart is to always walk by the Spirit, and it grieves me to admit these things. But I do admit them, and I want you to take courage from my example. I'm in process, but the dross doesn't release easily, does it?

One evening I went into Jack's office to hang some pictures. I had threatened his life if he ever hung them himself, knowing he'd have them in all the wrong places and at all the wrong angles.

After hanging the pictures, I dusted and straightened up his office. Then I noticed that his desk pad was a mess. It spoiled my lovely new decor! Jack had scribbled all over it. So I got out his address book and neatly and carefully wrote down every name and number I saw on that desk pad. Then I tore off that messy sheet. But I wasn't stupid; I didn't throw it away. Instead I folded it up and put it in his desk drawer. Then in beautiful script I wrote a note on the clean desk pad: "Surprise! I love you, Darling!"

I was so proud of myself.

Then I went home to resume my study of Philippians, the next book of the Bible I was teaching in our ministry. While I was at the desk in our bedroom, Jack walked in.

I proudly sat up, looked at him and beamed. *He's going to be so pleased*, I thought. My heart was filled with love. I just knew he was going to be so happy with me.

But he just walked in and looked at me.

I asked him, "You didn't happen to go by your office, did you?"

"Yes."

I sat a little straighter. "Did you notice I hung your pictures?"

"What did you do with my desk pad?" he asked, almost in a demanding way that brought a twinge of irritation to my "loving" spirit.

"Jack, honey, I hung your pictures. Didn't you notice?"

"What did you do with my desk pad?"

"Jack!" I said. "I'm not stupid! I didn't throw it away!"

"Well, I had lots of important numbers on there."

"Jack!" And suddenly I thought, *Why did I ever marry you?*

I had been so in love with him only a minute earlier. Now that old devil was knocking at my mind's door, talking to me as I flung it open: *You know, Jack's not very handsome*, he said, handing me a brick. The enemy was about to build a stronghold in my mind.

You're right, I thought. *Hand me another brick*—which he did rather quickly.

Not only that, but do you really think he's the best father for your boys? the devil hissed.

No, I don't. And I don't think he knows how to handle me either—and I need special handling.

I was taking the bricks as fast as I could, building a big case of "I hate Jack."

Jack walked into the bathroom, saying nothing more. Agitated, I had to move. Grabbing my Bible off the desk, I went to my rocker in the corner. I plopped down and started giving that old chair a real workout while trying to concentrate on my Philippians study: "How to Have Joy."

Mentally I rehearsed my outline for the first lesson I would teach the next day. Chapter One: "Joy despite imprisonment, because Christ is my life." And here I was imprisoned in my marriage.

Chapter Two: "Joy despite people, because I have the mind of Christ." It was Jack who was robbing me of my joy, and at this point I didn't want the mind of Christ. I was hurt, I was angry . . . and I knew I shouldn't be.

The rocker went faster as I clutched my Bible.

Chapter Three: "Joy despite things." That stupid desk pad was robbing me of my joy when Christ should be my goal.

Chapter Four: "Joy despite circumstances." My circumstances were awful, and at that point I wanted to wallow in them rather than allow Christ to be my peace.

Mr. Peace-at-Any-Price was still in the bathroom, brushing his teeth.

We have a closet between the bedroom and the bathroom, and I had to get something out of it. I walked into the closet, got what I wanted, and turned to walk back to my rocking chair. It was as far as I could get from Jack without leaving the room. Then Jack playfully grabbed my elbow and laughed.

I reacted. I jerked my arm away and went back to my rocker to study "How to Have Joy, No Matter What" so I could teach it the following morning.

So what did Mr. Peace-at-Any-Price do? He said nothing and went to bed. I shrugged, thinking, *It will be all right in the morning.*

And the Lord said to me, *Don't let the sun go down on your wrath.*

Jack was making z's by now. I couldn't wake him up, could I?

Finally, when I was sure he had passed from twilight into deep sleep, I joined him in our king-size bed. I was hanging off the edge on my side. I didn't want him to touch me.

My husband has always been an early riser, while I was magnetized to mattresses in those days before we had my thyroid problem under better control. The next morning Jack got up and went into the bathroom and began whistling. No one should ever whistle that early, especially after having done that to his wife. How could he whistle when I was still hurting, still chafing?

I arose and went to the rocker with my Bible to have my quiet time and to go over my lesson for that morning's teaching session.

As I sat there I could recognize my Lord's still small voice in the recesses of my heart: *Ask Jack to forgive you.*

I answered, *But Lord!* (Do those two words go together?) *He should never have laughed at me. He's got to become more sensitive. He doesn't understand me, Lord.*

I'm talking to you, the Lord said. *It's not about Jack. It's about you.*

I went into the bathroom and looked at Jack. "Will you forgive me for the way I behaved last night?"

He began to laugh. "That was so unlike you to act that way," he said.

"No," I answered, smiling weakly, "that's exactly what I'm like when I don't walk in the Spirit."

Finally Jack put his arms around me.

You know, as I recall this incident that happened years—and I mean *years*—ago, I don't think he ever did thank me for hanging his pictures in his office!

Another picture of meekness toward man is described in Ecclesiastes 10:4. Although the Hebrew word for meekness isn't used in this verse, we do see a good demonstration of it: "If the ruler's temper rises against you, do not abandon your position, because composure allays great offenses." *Composure* allays great offensc. The New International Version renders it, "If a ruler's anger rises against you, do not leave your post; calmness can lay great errors to rest."

In other words, if somebody over you—your boss or a public official—gets hot under the collar against you, we're taught that you're not to abandon your position. You don't let somebody's anger alter what you are, who you are, and how you're to behave under the Holy Spirit's control. In essence that was what I did with Jack, only it wasn't his anger I was reacting to, it was what I perceived as his lack of gratitude.

Composure and calmness will allay great offense.

Many Christians today are making a stand for righteousness and holiness and godliness, which is wonderful. But some of them are not doing it in meekness. Some of them seem as mean as a snake. And when they react that way they negate whatever they're trying to accomplish publicly as Christians.

WHAT THE MEEK DO AND ARE

Meekness toward both God and man is especially displayed in Psalm 37, a dynamite passage that shows us a full-rounded picture of how the meek act instead of react. Although I want to share with you some insights from Psalm 37, I want to I encourage you, beloved, to study it on your own.

This is what the meek do and are:

They *trust* God (verses 3 and 5). They trust in the Lord instead of being fretful. They "do not fret because of evildoers" (verse 1). They are not anxious about the evil around them and how it will affect them, because they know meekness is manifested in the face of affliction and trial and in the face of oppression and evil. They're not looking at the situation or the circumstances but at our sovereign God.

The meek *do good* (verses 3 and 27). When I trust God, I do good and not evil. I don't pay back evil for evil or nastiness for nastiness; instead I repay evil with good.

In verse 3 we see that the meek *dwell*. They don't run away. They don't abandon their position (Ecclesiastes 10:4). Lots of people react by saying, "I don't need to take this from you anymore; I've had enough of your lip, your guff." And they walk out. The same verse says that the meek *cultivate faithfulness*. They keep their vows, their promises, their friendships.

Before I was saved, I walked out on my first husband, Tom, who was truly a fine man. I believe Tom must have had a chemical imbalance. He had the symptoms of manic depression that played a part in his eventual suicide. But I was young, unsaved, and wanting so badly to be happy and to be loved that I missed what was going on with Tom. In those days all the manic depressives I knew were in an institution for the insane in Toledo, Ohio. This was more than forty years ago, and we didn't know what we know today.

Anyway, here was a man who in his private prep school had been voted most likely to succeed. Four major league baseball teams—the Pirates, Phillies, Indians, and Yankees—had offered him contracts to pitch for them. He was a natural athlete. He also knew his way around country clubs and had plenty of money. But his home life had been hellish. He had grown up having parents who carried on a private war, a conflict that was exacerbated by both having too much to drink.

After he and I were married, Tom would often come home from work, eat dinner, and go straight to bed because of his severe depression. And I would sit on the porch, look at the other women with their husbands, and feel incredibly lonely. My marriage wasn't what I had dreamed of or what I saw in movies or on television.

I found myself sleeping in, preferring to dream rather than face reality. I didn't escape with drugs or alcohol; I knew their destructive effects. But I went quickly into that Deadly D spiral, and I knew I was in trouble.

To get out of the pit, I got a job as a model for a local store. Tom wouldn't let me go back to nursing; nor would he let me study to be a doctor, but he liked the idea of saying his wife was a model. How I wish I had known the Lord then, that I hadn't been so self-centered, that I had been the wife I should have been and sought help for this man I had become one flesh with. Instead I began to enjoy some professional success—and that was hard on Tom, for he was miserable in his job.

One evening I came home from modeling, and Tom was sitting downstairs in his shorts on the couch. I can still picture him there.

He said something cutting to me. But I turned and walked upstairs.

Getting up from the couch, Tom followed me into the bedroom. I turned around and lashed out at him with harsh words. I didn't know the Bible's teaching that although the tongue is a small part of the body, it can set on fire the course of a person's life and is itself set on fire by hell. I verbally cut Tom to shreds—so much so that this man who normally was a perfect gentleman lifted his arm and backhanded me, knocking me to the bed. I felt and tasted a warm, salty liquid oozing onto my lip. I reached up and touched it then held my blood-marked fingers out in front of me.

"Tom, that's it," I said. "I've had it."

He begged me to stay as he followed me downstairs. In our family room I took off my ring—with its big diamond and the inscription inside the band that read "Our Love Is Eternal"—and threw it across the room.

And I walked out, just like so many people are doing today.

The meek *stay*, but I wasn't meek. I didn't stay. I wanted my way, my happiness. I took no thought for my future or the future of my two sons or the future of this man I had vowed to love unconditionally. And although two ministers counseled me to separate, I know now that they were wrong. I was wrong. None of us looked at the Word of God and allowed it to be our plumb line.

Not long after our divorce, in the midst of his depression, my capable, fine husband took his life. Oh, that I had been meek and submitted to God rather than walking in the pride of my own counsel! But I didn't, and because of that we all suffered in our own way.

Delighting and Waiting

The meek *delight in the* Lord, verse 4 of Psalm 37 tells us. The meek focus on the Lord, not on self. Their happiness is in Him, not in their circumstances. What a problem this is today, even in Christian circles! The focus is so much on *who I am* instead of who God is.

The meek say to God, "Lord, all I want in this life is to know You. I want to know You intimately. I want to know Your character, Your attributes. I want to know You in the power of Your resurrection and even in the fellowship of Your sufferings." The meek say, "I want to hide myself in all that You are."

"Delight yourself in the LORD," David said. Part of this delight in the Lord is a delight in His holiness, in His being set apart as someone infinitely greater and more pure and more glorious than we are. Our problem so often is that we don't understand the difference between God and man. We have a tendency to deify man in his human wisdom and understanding. And yet there's an infinite difference between God's wisdom and man's, and acknowledging this is where meekness begins.

That's why our society is in the trouble it is—because we don't know God. "Truth has stumbled in the street" (Isaiah 59:14); therefore we have very little knowledge and awareness and experience of the God of all truth.

A host of people will get the shock of their lives when they discover they're not going to heaven because they don't know God. They think they're "all right with the Man upstairs." But He is not a man, He is God, and He is not limited to "upstairs." The meek understand and delight in the fact that He is God and has no limits.

The meek also *commit their way to the Lord* (Psalm 37:5), entrusting Him with the ownership of the present and the future.

In a trial or affliction when they're tempted to react rather than act, the meek bow the knee before God and say, "Lord, I don't know how to handle this. I don't know how to respond to this person. I don't know what to do or which way to move. So I commit my way to You, and I trust You to lead me step by step." They trust that He's in charge.

The meek know that the Lord *will* lead. I've seen it in my own life countless times. He will lead—in our decisions, in all our responsibilities. I've seen it in His guidance for our ministry. You know, leadership is really hard, and that's why a lot of people don't want it. It's not just glory—not for godly leadership, that is. In ungodly leadership there's a lot of glory, though it's empty glory. But holy, godly leadership is hard, and the only way to be a godly leader is to commit your way to the Lord and then discover how He does indeed lead.

The meek *rest in the Lord* and *wait patiently for Him* (verses 7, 9, and 34). They *take refuge in Him* (verse 40). They're willing to allow the Lord to bring to pass what He wants to bring to pass in His own perfect timing.

A few months ago I received a letter from a woman expressing her joy and gratitude for life-changing discoveries she had experienced in Bible study. She said she had been saved for a number of years, "but until God did a great transforming work in my heart (and tongue!) my husband never saw me living a victorious Christian walk but more of a defeated one." As a result, she said, her unsaved husband was now able "to see the fruit of the Spirit lived out."

But then, three years ago, came a shattering development:

> My husband's seven-year-long affair was exposed by the woman's husband. This husband—my husband's "best friend"—had no clue. I had long had suspicions, but never any concrete proof; things were always explained away, and I didn't want to believe that my beloved was capable of such an immoral act. . . .
>
> When the truth came out about this affair, the truth about other women followed. It has been a habit of life for him for about 15 of our 17 years of marriage. . . .
>
> We stayed together another year. . . . The adulterous woman divorced her husband, then God hardened her heart against my husband (at my prayer). She met someone, and I prayed God would strengthen *that* relationship. He did, and they've been married over a year. My husband pined away for her. Then, on the rebound, he began seeing someone who looked a lot like her.
>
> We are not divorced, by God's grace and mercy! My husband's leaving me was a mutual thing. I knew he needed to chase whatever was calling him out in the world. He had said, "If I asked you for a divorce would you give me one?" I wanted to protest. But the Lord whispered, "He's an unbeliever; you must let him go." So I told him

what the Lord told me. I said lovingly and supportingly, "I'll even help you pack," and I did. Moving day was the hardest thing he said he'd ever had to do, leaving me and our two young teenage daughters. . . .

The day before he left, my husband said, "I don't want to get your hopes up; I might come home—but if I do it will be with a right heart."

I thought, *That is exactly how you will come home, with a heart right with God, cleansed by God!*

By the time the affair came out, the fruit of the Spirit had already been manifested, so my husband has never been judged or condemned by my mouth, nor seen any anger, resentment, bitterness, hatefulness, spitefulness, or jealousy in me. . . .

God has allowed no intimacy with my husband for several reasons that He has revealed to me, but He has totally preserved my heart and body, first for Himself, then for my husband, to be presented pure to him upon his return. When someone has a cousin they want me to meet because he's "perfect" for me, my heart feels betrayed at the very thought! No man has turned my head in my husband's two-year absence from my life!

Logically, I have no reason to wait for and to want this man; he's cheated through most of our marriage. I've never felt loved, cherished, admired, respected, or appreciated by him.

Why would I want him? Because God has a plan for us, because He's done something awesome in me and intends to in my husband, bringing honor and glory to Himself. He will be magnified to all who know our story and all who will know it in the future.

Since he left I've prayed that first, God would not allow a divorce in our marriage no matter what, because I reminded Him (and still do) that He says in His Word (Malachi 2:16), "I hate divorce." I've asked God also to save my husband and bring him home and to protect him, to put a hedge around him and not let anything happen to him except what can be used by God to bring him to God. Twice since he left there have been incidents where he should have been killed or severely injured, and God has been merciful and true in protecting my beloved.

Though my husband doesn't see us (or his parents, who live nearby) or talk to us often, he fully takes care of us financially—bills and groceries. This is God's provision for me and our daughters (who are also saved; they're 16 and 15 now). . . .

Please pray that soon, very soon, God will reveal Himself to my husband as He did to Paul on the Damascus Road and save him and lead him back home, totally cleansed, to his loving, waiting family.

This is a woman who has learned and is learning what it means to wait patiently for the Lord.

I received another letter from a woman who wants to get married to a man in prison, but her mother is opposed to it. "I'm writing to you because I can trust you," her letter said. "You know, my mother's friends are just a bunch of hypocrites. They're not forgiving him at all, and they're saying I shouldn't marry him."

The letter goes on to reveal that both have been married before, but otherwise they are from very different backgrounds. And even though he's in prison, they messed around in some way and did things they shouldn't have done. Now she seems bent on having her way.

I wrote back and said, "Don't marry him!" I told her that God could forgive this man, and I'm sure He had, but why should she rush into a marriage with a man in prison and try bringing two families together in an abnormal situation? I pointed out that while he was in prison (and she didn't know when he would be released), the man would not even be able to fulfill what Scripture says a husband must do. I told her, "I guarantee you that if you marry him in prison, you're going to be sorry."

Meekness is willing to wait patiently in the Lord.

While the meek wait patiently, they *cease from anger* and *forsake wrath* (Psalm 37:8). The meek refrain from anger at evildoers because they know, "Yet a little while and the wicked man will be no more" (verse 10).

And finally, the meek *look to the future*, with eternity stamped upon their eyes. They look not at present circumstances but at the things to come. They trust the Lord's promise that the meek who wait for the Lord will inherit the land (verses 9, 11, and 34) and "dwell in it forever" (verse 29). They know that "their inheritance will be forever" (verse 18), and that they themselves "will abide forever" (verse 27).

Search Psalm 37 in the presence of God, my friend, to discover for yourself what His gift of meekness means. And let your heart be ready to heed His Word of counsel, and to hear His Word of encouragement.

Who is wise and understanding among you?
Let him show by good conduct
that his works are done in the meekness of wisdom.

JAMES 3:13 (NKJV)

CHAPTER SIX

STRENGTH IN THE FACE OF STRESSES

Meekness in Action

MEEKNESS IS NOT weakness, and meekness is not apathy. The biblical meekness we're exploring does *not* mean you get slapped around and don't feel anything. Meekness does *not* mean you never have the spirit of a valiant warrior in you. Meekness does *not* mean you have no guts as a Christian.

Meekness is humble submission to God's sovereign will, yet it still knows to *resist* the devil—but *only after submitting to God*. Note the order in James 4:6-7: "God is opposed to the proud, but gives grace to the humble. *Submit therefore to God*. Resist the devil and he will flee from you." Then the focus goes back to God in verse 8: "*Draw near to God and He will draw near to you*." So both before and after resisting our enemy, your attention must always be on God, not on the devil. God never wants our focus to be on the enemy. He wants our focus on Himself. We're to always see the enemy in relationship to God and in relationship to who we are *in Christ*.

So you first submit to God. You come to Him and say, "God, You are sovereign. I come to You; I submit to You. I want whatever Your will is. If You want to afflict me, then I accept that because I know You do it only in love—for my good and for Your glory. Lord, I bow the knee and I say, Not my will but Thine be done."

Then you resist the devil. You pray, "God, in submitting to You I'm also telling You that I'll take my stand against the enemy." Then whatever comes from Satan, you refuse it. You resist it. You don't buy his lies.

Then again you draw near to God in submission and praise and thanksgiving and in the assurance that He'll draw near to you.

Meekness isn't weakness, and it isn't apathy. When you're meek it doesn't mean you're without passion or convictions. Look at Jesus' casting out the moneychangers from the temple. We see Him angry, but it was anger under control. Even there He was doing only and always what pleased His Father.

We also see Him calling the Pharisees "white-washed sepulchers"; he exposed these hypocrites for what they were. Likewise He was strong in the way He rebuked demons. Jesus was meek, but He never shied away from truth or responsibility or from holding others accountable. He stood for righteousness. In that sense He was never a doormat but always the Door! He was strong, in control of Himself and of the situation, because in perfect meekness He did and said only what was pleasing to the Father.

Meekness means you're in control—in the Spirit's control. You don't let the situation alter who you are or determine how you respond.

In meekness you acknowledge that affliction or oppression or humbling situations have come your way as situations permitted by God, yet you still do not let them rule over you.

WHEN PEOPLE SPEAK AGAINST YOU

Since Scripture describes Moses as the meekest man on earth, it's fitting to study closely an astonishing example of meekness from his life as we see how he responded in a stressful situation.

Moses and his brother Aaron and sister Miriam had come out of Egypt together with the children of Israel. Together they had seen great miracles of the Lord; together they had gone through the Lord's testings.

Then suddenly a relational conflict arose between them. It's described in Numbers 12:

> Then Miriam and Aaron spoke against Moses because of the Cushite woman whom he had married (for he had married a Cushite woman); and they said, "Has the LORD indeed spoken only through Moses? Has He not spoken through us as well?" And the LORD heard it. (verses 1-2)

Miriam and Aaron were being eaten up inside, and now they were reacting rather than acting. They were upset with Moses, so they made him a verbal target. They "spoke *against*" him.

And God heard it.

Have you ever had people speak against you? Have you ever had people misjudge your motives? I have. You can't be in leadership and not experience it. It can even happen in your family.

Sometimes what people are saying is so wrong and hurts so badly that I want to vindicate myself. I want to stand and shout, "Don't you know my heart?"

Years ago I went for the first time to teach a Bible class in the large and lovely Atlanta home of my dear friend Grace Kinser. Now, in Atlanta they dress differently than they do in Chattanooga, where I live. I walked into her home, and it was filled with truly wonderful women who were dressed to the teeth. I remember thinking I'd never seen so much gold in all my life—on their arms and their fingers and around their necks and hanging from their ears.

And I was wearing a plain, black missionary-barrel dress. I had tried to dress it up by wearing a beige jacket that didn't quite go with it. It was very cheap, but it was the best I had.

So that same day Grace handed me two new dresses. She wanted me to look nice. "And you know," she said, "it's just for the public, as far as not turning them off. But once they know you, it really doesn't matter." She loved me and didn't want these women to be distracted by my appearance and not hear my message. I was so thrilled. I could hardly wait to get home and try on those two new dresses. And Grace began to take me shopping and buy me clothes to keep me looking good.

One of the dresses she bought for me was very stylish with batwings around the sleeves and a slender cut. I'm slim through the hips, so I can usually get away with wearing that style of dress.

I decided to wear it to a book-signing party at Rich's Department Store in Atlanta. We were having several hundred people coming each week to our Bible study classes, and the store asked me to come and autograph copies of one of my books because they knew it would draw a lot of those Bible study women into their store.

Before I went, I checked that dress. "Now, does this look all right?" I asked the Bible study ladies. "It doesn't look too tight, does it?" And they assured me I looked all right. So I went to the store and had a wonderful time.

A few days later I received a letter from one of the Bible study women whose name I can't recall. (Don't feel bad if it was you, because I don't remember you anyway, darling.) In her letter this woman berated me for the way I had dressed at the book signing. She said I dressed like a harlot and asked what kind of example that was.

I read that letter and cried—first of all because I had dressed like that in my "BC" days—before Christ—and I certainly didn't want to look like a harlot now. I was horrified. "O Father, what have I done?"

Then, the more I thought about it, the more indignant I became. I thought, *Here you've been listening to my teaching all this time. Don't you know my heart? Why are you attacking me?*

I wondered why she didn't say, "Kay, darling, I've heard you teach and I know you want to be a woman of God. And I just want to tell you—because you probably didn't realize it—that the dress you wore at the department store is just a little too tight, and you need to get rid of it."

But she didn't come across that way with me, just as Aaron and Miriam didn't come across in a kind and gracious tone toward Moses.

So what do you do? You pray, "Lord, teach me to act rather than react."

I cried out to Him. "Lord, You know my heart. You know I don't want to look like a harlot anymore." That used to be what I wanted, believe me, before I got saved. But it wasn't my desire anymore. "And Lord, You know that I wouldn't disgrace You for anything in the world, and I wouldn't do a thing to bring shame to Your name."

I never wore that dress again. I gave it away to someone whose hips are slimmer than mine. And I refused to dwell on any negative thoughts about the woman who wrote the letter. I knew the Lord was teaching me a lesson about responding properly. I submitted to my heavenly Father, resisted the devil, and drew near to God to have Him draw near to me.

Numbers 12:2 tells us that "the Lord heard" what Miriam and Aaron were saying about Moses. There is a God who hears all and sees all and who knows it all, right down to the thoughts and intents of our hearts, because He looks not on the outward but on the inward.

And because He sees everything within, we discover His perspective on Moses in verse 3, which says, "Now the man Moses was very meek, above all the men which were upon the face of the earth" (KJV).

Why was Moses so meek? It certainly didn't seem to be natural for him. Before he left Egypt the first time, he was bent on delivering the children of Israel from slavery by the power of his own strength. And he was indeed a man of power. We read this about his young manhood in Acts 7:22: "Moses was educated in all the learning of the Egyptians, and he was a man of power in words and deeds."

He was a man of power. But what happened? Moses was broken. He had to flee from Egypt, and he lived in the wilderness for forty years as a shepherd. By the time God spoke to him from a burning bush, Moses was no longer powerful in deeds or words. He even questioned how he could be God's spokesman before Pharaoh, because as he put it, "I am slow of speech and slow of tongue" (Exodus 4:10).

God had brought Moses to a state of weakness, which many times brings forth in us a meekness we might not know otherwise. Thus when

God appeared to Moses at the burning bush and told him that he was going to deliver the children of Israel out of Egypt, Moses' response was, "Who am I that I should go to Pharaoh and that I should bring the sons of Israel out of Egypt?" Moses, now broken, was in the position where he could become a mighty man of God. God responded not by answering Moses' question but simply by letting Moses know who He is: I AM. "I am everything and anything you will ever need."

It is the meek who believe that God is everything, and they live accordingly, just like the Son who modeled such a lifestyle in the Spirit for us by doing only the works of the Father and speaking only the words of the Father.

Thus we read later of the meekness of Moses.

MEEKNESS AND HOLINESS

Then we come to an incident where Moses loses it. The sons of Israel began to complain. This time they were in the wilderness of Zin, and they lacked water. In the face of this adversity they became hostile toward Moses and Aaron as well as against God. And Moses did what he usually did: He fell facedown before the Lord in prayer. God responded and gave Moses His instructions for getting the water the people were crying for. Moses was to take his rod and speak to the rock, and water would come forth.

Those were God's orders. But it didn't quite happen like that. In anger Moses struck the rock twice with his staff instead of speaking to it as God specifically commanded (Numbers 20:1-13). At that moment, dear Moses—you have to feel sorry for the man when you see all it cost him to lead Israel's children for those forty long, hard years—failed to walk in the meekness that trusts God, the meekness that fears and delights in Him, the meekness that ceases from anger and forsakes wrath. And God said to him, "Because *you have not believed Me, to treat Me as holy* in the sight of the sons of Israel, therefore you shall not bring this assembly into the land which I have given them" (20:12).

The Lord's promise was that "the meek will inherit the land" (Psalm

37:11, NIV), and in His wise and loving sovereignty He chose to disqualify Moses for that inheritance because of this one failure to be meek. The first time that really hit me, I wept. How devastated Moses must have been! Yet it's in a circumstance such as this that we truly see the holiness of God and understand how serious He is about our meekness before Him. Without meekness, we can't and won't treat God as holy.

God made this clear again as He spoke later with Moses: "In the wilderness of Zin, during the strife of the congregation, *you rebelled against My command to treat Me as holy* before their eyes at the water" (Numbers 27:14). More than once Moses begged God to change His mind and let him enter the Promised Land. But God said, "Enough! Speak to Me no more of this matter" (Deuteronomy 3:26).

At the very end of Moses' life, God once more made clear His dealings with Moses over this incident. God told him to climb Mount Nebo so he could take a dying glimpse of the Promised Land. And He added:

> Then die on the mountain where you ascend, and be gathered to your people . . . because *you broke faith with Me* in the midst of the sons of Israel at the waters of Meribah-kadesh, in the wilderness of Zin, because *you did not treat Me as holy* in the midst of the sons of Israel. For you shall see the land at a distance, but you shall not go there, into the land which I am giving the sons of Israel. (Deuteronomy 32:50-52)

So did Moses discredit God or complain about the treatment he was getting from God's hand? No, in meekness again Moses sang praise to God for His perfect fairness. How I love the way Moses, without hesitation or any bitterness, called God "the Rock":

> The Rock! His work is perfect,
> For all His ways are just;
> A God of faithfulness and without injustice,
> Righteous and upright is He.
>
> (Deuteronomy 32:4)

Moses knew His God. He had slipped away from meekness in the incident at the rock, but we see his meekness in Deuteronomy at the end of his life, just as we see it back in Numbers 12.

OUR MEEKNESS WHEN GOD IS ANGRY

Consider how Aaron and Miriam must have trembled when they heard God's voice calling them after they had spoken harshly to Moses. Numbers 12:4 says:

> And suddenly the LORD said to Moses and Aaron and to Miriam, "You three come out to the tent of meeting." So the three of them came out.

Can you imagine the scene? Can you just hear the sound of His voice? *"YOU THERE COME OUT TO THE TENT OF MEETING."*

God knew what was going on. And now He would deal with it.

Moses had a tent where he would go and meet with the Lord, and a cloud would come down, and the *shekinah* glory of the Lord would descend and hover over the tent. We learn in Exodus that whenever this happened, the people of Israel would stand in the doorways of their own tents and watch. God loved Moses and met with him, and Moses loved God—and God knew Moses' heart. He knew Moses was a meek man.

> Then the LORD came down in a pillar of cloud and stood at the doorway of the tent, and He called Aaron and Miriam. (verse 5)

Picture yourself in their place, and hear their summons: *"STEP FORWARD, AARON. STEP FORWARD, MIRIAM."*

> When they had both come forward, He said, "Hear now My words: If there is a prophet among you, I, the LORD, shall make Myself known to him in a vision. I shall speak with him in a dream.
> "Not so with My servant Moses. He is faithful in all My

household; with him I speak mouth to mouth, even openly, and not in dark sayings, and he beholds the form of the LORD. *Why then were you not afraid to speak against My servant, against Moses?"*

So the anger of the LORD burned against them and He departed. (verses 5-9)

Aaron and Miriam, along with Moses, heard God's own commendation here of Moses' faithfulness and of the extraordinary relationship God had with him—and only with him. It was something Miriam and Aaron already knew about, and it should have made them meek before God and meek in their relationship with Moses. But they weren't.

Therefore God was angry—*burning angry.*

And you know, it helps me to realize that God gets angry. Does it help you? As a matter of fact, in the Scriptures the word *anger* is connected with God more often than with anyone else.

One day after teaching a session on forgiveness, a woman walked down the aisle, and I stepped forward to meet her. She was extremely overweight and unkempt, with greasy hair and no makeup. She wore tight jeans and an old sweatshirt. There was nothing feminine about her.

Her teeth were clenched, and her lips were tightened. "I cannot forgive my father," she said.

"Oh honey, come here and talk to me," I said. We sat on the steps leading to the speaker's platform. "Tell me," I asked her, "why can't you forgive your father?"

She told me her story. Her father had molested her and gotten her pregnant and forced her to have an abortion. Then he got her pregnant a second time. He let her have the baby, but it was born deformed and died. Then he got her pregnant a third time, and she moved out. "I couldn't take it anymore," she said.

The baby was born—a little girl—but it was deformed and lived only a year.

So the young woman tried to take her life. She ended up in a mental institution. In a group therapy session, they brought her parents in. When she told her story, her father jumped up and called her a liar and a harlot and a tramp—and worse. So she shut her mouth and said nothing more.

As we sat there and I listened, she spoke through clenched teeth and taut lips.

I looked at her and said, "Honey, that makes me so angry."

Her mouth flew open, and her eyes grew wide. "No one's ever said that before!" she said.

"Oh, honey," I answered, "not only does it make me angry, but it makes God angry."

Yes, there is a righteous anger. God communicated it here to Moses and Miriam and Aaron. And once God had gone from their presence, the evidence and result of His anger remained:

> But when the cloud had withdrawn from over the tent, behold, Miriam was leprous, as white as snow. As Aaron turned toward Miriam, behold, she was leprous. (verse 10)

Miriam had instantly become a leper, already in the advanced stages of this awful disease.

Her brother Aaron immediately pleaded to Moses for help on his sister's behalf:

> "Do not account this sin to us, in which we have acted foolishly and in which we have sinned. Oh, do not let her be like one dead, whose flesh is half eaten away." (verses 11-12)

God was angry with a righteous anger. So did Moses also react in human anger? He easily could have said, "Lord, she's hurting the ministry. Get her out of here!"

While I was teaching Bible classes in Atlanta, a woman began coming up at the end of each class and criticizing my teaching. She had studied biblical Greek while I got my Greek through *Vines Expository Dictionary*, the same way I was teaching our students to get it. With a face like cast iron, this woman would come up when the class ended and let me have it about my teaching.

I began to pray: "Lord, I'm sure this woman is a hindrance, and you need to remove her from this class."

What was I doing? I was reacting to a difficult situation instead of acting. There's nothing meek about that kind of prayer.

Finally the Lord brought me to the point of praying, "Lord, You're in charge. You've allowed this woman to keep coming. What do You want to teach me through her?"

Then He let me find out how badly this woman was hurting. When I heard about her problems, I realized she was in such a mess that she probably belonged in a mental institution.

As I prayed, the Lord impressed me that I was to begin loving her.

So I started hugging the woman. Have you ever hugged a plank? She would jerk her head to the side and her body would stiffen. And the Lord said, "Keep hugging, keep hugging."

So I kept hugging—but it wasn't much fun until I noticed that she was becoming less like a plank and more like plywood—still firm but with a little more give. And then she began to change even more.

Thanks be to God, I saw Him soften that woman and heal her. When I received a letter from her saying how much she missed me, I could answer, "I really miss you, too." God could and did change her, just as He changed this mess called me.

MEEKNESS IS MINE

So how did Moses respond to Miriam's leprosy?

> And Moses cried out to the LORD, saying, "O God, heal her, I pray!" (verse 13)

Moses was meek. God heard his prayer, and eventually He did heal Miriam, but only in such a way and timing that the lesson He wanted to teach wasn't lost.

As far as we know, Moses himself wrote the first five books of the Old Testament, including the book of Numbers, where we find the verse about his being more meek than any other person alive. He was being honest, under the inspiration of the Holy Spirit.

And, beloved, what about you and me? Under the Spirit's power and control, can we say, "By the grace of God, *meekness is mine*"?

His sovereignty rules over all.

<small>PSALM 103:19</small>

<small>CHAPTER SEVEN</small>

FACING THE PAIN

The Safety of His Sovereignty

I AWOKE EARLY but rolled over to get another hour of sleep. I knew that my travel—a flight from Israel to Saint Petersburg, Russia—would keep me up all night.

Forty-five minutes later I was awakened in pain. Nausea overwhelmed my aching body, demanding that I rise. I knew in my spirit that I wasn't going to Russia as planned. All I could assume was that for some reason, the Lord wanted me to stay in Jerusalem.

All through the day my body groaned, longing for the sweet respite of sleep. Meanwhile, I couldn't help but think of five brothers in the Lord whom I'd never seen or known—but whose situation the Lord had earlier brought to my attention. These five were pastors of "house" churches in China. They were now in prison, and one of them had been sentenced to death by the authorities.

I was in a comfortable bed; they were in a prison cell. I could go to the hospital to receive the needed fluids lost in my bout with this virus while in all probability these five men were being denied even a cup of cold water. I had the love and attention of my husband and friends and the care of a personal physician; they were left to the wiles of their enemies where the tender hands of friends and loved ones could not reach or comfort them.

I prayed for them. My own sudden onset of pain, in a sickness I'd never before experienced and which would pass in only two days, awakened a consciousness of the more enduring pain of others. I was flooded with an empathy that seeped deep into the cracked and parched condition of my dried-up heart. And I was newly aware of the fact that when you're without pain, it's so easy to forget the pain of others.

WHEN THE PAIN IS DEEPEST

King Solomon wrote, "I looked again at all the acts of oppression which were being done under the sun. And behold I saw the tears of the oppressed and that they had no one to comfort them; and on the side of their oppressors was power, but they had no one to comfort them" (Ecclesiastes 4:1).

We, too—probably even more than Solomon—live in an age of oppression and incredible pain. If we had access to the naked truth, our times would probably be recognized as having unprecedented anguish. More people have been martyred for their faith in Jesus Christ in our days than in all the previous centuries combined. Besides these persecuted believers, multitudes more can be added to the rolls of suffering souls—each precious one a victim of those who have no fear of God and who in their consuming, unbridled lust brutally inflict and wound others in the rage of their passions. Think of the children and women and men who have suffered unspeakable emotional, physical, and sexual abuse.

Perhaps you too have experienced such pain—enough to be awakened, sympathetic, and sensitive to the hurt of others.

You might at times feel lonely in your pain. Or maybe your pain is actually born of loneliness, which is one of the most common hurts people deal with today. This shouldn't be true of those in the body of Christ, but unfortunately it is.

But you're *not* alone. Pain is everywhere. Its victims may camouflage their inward suffering by external decorum, but "even in laughter the heart may be in pain" (Proverbs 14:13).

Life is fraught not only with stress and tense relationships and everyday disappointments but also with acute, piercing *pain*. It's part of the trials and tribulations bred into our lives, like weeds in what would otherwise be a garden. Pain is here (and will be until Jesus comes) because of sin and sinful men, and essentially there's nothing we can do to change that.

If you're going to respond to this inescapable pain in meekness, without murmuring or disputing, if you're going to act and not react, if you're going to trust God and not try to control and manipulate, then you have to know two things:

You have to realize that God is in control, that He is sovereign.

And you have to understand who He is. You have to know God's heart, His character, His attributes.

For those reasons alone, you can act in meekness and in the power of the Spirit rather than react in the passion of the flesh.

And when the pain is deepest and sharpest—engulfing the world around us and infiltrating our own hearts and lives as well—it becomes a testing and proving ground both for our belief in the sovereignty of God and for our understanding of His heart.

THE MOST POWERFUL TRUTH

The single most powerful, liberating, peace-giving truth I've ever learned in God's Word is the fact that He is sovereign. It has been a mainstay in my life. Resting in the sovereignty of God has held me through all the trials, all the pain—everything. *God is in control*, and therefore in *everything* I can give thanks—not because of the situation but because of the One who directs and rules over it.

We find our joy *not* in the heat of the flame but in the fact that the

Refiner is right there controlling it. The fire is a *controlled* fire. It isn't a purposeless fire, and it isn't a fire to destroy us. It's a purifying fire.

Therefore we don't focus on the flames or stare at the fuel being added to make the blaze hotter. If we did, we would only want out of the situation. But by keeping our eyes on the Refiner, who never leaves the silver and the crucible unattended, we can endure, because we trust Him.

I can look back at every single trial and tragedy, at every hurt and every suffering in my life, and I can say, "God, You've used this to make me more like Jesus." From the picky little things like having to stand in line when some salesclerk is inefficient, to the piercing pains like my husband's committing suicide or my father's death—I can hold on to those things in the light of the knowledge of God's sovereignty. I can walk in meekness in submission to God, knowing He has used these disappointments and *will* use them to make me more and more like Jesus.

LOOKING BACK

I used to cry and moan and groan over the fact that I was already twenty-nine by the time I was saved. I once prayed in bitterness, "God, why couldn't You have saved me when I was a teenager? Why do I have to have these negative memories from my past? Why do I have to battle with my thought life over these awful things I've done? Why couldn't I have known one man instead of many? Why couldn't my kids have had one father instead of two? Why couldn't I have a model life, a dream life, the kind of life I planned? *Why?*"

And God showed me: "Kay, if you'll quit moaning and crying, I'll use these things to make you into someone I can use in the lives of others to show them that no matter where they've been, no matter how deep the hole, no matter how painful the trial, there's hope. There is victory."

God knew, and God was in control.

Before the foundation of the world, He knew the day I would be born and the day I'd be born again. He wasn't shocked when this divorcee with two sons suddenly got saved, when she went down on her knees for the first time in her life in genuine, heartfelt prayer. God wasn't saying, "What am I going to do with her?" He knew, He was in control, and I was there at His timing, at the time that pleased Him, according to Galatians 1:15-16.

Before time began God knew the personality I would have—my nature and disposition and temperament that He Himself planned and put together. When I've complained about it, my husband has told me, "Honey, God made you *you*. That's what makes Kay *Kay*." Knowing and believing that God wants to express Himself through me, I can say with David (just as you can), "I am fearfully and wonderfully made" (Psalm 139:14).

Especially in my youth I wanted to change my personality. *Yuck, I can't stand you*, I thought about myself. *You're so awkward.* So often I opened my mouth and stuck my foot in—and what a long skinny foot it was.

So many times I found myself reliving a situation where I'd blown it and telling myself, "If only I'd done this or that." In my mind I could see myself doing what was right—and making it big. I pictured myself as a beauty queen. I thought I'd look so good riding on a float. (I could cover up those skinny, awful feet with a long dress.)

I just wanted to be discovered. I wanted somebody to notice me, to say, "This kid has potential."

I went to twelve grade schools and four high schools. Only six months before I was to graduate we moved again, this time from New York to Ohio. We hadn't been in New York that long, but I had worked like a dog so I'd have a list of wonderful achievements under my yearbook picture and everyone would be quite impressed. But we moved, and in Ohio I was lucky to get even my picture in the yearbook.

God knew, and He was in control.

He knew when and how I would meet my first husband. And He knew Tom would commit suicide.

Tom used to tell me that he was thinking about killing himself. And thinking I could bluff him out of it, I'd say, "Do a good job, so I get your money."

God knew the depth of the darkness I was in, and He knew He would save me from it.

God also knew everything that would happen afterward. He knew He was holding Jack out there on the mission field, keeping him eligible even with all those single missionary women drooling over him. He was reserving Jack for me, waiting to bring him into my life at a special time. He always knew at what moment He would put us on the same street corner at the same time so we could meet.

God knew all that—but I didn't. Even when I became a new child of His, He didn't inform me. He gave me His promises, but He didn't tell me what would happen to me.

HELD IN GOD'S HANDS

One evening when I was a brand-new believer, I was talking with a single Christian man I'd met, David Pancer. At the time I was working on a research team at Johns Hopkins University, and earlier that day, while I was typing, a shocking thought came to my mind: *All this stuff about Christianity is just a bunch of bull____.* I was horrified.

I burst into tears as I told Dave about it. How could such a terrible thought enter my mind? Dave explained to me that this was from the devil. It was an enemy attack that I was to resist and that God had allowed in my life to teach and strengthen me.

Dave leaned forward, took off his college ring, held it out in his palm, then clenched his fist tight. I can still see his blanched knuckles. He said the ring so tightly wrapped in his hand was like me in God's hands now that I had come to know Jesus Christ. And he said, "No one can touch you without God's permission."

I understood—and I kept growing in my understanding over the years as I studied God's Word and as I remembered that ring hidden in Dave's hand: No one could touch me or speak to me or do a thing to me unless God allowed it, because He is sovereign. Nothing could reach me unless it was filtered through His fingers of love.

I'd never seen a real man like Dave who knew the Bible the way he did. And I wanted to be his wife. But Dave received counsel that he shouldn't marry me because I was divorced. With all my being, I believe God used that counsel for my good. But at the time I thought I would die.

The day Dave told me he couldn't marry me because of my divorce, I thought, *That is so un-Christlike! It's so contrary to God's Word! Has God forgiven all my sins except that one?*

I jumped out of his car (leaving him sitting there), ran into my townhouse, and raced up the stairs. *I'll just jump out the window,* I thought. *That will serve him right, and it will make a good scene.* (I knew it wouldn't kill me, since it was only the second floor.)

But I flung myself on the bed instead of out the window, and I bawled like mad. I decided not to control myself. I sobbed and sobbed until this thought came to me as a question from the Lord: *You've been telling everyone that I am adequate for anything. Am I?*

My response was, "Yes, Lord," and I blew my nose, got off the bed, and went downstairs. God was adequate.

I would accept this without murmuring, without disputing, without resisting anymore. I humbled myself under the mighty hand of God.

Eventually God brought me to the place where I could say, "Father, if You want me to go back to Tom, I will. If You want us to be married again, even though I don't love him, I'll do that. I'll do what You tell me to do."

I had it in my heart to write Tom a letter and tell him how I felt. But before the letter was written, I received a phone call informing me that Tom had hanged himself in his apartment.

Immediately I tried to call my pastor, but he wasn't home. So I talked instead to the One who is always home.

I fell to my knees beside my bed and cried out, "Father!" That was all.

God said three things to me in those moments.

First He brought to mind a verse I hadn't purposely memorized and for which I didn't know the reference. It was this: "All things work together for good to those that love God, to those who are called according to His purpose."

The second thing He brought to my mind was, "In everything give thanks, for this is the will of God in Christ Jesus concerning you."

And the third thing was this thought: *I will not give you anything you cannot bear*. It wasn't a Scripture verse, but later I learned the truth of 1 Corinthians 10:13—that no temptation (or trial or testing) has overtaken us "but such as is common to man; and God is faithful, who will not allow you to be tempted beyond what you are able."

I was learning that meekness *is* possible as an inwrought grace of the soul. We *can* walk in it.

And for me to allow God to produce it in my life—especially with my take-charge kind of personality—I've had to keep growing in understanding who God is and the fact that He's in control.

GOD IS GOD

God is sovereign. When you spell out that word, you also find the word *reign*. God reigns. He rules over all. He's the ultimate ruler of everything that goes on in the universe. Nothing—*nothing*—anywhere or at any time is outside His sovereign rulership.

Understanding the sovereignty of God isn't easy unless you just see that *God is God*. Years ago the Lord gave me the gift of meeting Addy, a godly woman nine years older in the Lord than I am (and it shows). She was raised in a Christian home but rejected those roots and was totally opposed to what the Word of God had to say—until one day God brought her to Himself. "I knew from the day I got saved that He was Lord," she said. "I understood that He was God, period." *God, period*. Nothing else needed. No debate.

Addy said she lifted her hand in a kind of salute that day and told Him, "Lord, even if You want to send me to hell, that's all right, because You're God."

He is God, and He is sovereign. And when we stay close to Scripture to measure our understanding of this concept by the plumb line of His Word, we see again and again how God is in supreme and total and complete and absolute control.

David said in Psalm 103:19, "The LORD has established His throne in the heavens; and *His sovereignty rules over all.*" In the next two verses we see how even the angels fit into this:

> Bless the LORD, you His angels,
>> Mighty in strength, who perform His word,
>> Obeying the voice of His word!
> Bless the LORD, all you His hosts,
>> You who serve Him, doing His will.

The angels obey the Lord because He's the sovereign God of all the universe. "*All* His hosts" serve Him, doing His will. Both good angels and fallen angels do the bidding of God. His sovereignty rules over all.

Nothing can stop God from carrying out His determined will. "The LORD of hosts has sworn saying, 'Surely, just as I have intended so it has happened, and just as I have planned so it will stand. . . . For the LORD of hosts has planned, and who can frustrate it? And as for His stretched-out hand, who can turn it back?'" (Isaiah 14:24,27).

God, and *only* God, is able to be sovereign. Only God is omniscient—all-knowing. Only He is omnipresent—present everywhere so that He's never busy in one place to the neglect of the situation somewhere else. *He is always there.* And only God is omnipotent—all-powerful.

Only God is in charge, and if you and I understand this, we can bow the knee before Him.

Sometimes the only way we can learn this is the hard way. For a time King Nebuchadnezzar of Babylon, the most powerful man on earth in his day, was quite impressed with himself and with his kingdom, which he assumed had been brought into being with his own hands. He had forgotten *El Elyon*—God Most High. So through the prophet Daniel, God pronounced His judgment upon Nebuchadnezzar: he was to lose his mind and live like an animal until he recognized "that the Most High is ruler over the realm of mankind" (Daniel 4:25).

By the time his humbling punishment ended, Nebuchadnezzar had learned a rich lesson that all of us need to ponder:

But at the end of that period I, Nebuchadnezzar, raised my eyes toward heaven, and my reason returned to me, and *I blessed the Most High* and praised and honored Him who lives forever; for His dominion is an everlasting dominion, and His kingdom endures from generation to generation.

And all the inhabitants of the earth are accounted as nothing, but *He does according to His will* in the host of heaven and among the inhabitants of earth; and no one can ward off His hand or say to Him, "What hast Thou done?" (4:34-35)

God does according to His will. He does it in the host of heaven as well as among the inhabitants of the earth—with everyone, whether kings or commoners, great or small, whether angels or demons or Satan himself. No one can hold back God's hand or stop His plans, and no one has the license or prerogative to question Him with, "What hast Thou done?" He is the Most High, He is sovereign, and He's in control. Nebuchadnezzar finally recognized that the only permanent power and the only absolute power belongs to God.

God is sovereign, and He bestows positions of authority and power over the nations to whomever He wishes—even to dictators and corrupt officials, even to those who deny His very existence. In His greatness He allows them a time of prominence and power, yet ultimately even their wicked abuse of authority will be seen to serve God's purposes and will result in His glory.

I once went to an election-night party for a godly man who was a congressional candidate and who seemed to have a good chance of winning. But as the returns came in, the story was otherwise. It was a disappointing night. He knew God had called him to run, and he had stated that publicly. But God did not allow him to win.

There was a woman at the party that night who had been in a Sunday school class I taught. When a TV news crew arrived for interviews, she began lashing out at the media people. Someone tried to stop her, but she said, "I don't care! They didn't treat him right, and I'm going to make a scene."

I called out her name, and she turned and said, "Oh, Kay—I didn't see you there." Then she said, "I'm mad."

"I understand," I told her, "but you and I know that God is sovereign. He's in control. We don't know why, but for some reason God didn't allow our man to get elected. And you can't act this way, because you'll hurt that young man's cause, and even more importantly you'll hurt the cause of Jesus Christ."

BUT WHAT ABOUT TRAGEDY?

But you say, "What about those truly horrible and cruel things that happen? You can't tell me God permitted a tragedy. You can't tell me He allowed something that's absolutely evil. Don't tell me God permitted this catastrophe, this disaster, when He's omniscient and omnipresent and omnipotent. Don't tell me He knew all about it beforehand and could have stopped it."

And I say, Reason with me, beloved. Let's follow out your thinking. Let's see where it leads.

Let's assume God did *not* permit it, that God in His nature would not allow such a thing to happen. And yet it did happen. So by saying God didn't permit it, you're saying something or somebody is greater than God.

If God didn't permit this tragedy, who did?

Was it just an accident? Was it fate—just "whatever will be, will be," or whatever fate is? Are we left abandoned in an orderless world, where nothing can fulfill God's promise of all things working for good?

Or was it Satan? If bad things come only from Satan and God has no power to stop them and no authority over Satan, then whose hands are we really in?

Was it some other person? A drunk driver causes an accident in which a child is killed—did that drunk driver in that situation have more power than God? Does God have no ultimate power over that which He has created?

In this line of thought, whether it was an accident or fate or Satan or man that caused the tragedy, one of those had to overcome God to do it. And if it overcame God, then God is really not God.

When you start thinking, "There's no way the God I know and love could allow this if He's the God I think He is," you're on track to the obvious outcome that God *isn't* who you think He is. In fact, He isn't God at all. That's the only conclusion this line of thought can yield—and it's an impossible conclusion.

So *there is no other cause* behind it all. There is only God behind it. Whatever the part that Satan or man played in the tragedy, neither could have done it unless God gave permission.

Even killer storms and natural disasters are not from mother nature, whoever that could be, but only from Father God. Read the Old Testament; you cannot escape the sovereignty of God!

There is no other cause, and there is no other god. Our sovereign Lord tells us, "See now that I, I am He, and *there is no god besides Me*; it is I who put to death and give life. I have wounded, and it is I who heal; and there is no one who can deliver from My hand" (Deuteronomy 32:39). He gives life, and He also puts to death. He heals, and He also wounds. Over all of it, over everything, God is in charge.

Every disappointment—even if it's tragic and evil—is *His* appointment. I may not like His appointment or agree with it, but God is in charge. Nothing happens apart from His permission. He is the ultimate authority, the ultimate cause, and He has the ultimate responsibility for all that goes on. That's why He commands us, "In everything give thanks; for this is God's will for you in Christ Jesus" (1 Thessalonians 5:18). What possible reason could there be to give thanks in everything if God isn't sovereign? Why should we thank Him if He isn't responsible, if He's not in control?

If God is not sovereign, we're in trouble. We'd better panic, because Satan, the prince of this world, can do anything he wants to us. But God *is* sovereign, and therefore whatever happens to us has been filtered through His fingers of love, designed for our good and for His glory.

Pain and tragedy are the proving grounds of our belief in this. So often you hear people say, "I was fine with God until He let *that* happen." You see their bitterness, their anger, their resentfulness, and the spiritual self-destruction and defeat that result. When tragedy struck, they cried, "No, God! No!" and then walked away from Him, because they wrongly thought of Him only as a cosmic Santa Claus.

But other people, going through the same kind of tragedy, come through it stronger than ever and more faithful than ever because they cling to the sovereignty of God.

On Interstate 35 in north Texas on a rainy July morning just a few years ago, a proud grandfather was driving toward Dallas with a precious cargo: four of his grandchildren. The children had just enjoyed a family vacation at their grandparents' farm. (Their parents and their ten-year-old brother had earlier returned home to Dallas for the boy's Little League baseball game.)

Thunderstorms that began the night before still rumbled in the skies. Heavy rains made the highway's surface slick. Suddenly the car hydroplaned out of control. It crossed the median and slammed into another car.

The grandfather and three of the children—twelve-year-old Rebecca, eight-year-old Sarah, and five-year-old Mary Catherine—were killed at once. The fourth child, three-year-old John, died the next day in a Dallas hospital.

What more piercing tragedy could there be for a family?

But the mother—who lost her father as well as four of her five children—had been a student under our ministry, and she understood the sovereignty of God. The children's obituaries in the *Dallas Morning News* reflected their parents' trusting faith.

John's included these words:

> Boy of all boys, lover of nature, climber of trees, cowboy, son, and brother is now resting in the loving arms of his Master in eternity. . . . John loved and protected his sisters, Rebecca, Sarah, and Mary Catherine, and joins them in glory with their grandfather, face to face with their Lord and Savior. John was a foot soldier and servant

of others. This boy loved to rock in his mother's arms and now he is rocking in the arms of Jesus. He was a gift to all who knew him. We will miss you greatly, beloved son. . . .

Mary Catherine's obituary described her as "full of joy," and added:

Mary had the gift of hospitality and will be remembered for her ready smile. She was always the first to greet her daddy at the door. Her heart poured forth in song, worshiping God, and she encouraged others to love God for He truly was her God. All God's creation—animals, flowers, and His people—found refuge in her tender care. . . .

Sarah was described as "tenderhearted" and "full of mercy."

Sarah . . . loved God's creation and all things that needed tending. Sarah, in her quiet way, is now tending God's gardens. We will always remember the fullness of joy in Sarah, with her gift of help and serving. We treasure her faithful prayers for all she loved. We picture you, sweet Sarah, at the feet of Jesus and we know it is well with your soul. . . .

Rebecca, the oldest, was commended for having led all her siblings to the Lord. Her parents called her "a sister in Christ, a friend, and companion."

At her tender age Rebecca possessed an extraordinary depth of character and spiritual maturity. Jesus was not only her Savior, but her Lord. She had answered His call to commitment and walked in both the nobility and beauty of conviction. She was not a creature of this earth but truly a princess of heaven. . . . Gifted with discernment, Rebecca used her wisdom to encourage others to godliness. . . . Those of us who knew this outstanding young woman can truly picture her enjoying the delights of her new home. . . .

Also included in each child's obituary were these words:

> This family is so grateful to have had this blessing from God, even
> for such a fleeting time. . . . The Darby family looks forward to
> being together again in eternity with the Master and Shepherd. . . .

A heart-wrenching tragedy, yes. A thousand mourners gathered at the family's memorial service, many in tears.

The parents wept as well under the enormous pain and loss. They knew that it's all right to weep in the tragedies, to feel the pain, to hurt from the loss. But they demonstrated that we're not to be controlled by it or overwhelmed or demolished—because the Refiner is there.

THE REFINER UNDERSTANDS

He is there, and He sees our tears and feels our grief. In fact, Jesus weeps with us, just as He shed tears when He saw Martha's weeping over her dead brother, Lazarus.

And remember, beloved, that God *personally* knows all about tragedy. There has been no greater tragedy in history than the crucifixion of His perfect and sinless Son. Yet only weeks later, God's children understood His sovereignty even in this. In the prayer recorded in the book of Acts, they acknowledged before God that when Herod and Pilate and the Jews and Gentiles put Jesus to death, they were doing only "whatever Thy hand and Thy purpose predestined to occur" (4:28).

Peter proclaimed the same thing on the Day of Pentecost: Jesus was "delivered up by *the predetermined plan and foreknowledge of God*" to be "nailed to a cross by the hands of godless men" (2:23).

God sees us in our grief, and He knows and understands. And in His loving sovereignty He does not expect us to go through these trials with stoic coldness. He doesn't say, "Quit your crying," or, "Stop feeling that way."

David prayed, "Put my tears in Thy bottle; are they not in Thy book?"

(Psalm 56:8). And God does that for us. He collects our tears. And so we can say as David did,

> This I know, that *God is for me.* . . .
> In the LORD, whose word I praise,
> In God I have put my trust,
> I shall not be afraid.
>
> (verses 9-11)

One of the letters I treasure most was written a number of years ago by a woman in our ministry's Bible studies. It's faded and worn from my having read it so often to others because of its testimony to the victory that can be ours when we hold fast our borders of faith. Let me share it with you.

I received a call from the president of our son's Bible college about 11:30 P.M., telling us that our son was missing and thought to be dead. The night that followed is lost somewhere in my subconscious, but by morning my husband was on his way to our son's school. My house was full of bodies and faces. The next call came around 10:30 A.M. They had found our son's body. He was—is—with the Lord.

The day before I had spent a wonderful time with the Lord. Now I prayed, "If You aren't as real today as You were yesterday, I don't need You tomorrow."

I wish I could express how very real He was and is. . . .

I had to lie in bed that day, for my body could not hold me. But, Kay, I was strong in spirit. . . . When I couldn't trust my thoughts, I would cry out, "I TRUST YOU."

I remember when Daddy died, you were teaching Romans— daring to say God was sovereign. I had been taught this doctrinally, but you made it so personal. I was so mad at you, but I wanted it to be true so badly. You said, "The events of our lives are filtered through fingers of love." Week after week, you pounded away— "filtered through fingers of love." It rang in my heart: HE LOVES ME!

I have said time after time: "He doesn't test us to see if we will fail but to show us how strong we are. He proves us."

I didn't realize how much He had built into my life the safety of His sovereignty until He asked me to see our son's death as an act of love. I am free in His love. Free to feel pain. Free to know joy.

This dear sister found freedom in the safety of God's sovereignty—a freedom that overflowed in joy because she would not allow the enemy to invade her faith or to take captive her thoughts and chain her in bitterness.

I know the topic of God's sovereignty can seem so heavy—especially if you don't study God's Word on your own and if you believe only what you've been taught from the Word by someone else. But take what I am saying and test it with what you read through the whole Word of God. If it meets the test then live by it, and you'll know how to handle every disappointment, no matter how painful. You'll rejoice not in the tragedy itself but in the fact that *God is with you in it*. You'll know that He'll never leave you nor forsake you, and that He'll not give you more than you can bear. You'll know that this tragedy has a purpose and that it's God's will for you to respond in this way.

GET THE WHOLE PICTURE

Those who say God wouldn't allow bad things to happen to good people are not seeing the whole picture.

A passage that's so helpful to me is Isaiah 45:6-7, where God said, "I am the LORD [the word for Jehovah, the self-existent One], and there is no other, *the One forming light and creating darkness, causing well-being and creating calamity*. I am the LORD who does *all* these."

God is behind both the light and the darkness. He causes both the good things and the calamities. The Hebrew word here for *calamity* can also be translated as "adversity." The King James Version renders it as "evil." God is behind it *all*.

At times this may not square with my feelings about God. So I must go beyond my feelings and look to God Himself and see who He is in His Word.

That's why we need to know the character of this One who gives life and who puts to death, who wounds and who heals. We need to know His attributes. We need to know His names, because His names express His character, and the name of the Lord is a strong tower that the righteous can run to and be safe (Proverbs 18:10).

Isaiah 45:7, by the way, is from a prophecy given to Cyrus, king of Persia, but it was written well over a century before he came to the throne—more evidence of the sovereignty of God.

"Consider the work of God," we're told in Ecclesiastes 7:13-14, "for who is able to straighten what He has bent? In the day of prosperity be happy, but in the day of adversity consider—*God has made the one as well as the other....*" Our days of adversity are from God just as much as our days of prosperity.

One year, a few days before my birthday, I opened a box that included a thank-you letter from a woman who had been studying under our ministry for years. The letter told this story:

> Kay, I watched my mother suffer and die this summer from colon cancer. She had cancer six different times.... The last five years she had many doses of chemo and test after test and five major surgeries. Kay, I would have fallen away without the teaching that I had from you. Time after time the Lord brought to my heart Scripture that had been implanted. The sovereignty of God held me and still does in the low times, for I miss her so much....

She then recalled a time when she and her mother had attended our Bible study classes together.

> What a special gift the Lord gave me to study the Word with my own mother. I never dreamed that would come about. He is so good. He gave us such special times, close intimate sharing.

Mother and Dad lost a child four years old before my birth. He was run over and was buried on Christmas Eve. One day, a special day, Mother had been studying about anointing with oil, and she asked me to anoint her and pray for her. Afterwards she asked me why God took Jimmy. Was it His will? She didn't understand.

I prayed so much for an answer. No pat answers will do, but somehow I told her God loved Jimmy and He was in control and knew what awaited him, and decided to take him home early.

Kay, I believe that this began an inner healing in my mother. About a year before she died, she told me she burned Jimmy's clothes. You see, she had kept those clothes he died in for forty years.

Although Mother wasted away physically, from 117 pounds to 60, I believe she grew in her spirit until the day she went to heaven.

Along with her letter, inside the box, was a white handkerchief trimmed in lace and two sown pearls. "Kay, the handkerchief was my mother's," the letter explained, "and I want you to have it."

Yes, we're truly able to grow in spirit when we understand both the sovereignty of God and His loving character.

Though I know these truths, I still have to keep reminding myself of them when I meet with disappointment: We can act rather than react, we can trust rather than mistrust, because God is sovereign. When we say to Him, "I give You complete control," we're giving that control to the One who rules over all the universe. We may not see it and understand it now—but then, we really can't see beyond the end of our noses, can we? We can only see this minute, and not the eternal future.

But that's all right, because God can and does see the future. He sees and knows it all, and He is all-powerful, and He is here, and therefore we can act in meekness. We don't have to try taking control of the situation. We can bow the knee and submit to Him and say, "Lord, if it pleases You, it pleases me."

You may need to ask now for His forgiveness for not submitting totally and completely and absolutely to Him in some painful trial you've encountered or for reacting in the flesh instead of responding in meekness. You may need to let go of some things. Whatever you seek forgiveness for, beloved, He will hear your prayer.

Then you can say, even as Job said in his pain, "The LORD gave and the LORD has taken away. Blessed, blessed, blessed be the name of the LORD" (see Job 1:21).

WHAT KIND OF GOD IS HE?

But still you say, "If He's truly a God of love, how can He even allow adversity? If He's a merciful and long-suffering God, how can He permit people to suffer? If God authorizes such tragedy, what kind of a God is He *really*? *Why* does He allow such tragedy? Is God cruel and uncaring? Is He vindictive and merciless? Is He a destroyer?"

What kind of God is He? What is He like, this One who rules over all?

So often we have such a warped opinion and understanding of Him.

When people say to me, "I'm afraid to give my life to God" then I know immediately, *You don't know God.* Because when you know and begin understanding His character, you're not afraid to give your life to Him. In fact, you're afraid *not* to—not because You think He'll smack you down but because of what you know you'll miss if you don't let Him be in control.

Look in the Scriptures and see that He's a God of love. He can never take off His love and lay it aside. His love is not clothing. It is His being. It's something He is. "God *is* love" (1 John 4:8). It's a love He can never divorce Himself from. *Everything* that comes into your life as a child of God is filtered through His fingers of love. He loves you with a perfect love that desires your highest good.

God is not a destroyer of us. Even when He allows us to self-destruct because of our wrong choices, even then He intervenes in His sovereignty for His children.

Look in His Word and see that He's a God of righteousness. He is totally and absolutely right in all that He does.

Look and see that He's a God of justice, a God of mercy, of long-suffering.

Look in His Word and see that He's a faithful God, faithful to His promises. His thoughts toward me are the same as they were toward Israel when He said to His people, "I know the plans that I have for you, . . . plans for welfare and not for calamity to give you a future and a hope" (Jeremiah 29:11). After the people of Israel had endured the destruction of Jerusalem and then their captivity in Babylon, they never went back into idolatry because they found out God means what He says, that He is faithful, that He is just.

And because He was faithful with Israel, I know He'll always be faithful to you and to me.

Because of God's faithfulness, you, too, are like that ring wrapped tightly in Dave Pancer's fist. You're in God's hand, and Jesus says no one is able to snatch you out of the Father's grasp (John 10:29). He holds your life in the palm of His omnipotent hand.

In His love and faithfulness and righteousness He weaves the events and circumstances of our lives like silk in a tapestry. If you look only at the back side of a tapestry, you see only a tangle of threads. That often seems like all we can see in our lives—a tangle of trials. But now and then God lifts us up so we can peek over the top. "Let Me show you what I'm doing," He tells us, and we get a glimpse of the beautiful design He's making, in which the dark threads give dimension and needed contrast to the light.

This is our God who rules over all. This is the One who sits on the throne.

Therefore when tragedy and pain come our way, beloved, the only place to hide and rest secure is in the sovereignty of God.

Rest, beloved, rest. Your Father is in control. He will not leave His throne.

CHAPTER EIGHT

PEACE AMID THE PAIN

Profiles of Trust in God's Sovereignty

PAIN WAS HIS constant companion—pain from malaria that he battled in conditions far from ideal for his recuperation. He had been captured by South American Marxist guerrillas and dragged for three days and nights to an isolated camp in a Colombian jungle. The likelihood of being shot to death loomed over him. Little did he know that his captivity and the ever-present threat of execution would last for most of the coming year.

Bruce Olson—whose amazing story of miraculous missionary service among jungle Indians is told in the book *Bruchko*—now faced another ordeal and another opportunity to see God's sovereign hand at work. He sets the scene in these words:

> In all of the twelve camps I lived in during the nine months of my captivity, I would be guarded 24 hours a day by at least two heavily armed men. The guards were usually changed every hour, so there

was no possibility that one might fall asleep or become too relaxed in my presence. Much of the time my hands were kept bound behind my back, even when I was very ill and in extreme pain.

The rains were relentless and demoralizing. A crude makeshift shelter was constructed over my hammock in the first camp, but it offered virtually no protection from the elements. I was always soaking wet, even when the rain let up for a few hours, as it did only occasionally. It was so humid, even on sunny days, that shoes and clothes never dried.

To endure, he had to rely on what God had taught him through years of jungle hardship:

I knew the malaria wouldn't kill me, but the disease has a way, sometimes, of making you almost wish it would. Yet it wasn't unbearable. I had learned years before, when I had injuries and illnesses in the jungles, to separate myself from the physical discomfort. When you're miles from help and your arm or leg is dislocated on a jungle trail, you can't sit down and agonize over it. You have to keep going. I'd say to myself in such moments, "I'm in pain, yes, but this pain exists only in my body. I am not my body. My mind and spirit are above this, not part of it." This technique worked for me, and I would use it to get through some of the worst experiences of my captivity.

Those "worst experiences" would include his own torture, as well as having to witness the abuse and death of other prisoners. How did he endure? Did he long for and even plot his escape?

It may seem bizarre to some people, but the truth is that it never once occurred to me that it was God's responsibility to rescue me miraculously from this situation. Instead I believed it was my responsibility to serve Him right where I was.

What I asked of God from day to day was very simple, very practical, and I suppose quite typical of me: *Father, I'm alive, and I want to use this time constructively. How can I be useful to you today?*

This was to be my prayer, as well as my "strategy," throughout the long months of my captivity. But it was nothing new; it was how I approached every day of my life. Why should my prayers or my outlook change now, just because I was in the hands of guerrillas?

I knew that God was subtly orchestrating His plan in the jungles—not only among the Motilones and the other 14 tribes we'd been working with, but also among the guerrillas. I assumed that this situation was part of that orchestration, and I wanted to be open to whatever God might have in mind. I've always felt that I could serve God in *any* situation, and this one was full of intriguing possibilities. As a result, I wasn't terrified or even particularly anxious about my fate. I knew it was God—not my captors—who would control the outcome of the situation. . . .

In whatever painful situation you may be facing today, beloved, can you believe and affirm the same truths that Bruce Olson did in the jungle? Are you convinced that God is in control, that He's orchestrating His plan even in unexpected and unpleasant circumstances, and that your own responsibility is simply to serve Him right where you are?

Or do you long for or even plot some kind of escape from the difficulty?

QUIET ENOUGH TO HEAR HIM

Bruce Olson described another critical lesson he learned years earlier in the jungle. One day he and his Indian friends were deep in the jungle when the noise level—from countless insects, birds, monkeys, and other creatures—reached a clamorous level. Amid the riot of sound, one of the Indians remarked that he could hear a piping turkey. "His remark stopped me in my tracks," Bruce recalled. "How could anyone notice the voice of one lone turkey in the midst of this din?"

His companion signaled Bruce to stop and listen quietly.

> Slowly, the separate voices became more and more distinct. Finally,
> after more patient listening, I heard it. Behind the hue and cry of the
> jungle . . . was the haunting, reedy voice of the piping turkey. . . .
>
> It had been a poignant moment for me. . . . It had made me
> wonder what I'd missed—not only in the jungles, but in my own
> spiritual life. How much had I overlooked when I'd failed to
> patiently "tune in" to God's subtle voice in the midst of life's clamor
> and activity?
>
> In the years that followed, the piping turkey had come to mind
> many times as I'd struggled to discern God's voice and sense His
> quiet, often barely detectable presence in the seemingly chaotic
> situations I encountered. But over time, I learned enough patience to
> be able to see God in the *subscripts* of life. And I'd learned from
> experience that even when I couldn't see or hear what He was doing,
> I could trust that He was always there, always working out His
> sovereign will, even when I was too overwhelmed by the "noise" to
> notice or appreciate His complex orchestrations.
>
> So it was natural for me, when I was kidnapped, to assume that
> God was there working in His usual way, and that I was there for a
> purpose.

God is there. For you, beloved, and for me as well, God is there in
whatever the present difficulty, working out His sovereign will.

But are you quiet enough to see Him . . . to hear Him . . . even, as
Bruce Olson put it, in the "subscripts of life"?

Bruce Olson concluded, "So the question was never, *How could I believe that God was in control? The question was, How could I doubt it?*"

When we listen, when we learn, when we submit to the Lord in meekness, we move beyond question and doubt to the sure faith that His sovereign hand is always at work.

Under the Lord's guiding hand, Bruce Olson faithfully served God in the prison camps by quietly and calmly serving his captors. He taught many to read, helped meet their medical needs, and led dozens of the young guerrillas to faith in Jesus Christ. He won the respect of them all and the deep friendship of many—but painful challenges continued.

> By far the worst moments of my captivity came when I had to watch the executions of the other hostages—people who had become friends. As their bodies were ripped apart by the guerrillas' bullets I was told, "This is what will happen to you unless you sign a confession." The experience was inexpressibly painful.

Again and again, he refused to sign the confession the guerrillas demanded of him.

> "Then we'll kill you," they said.
> "The truth is a good thing to die for," I told them. Then I looked each of them in the eye and said, "I can die only once. But you, my friends, will die a thousand times, because you'll know you've killed an innocent man."

For psychological torment, the guerrillas repeatedly told Bruce Olson that he had been forgotten by the Motilone Indian friends he had served and lived with for twenty-eight years, almost all of whom were now Christians. "I began to have small doubts," he remembered. "Was it possible? Had I been abandoned?"

His physical torture continued as well. "Many things that happened during this time were so terrible," he wrote, "that I will probably never be able to talk about or forget them."

THE QUIET WORKING OF HIS WILL

There was also more illness.

> During the latter part of my captivity I suffered a severe attack of diverticulitis—one of several attacks that involved severe

hemorrhaging. I lost about two quarts of blood this time, was in excruciating pain and eventually lost consciousness.

When I awakened I was being examined by a doctor the guerrillas had brought into the jungle. He said only a blood transfusion could save my life.

Immediately a fight broke out among the guerrillas over who would win the "honor" of giving their blood for me. A young Christian guerrilla was one of those chosen. After the transfusions were completed, he sat with me for a while. "My blood now flows in your veins, Papa Bruchko," he told me. There were tears in his eyes. And in mine, too.

That night Bruce's pain intensified to a level beyond any he had ever known. This time, because of his weakness, the technique of separating himself from his pain wouldn't work. "I had never experienced such total anguish," he wrote.

Then an absolutely amazing thing happened: A bird known in Colombia as the *mirla* began to sing. I looked up and saw the full moon pouring down through the thick jungle vegetation and felt inexplicably that it was shining for me. The mirla's song was the most hauntingly beautiful sound I'd ever heard.

The music was also profoundly familiar and reminded him strangely of the resurrection of Christ. Wondering why, he drifted again into unconsciousness. When he came to, it was dark, and he was surprised to hear the bird once more because mirlas normally don't sing at night. He thought he might be hallucinating.

But what I was more intent on trying to understand was why this song—real or imagined—was having such an amazing, restorative effect on my spirit. I could feel myself coming back to life with each note.

Finally he recognized why the song was so familiar. The mirla was accurately mimicking one of the beautiful minor-key chants Bruce's Motilone brothers and sisters used in their worship.

> I could almost hear their words, could almost see my friends . . . singing the prophecies of the resurrection of Christ in the timeless Motilone way, our hammocks swaying together in the rafters of a communal home in the jungles as they had for the 28 years I'd lived among them. . . . And I was going to survive to be with them again, because God had used the mirla's song to transfuse His lifeblood into me.

Bruce Olson concluded that "the greatest victory in this long drama" of his captivity was not his actual release but "the song of the mirla in the moonlight." It reflected the quiet victory he discovered in other times as well during those months:

> . . . in the sweetness of the moments when I caught glimpses of the "subscript" in God's complex orchestration of lives and events. In those moments I knew that He was quietly working out His sovereign will, not only in my life, but in the lives of everyone involved.

Is this your own sure knowledge as well, beloved—that God is quietly working out His sovereign will in your life and in the lives of those around you?

WHY, GOD?

The prophet Habakkuk is someone else who knew pain—the pain of seeing unavoidable and horrible and unexplainable trials both in the present and in his immediate future. And his experience of bringing his pain before God offers us more lessons in God's sovereignty.

Habakkuk's theme was the aching cry of "Why, God?"—a question so many of us have asked. God, why aren't You doing anything when I ask You to? I pray for deliverance from this trial, yet You don't deliver—*Why?*

In the opening verses of the conversation between the prophet and his Lord, Habakkuk cried out to God about what he was being forced to see: Violence. Iniquity. Wickedness. Destruction. Strife. Contention. All this was happening to God's people.

God—*why don't You do something?*

Then God answered. "Look!" He said. "Observe! Be astonished! Wonder! Because I am doing something in your days—you would not believe if you were told" (1:5).

I am doing something, God said. You just can't see it right now—and you wouldn't believe it if you could!

In our every painful trial, God *is* doing something about it, but often in the drama of life it's happening offstage, behind a curtain of time.

God told Habakkuk more: Yes, He was doing something, and Habakkuk soon would see—but it would not be anything Habakkuk would like. God was raising up the terrible Chaldeans (the Babylonians) to be His rod of judgment against Israel. He was bringing in "that fierce and impetuous people . . . dreaded and feared" to attack and devour His chosen nation. Of course this would in no way seem fair to Habakkuk, because the very people God was using as His instrument were more wicked than those He was correcting. But their attack was inescapable, God said:

> All of them come for violence.
>> Their horde of faces moves forward.
> They collect captives like sand.
>> They mock at kings,
> And rulers are a laughing matter to them.
>> They laugh at every fortress,
> And heap up rubble to capture it.
>> Then they will sweep through like the wind and pass on.
>>> (1:9-11)

So how would Habakkuk respond?

How would *you*?

First, Habakkuk praised God. "Art Thou not from everlasting, O LORD, my God, my Holy One?" (1:12). And then in light of God's holiness, Habakkuk accepted the prospect of judgment. "God, I know You're going to judge," he was saying, in essence, but with the same breath and in the same verse Habakkuk also expressed this confidence: "*We will not die.*"

Why could Habakkuk say this? Because he knew the promises of God. He knew God's everlasting covenant with Israel, and in light of it he knew Israel as a nation would live forever.

Do you, beloved, know the promises of your God well enough to confidently cling to them as you face up to whatever refining trial He brings?

In this confidence Habakkuk acknowledged the truth about the Babylonians: "Thou, O LORD, hast appointed them to judge; and Thou, O Rock, hast established them to correct" (1:12). Habakkuk knew the Babylonians were a rod of correction, *not* an instrument of destruction.

For us, and for every child of God, that's what our trials are—not a means to defeat and destroy but a way to discipline and correct. The Refiner's fire doesn't destroy; it purifies.

Habakkuk responded by thinking about his God, and those thoughts brought more *why* questions:

> Thine eyes are too pure to approve evil,
> And Thou canst not look on wickedness with favor.
> Why dost Thou look with favor
> On those who deal treacherously?
> Why art Thou silent when the wicked swallow up
> Those more righteous than they?
>
> (1:13)

Habakkuk asked—then he waited for an answer:

> I will stand on my guard post
>> And station myself on the rampart;
> And I will keep watch to see what He will speak to me.
>
> (2:1)

So many times in a trial we inquire of God, but we don't wait for an answer. How often do we really give Him the opportunity to respond? How often do we really wait and listen?

Habakkuk did, and the answer came. This time in the Lord's response there was a beautiful gem of gracious truth that is the key to enduring the fire: "The righteous will live by his faith" (2:4).

I want you to live by faith, God said. Living by faith is the way to get through the trials and the pain; living by faith keeps us looking at God in His Book. Faith comes by hearing, and hearing comes through the Word of God—through reading it, spending time in it, meditating on it, listening to God as He speaks to you.

The answers for our trials are always right there in the Book.

As His fire burns, where will I see the Refiner? In His Book. *"Open My Book,"* God says. "I'm speaking to you there. I'm telling you what will happen. I'm telling you it will work together for good. I'm telling you that you *can* give thanks. I'm telling you that you *can* count it all joy. I'm telling you that My goodness and mercy will follow you all the days of your life.

"All this I'm telling you," He says, "and you must believe it—you have to live by faith."

In our response to all our disappointments and trials, it's *faith* we're after. It's *faith* we want to get to. You may ask, "God, why are You doing this? I want to hear. I want to know." And He may answer—or He may not. However, either way, beloved, He wants you to live by faith—by every word that came from His mouth and has been preserved in His Book, the Bible.

PEACE INSTEAD OF ULCERS

People who live by faith have the greatest calmness, the greatest peace, the greatest equanimity of spirit when they face tribulation. For Christmas a friend gave me a mantle plaque that reads, "In His Will Is My Peace." Yes, beloved, that's where we find it.

By believing and understanding the sovereignty of God you'll have rest for your soul. You won't want to straighten out the whole world; you'll let God do it.

If I didn't grasp the sovereignty of God, I'd get an ulcer over the fact that our country, which was once so great, is now self-destructing. If I didn't understand the sovereignty of God, I would be completely frustrated at our government's corruption and mishandling of our tax dollars. But I know God is allowing all this. He's letting us self-destruct, and I know where we're headed. So I don't have to get an ulcer over the condition of our nation or the world. God is in control everywhere, just as He is of my own life.

Those who know this and who enjoy the peace that comes as a result of it are listening to the Refiner's words, embracing them, believing them, clinging to Him, and living righteously.

In their trials they don't fall to the temptations that can be so strong—the temptations to run, to sin, or to get out of the difficulty in their own way. That's why in James 1, where we're instructed to count it all joy when we encounter various trials, we're also told, "Let no man say when he is tempted, I am tempted of God." When the fire comes, it's an opportunity either to rest in the Lord or to face increasing temptation.

When the heat gets hottest, so many people say in their hearts, "God, You haven't done what I asked You. You haven't responded the way I wanted. I'm closing the Bible." They close God's Book and walk away. And when they do, they've just shut off the one source of all the answers, answers they've turned their back to without even hearing them.

But look ahead with me to the conclusion of Habakkuk's story at the end of chapter 3. Habakkuk was shaking, quivering. He was weak within, decaying, in danger of collapse. Yet he said,

Though the fig tree should not blossom,
  And there be no fruit on the vines,
Though the yield of the olive should fail,
  And the fields produce no food,
Though the flock should be cut off from the fold,
  And there be no cattle in the stalls,
Yet I will exult in the LORD,
  I will rejoice in the God of my salvation.
The Lord GOD is my strength.

(3:17-19)

He rejoiced in God—this was Habakkuk's will, his determination, his decision: *This is what I'm going to do.* Though his body trembled and decayed, he knew the Lord was his strength.

Then he added,

He has made my feet like hinds' feet,
  And makes me walk on my high places.

(3:19)

God will cause us to walk on *our* high places—not on someone else's. So often we glance at others, and their high places look so much better than ours. They have it made. Their families seem so all-together, their children so well-behaved, their marriages so peaceful, their ministries and work so ideal. But we don't know. We really don't know the heartbreaking struggles they face.

If you're asking God *why*, may I urge you, my friend, to turn to Habakkuk and read and meditate on these truths. Be bolstered in your faith, and walk confidently on your high places. Trust Him. Thank Him, and exult in the God of your salvation.

And in the peace that He will surely give, know that He loves you.

SOMETHING TO ACKNOWLEDGE

If he had wanted to, Habakkuk could no doubt have continued asking *why* questions of God. But in meekness he instead chose a better response. Even in affliction and with the prospect of far worse pain and tragedy, Habakkuk acknowledged God's sovereignty and rejoiced in His salvation.

God's sovereignty is always something to ponder and study and learn about, but even more importantly it's something to *acknowledge* before Him.

Whether you've got all this figured out doesn't matter. We don't have to figure it out. We don't have to understand it all. All we have to do is submit to its truth.

Bow the knee and say, "God, if that's what You say, then I believe it and I trust it. And I know, O Lord, that whether I understand them or not, Your ways are just and fair, exactly as Your Word tells me."

Remember that it's God's right to do with us as He pleases, and it's never our right to chafe at this. Paul said in Romans 9:20-21, "Who are you, O man, who answers back to God? The thing molded will not say to the molder, 'Why did you make me like this,' will it? Or does not the potter have a right over the clay?"

Oh, little pot of clay, don't argue back to God. Submit to Him!

Meekness says, "Father, You are the Potter, I am the clay. Glorify Your Son in me however You want to do it, in whatever way You desire, whether it's by my life or my death. I trust You, God my Savior."

Someday we *will* better understand this mystery. In Revelation 10:1-7, there appeared to John a mighty angel clothed with clouds and with a face like the sun and a voice like a lion's roar. He lifted his right hand to heaven and swore "by Him who lives forever and ever, who created heaven and the things in it, and the earth and the things in it, and the sea and the things in it." Then he proclaimed that *"the mystery of God is finished."* The mystery was over.

Someday when the trumpets sound and everything is brought full-circle, we'll better understand His answers to all the *why* questions we've ever asked. We'll understand why He didn't move sooner to quell the forces of evil and why iniquity ran such a long course.

But for now we want to trust God's sovereignty. We want to accept every disappointing circumstance in the meekness that says, "You are God. You're in control. You wound, You heal, You kill, You make alive, You do according to Your will among the hosts of heaven and among the inhabitants of the earth."

Then even now we'll know with absolute certainty—we'll *really know*, and we'll know that we know—that "all things work together for good to those who love God, to those who are called according to His purpose." We'll know God has a purpose in our lives. We'll know we were created to bring Him glory and that God will use even evil and pain and tragedy in our lives to draw that glory to Himself.

Remember again: God's Word doesn't say that *all things* are good, because in themselves all things aren't. But God causes them all to work together—and He *keeps on* causing them all to work together—for His higher purpose, a purpose that *is* infinitely good: our becoming like Jesus.

The New Testament is passionate about saying that Christ is being formed in us, that we're to become Christlike, conformed to Christ's image. If I'm being conformed to His image, then God is achieving His goal and I can rest, knowing all is well.

So we shouldn't forget that to make us like Jesus—to make us meek, because He is meek—God is taking us through afflictions, difficulties, oppressions, and humblings, and all of them are working together for our good and His glory.

Therefore in every situation of life, meekness bows the knee and says, "Bless the LORD, O my soul: and all that is within me, bless his holy name. Bless the LORD, O my soul, and forget not all his benefits" (Psalm 103:1-2, KJV).

I have heard of Thee by the hearing of the ear;
but now my eye sees Thee.

JOB 42:5

CHAPTER NINE

A TRUTH TO BUY

Deeper Discoveries in God's Sovereignty

I KNOW, beloved, that when you look at all the unspeakable tragedies that people must endure, all this teaching about God's sovereignty can be hard to buy. But listen—and I don't mean to sound hard but only to be realistic: You either buy it or you don't. Either God is *in* control, or He's *not*.

God's Word is true, or it is not true.

God's sovereignty is a hard lesson for many of us at different times in our lives, in different situations. It's hard and I understand, and I'm not trying to jam it down your throat. I would if I could, because it's very effective medicine. But I can't.

If you will open yourself to this truth—if you'll read through the Word of God, beginning in Genesis, and mark a triangle by every reference to God that tells you something about Him or His ways, His dealings with individuals and nations, His power and control over nature, man, nations, angels, and more, and if you'll record in the margin of your Bible what you learn about it as you grasp it in its plain sense—then He will make His sovereignty clear to you. And when He does, the will of God will seem good and acceptable and perfect to you.

There's a proverb that says, "Buy truth, and do not sell it. Get wisdom and instruction and understanding" (Proverbs 23:23). So buy the truth and wisdom of God's sovereignty, even though it seems costly to your human reasoning, for it is well worth the price.

On the other hand, if after reading this far you disagree with what I've said about God's sovereignty, if it's hard for you, then simply tell that to God. Say to Him, "This is hard for me," or "I disagree with this." Then tell Him, "But I want the truth, and it's the work of your Holy Spirit to guide me into all truth."

Then thank Him for the power of His Word, and receive it with meekness.

FOLLOW ME

Paul could say, "Be imitators of me, just as I also am of Christ" (1 Corinthians 11:1). And I can tell you confidently, my friend, that if you want to, you can follow me in believing in the sovereignty of God. You can follow me, because I'm following Jesus and because I believe the Word of God.

Paul said in 1 Thessalonians 1:5, "For our gospel did not come to you in word only, but also in power and in the Holy Spirit and *with full conviction*; just as you know what kind of men we proved to be among you for your sake." This "full conviction" here doesn't refer to the Thessalonians' response after Paul spoke to them. No, it was *Paul's* full conviction. He was saying, "*I am totally convicted and convinced* that what I'm testifying to is absolute truth."

And beloved, so am I. I am totally convinced. The teaching on these pages comes to you not in word only but in power and in the Holy Spirit and with full conviction. I know that meekness is the key to acting rather than reacting, and I know that the key to meekness is understanding the sovereignty and the character of God.

I know that I know that God is sovereign, and I know He's sovereign because I've done my homework in His Book. This is where I get my bread to live.

I believe with all my being that between the covers of the Bible is the answer to every situation in life. We don't need any other book in all the world. We simply make the Bible a part of us and allow His Word to come into our lives. If we receive this implanted word with meekness then you and I will be all God intends us to be.

I want you to know that I *do* walk in obedience to God. Most of the time I walk in meekness. I've told you in this book about many times when I haven't, so you can see I'm not perfect. But I have found that by His power, by believing and trusting in His control, we *can* walk in meekness.

To keep walking this way, then, just like you I have to go beyond my feelings and simply see who God is and what He's like and what He has promised.

I remember one day when I was feeling so totally, absolutely defeated as a mother in respect to our oldest son, Tommy. As I was driving home I was raking myself over the coals. I'd really tried to be a good mother to my boys, and I thought I was. But when children struggle as Tommy did, all you see and think about is that you've been a failure. This was in the days when so many books were telling parents how to be the right kind of parent and produce the right kind of child in a perfect, happy family. It was as simple as A plus B equals PC (Perfect Children).

So I felt I'd only failed. But the Lord kept bringing me back to where He said, "I came not to bring peace but a sword." The sword for me in our family was the fact that I was walking with the Lord and my son was not. I was saved, and my son was not. And he knew how to attack, and he did.

Then that day as I drove home—and I still remember the exact place on Highway 153 where it happened—I heard in my mind the Lord asking me, "Am *I* a perfect Father?"

"Yes," I said.

"Are all *My* children perfect?"

And of course I answered, "No," and I understood. "No, because all Your children have a choice."

I think this is part of the fellowship of His sufferings: He lets our hearts break for our children who walk in rebellion and who may even turn and accuse us, so that in our hearts we better understand what it's like for *Him* when *His* children rebel and then turn and accuse Him.

With my heartbreak over Tommy, I came to the point where I thought I might never live differently. Then God delightfully surprised me and turned him around at the age of thirty-eight.

NEVER TO DENY HIM

Let's take a look at someone else who was no stranger to pain.

The man in Scripture we probably associate most with painful trials is Job. And in his experience too we encounter penetrating and practical truth about the sovereignty of God.

Let's go to Job 1, where Satan had come from roaming the earth and appeared before the Lord. God directed Satan's attention to His servant Job, whom the Lord described as "a blameless and upright man, fearing God and turning away from evil."

But Satan countered, "Does Job fear God for nothing? Hast Thou not made a hedge about him and his house and all that he has, on every side?"

Think with me: Just how did Satan know that God had placed a hedge around Job? Obviously Satan had tried to penetrate it but was *unable* to get through.

The only way this hedge could be taken away was by God Himself removing it. Satan could never have said, "I'll touch Job whenever I want to," because God is the ultimate authority and even Satan is subject to God. Satan had to get God's permission to touch Job with affliction, just as no affliction can come to you and me without God's permission. Isn't that wonderful!

Remember what Jesus said to Peter about Satan's desire? "Simon,

Simon," Jesus told him, "behold, Satan has *demanded permission* to sift you like wheat" (Luke 22:31). Satan had to ask. Satan could never attack Peter (or us) without God's consent. Don't miss this point, beloved!

Satan's words about Job were an acknowledgment of this. But then Satan, ever the accuser, postulated what would happen if he *did* have the freedom to attack Job. He told God that Job would certainly react instead of act: "He will surely curse Thee to Thy face" (Job 1:11).

God, in His sovereign wisdom, agreed to take the hedge away. "Behold," He said to Satan in 1:12, "all that he has is in your power, only do not put forth your hand on him."

As you know from the biblical account, Satan wiped out everything Job had—except for Mrs. Job (and Job might have been better off without her, since she was anything but meek).

When Job heard the news that he'd lost everything—his children and his possessions—he arose, tore his robe, shaved his head, covered himself with ashes (a sign of repentance and sorrow), fell to the ground—"and he *worshiped*" (1:20). He looked at God's "worth-ship." In other words, he looked at God as He really is; he acknowledged God's attributes and qualities. That's meekness. Job was taking disappointment—crushing, overwhelming disappointment—and changing it into "His appointment."

"Naked I came from my mother's womb," Job said, "naked I shall return. The Lord gave and the Lord has taken away. Blessed be the name of the Lord." And Scripture tells us, "Through all this Job did not sin nor did he blame God" (1:20-21).

All this was just the beginning of Job's ordeal. But God, who creates good and who creates adversity, who wounds and who heals, who puts to death and who gives life, permitted Job's every trial.

God had a purpose.

In the second chapter of Job, God for the first time allowed Satan to touch Job's body but not to take his life. Job's misery knew no end as boils covered his body from head to toe. He longed for death. To top it off, Job's comforters became thorns in his side.

Did God permit all this suffering just to prove to Satan that Job truly did fear Him? Was this God's only purpose for Job? Was Job a mere pawn in a chess game between God and Satan?

Job didn't think so. When we read the last chapter we find him proclaiming God's sovereignty: "I know that Thou canst do all things, and that no purpose of Thine can be thwarted" (42:2).

We also see how God "restored the fortunes of Job . . . and the Lord increased all that Job had twofold. . . . And the LORD blessed the latter days of Job more than his beginning" (42:10,12). Job's end was better than his beginning.

All that happened to Job worked together for his good, even in this life. And Job understood that everything in this life—from severest affliction to brightest prosperity—was by sovereign appointment from the Lord's almighty hand.

Look closer at Job's attitude, even in the depth of his misery. Job once cried out, "Oh that my request might come to pass, and that God would grant my longing! Would that God were willing to crush me; that He would loose His hand and cut me off!" (6:8-9). In other words, *just let me die.*

Then immediately Job added these words, in a verse I love: "But it is still my consolation, and I rejoice in unsparing pain, that *I have not denied the words of the Holy One*" (6:10).

Isn't that wonderful? Job was in "unsparing pain." He wanted to die. He wouldn't take his own life, but he wanted God to take it, and God wouldn't. Yet even then Job possessed a consolation that can be ours as well in our own unsparing pain: *I haven't denied God's Word.*

Job knew about God's sovereignty and was deeply learning far more. Meanwhile he stayed true to his own responsibility to obey and serve God.

GOD'S SOVEREIGNTY AND MY ACCOUNTABILITY

Whatever the difficulty and pain we encounter, we're not to be like a feather in the wind but like an oak sinking down its roots.

God is totally sovereign, but we don't shrug and say, "Whatever will be will be." A true understanding of the sovereignty of God (in light of all of God's Word) will not put us in a passive mode. According to the Word of God, we are accountable, and someday we'll stand before Him and give an account of how we have lived as His children. Second Corinthians 5:10 and Romans 14:10 affirm this. And I believe that according to our faithfulness we will see and receive an inheritance, a rulership on the face of the earth.

So on one hand is the sovereignty of God, and on the other is the accountability of man, and there's a healthy tension between the two. We can't fully explain or comprehend how they work together. They're like two parallel lines, like the two rails on a railroad, and what makes them parallel is that they never meet. The sovereignty of God and the accountability of man don't fully converge in our understanding, but both of them continue side by side in reality and in our experience.

We can't comprehend it because God's ways are so much higher, His thoughts so infinitely superior and greater. We have a very narrow and limited human concept of love and mercy and long-suffering and all the factors that undergird His sovereignty.

So in our humanity we bow in humble submission and faith and acquiescence to his control. We realize that God's wisdom and understanding are infinite while ours are only finite. For there *will* be times when we feel we just don't understand. I have been there!

WHEN YOU DON'T UNDERSTAND

My father called me one day to tell me he was going into the hospital for heart surgery. He was sixty-eight.

I went to the hospital to be with him, and I asked God that day to give me a word about him. His answer, I believed, was a psalm whose words assured me that my father was going to live.

It was supposed to be one surgery. But because of very serious complications, he had two that first day and a total of five within twelve days.

Very late one night, my mother and I received a phone call from the hospital. Daddy had stopped breathing, and they had to place him on a respirator.

My body went crazy on the inside in a way I've never had happen before. I got down on my knees. "Father, I believe You told me he's going to live!" I cried. "This is what You told me!"

In fog that was so thick we could hardly see, I drove Mother to the hospital. And I was wrestling with God the entire time.

Because of a problem caused by blood clots, the doctors decided to amputate one of Daddy's legs. "God," I prayed, "I know You can speak a word and bring circulation back into this leg. I know You, God. I know You can."

But God didn't. And they cut off Daddy's leg.

Finally he seemed to be doing better. I left to go back home. Mother was concerned that I didn't stop by the hospital on my way out of town to say good-bye to Daddy. But I was sure I would see him again.

Shortly afterward we were having a big banquet in Atlanta to launch the beginning of our television ministry, and Jack and I were at Grace Kinser's house. While I was there, a phone call came through from my mother: Daddy was dead.

What is meekness in a moment like that? Meekness is bowing the knee and saying, "Lord, You're sovereign. If it pleases You, it pleases me."

I told God, "You did not fail me. I misunderstood You. I didn't have Your word, or Daddy wouldn't have died."

I wrote down my experiences of this time in a devotional. One woman who read it contacted me to say she had claimed healing for her own father when he was ill. When he stopped breathing in his hospital room, she shut the door and put her Bible on his chest and said, "God, You promised me!" And she said her father came back to life.

Weeks later she received a call from the hospital saying her father had died. She told them not to do a thing and to stay out of his room until she got there. She put the Bible back on his chest and said, "God, You promised me." She waited and waited—for hours. But God didn't raise him up. And she said that from that day forward she hadn't had anything to do with God.

In her mind, God did not keep His promise. But reading my experience, she realized that it was *she* who had been mistaken. She had misunderstood God, even as I had. And her restoration to fellowship with her heavenly Father was sweet indeed.

Meekness is bowing the knee whether or not you understand, whether or not you've got it figured out, whether or not you agree.

"You are God," the meek say. "You're in control. You wound, You heal, You kill, You bring to life. You do according to Your will in the host of heaven and among the inhabitants of earth, and no one can ward off Your hand or say to You, 'What hast Thou done?'

"You are God. You gave me breath. You numbered my days before there was yet one of them. I live and I exist because of You. You are fair and just in all Your ways.

"You are God!"

And in that submission, we find more than enough grace to keep going. That was what my new friend discovered.

His Grace Is Sufficient

In 2 Corinthians 12, Paul touched on the incomparable experience of having been called up into heaven, where he saw things that weren't permissible to be uttered. Then he told how God gave him a thorn in the flesh, "to keep me from exalting myself." Paul described it as "a messenger from Satan to buffet me" (12:7).

Now where did Satan get permission to put that thorn in Paul's flesh? Paul knew it came from God, because God is sovereign and He rules even over the devil.

Therefore Paul entreated God three times to take the thorn away. But Paul didn't ask beyond three times. Why? Because God said to him, "My grace is sufficient for you, for power is perfected in weakness" (12:9).

Paul responded in meekness and found strength in God's grace: "Most gladly, therefore, I will rather boast about my weaknesses, that the power of Christ may dwell in me. Therefore I am well content with weaknesses, with insults, with distresses, with persecutions, with difficulties, for Christ's sake; for when I am weak, then I am strong" (12:9-10).

You may be crying out, "God, deliver me from this trial!" And God has answered, "No," because He's using this painful difficulty to make you perfect and mature, and to keep you from pride—to make you like Christ. So you can say with Paul, "Therefore I am well content, for Christ's sake."

No matter how weak you are in your trial or because of your trial, you can rejoice because God's grace is sufficient. His power is perfected in your weakness. Your very pain will cause you to cast yourself on God and to depend on Him rather than on your own strength.

A BRIGHTER LIGHT TO OTHERS

And even in your weakness, you'll find that trusting in God's sovereignty will energize your testimony to others for a brighter light of witness.

In Philippians 1, Paul said that we have been granted not only to believe in Jesus Christ but also to suffer for His sake. We will suffer, often at the hands of those who attack us in one way or another. But Paul also said that we're to be "in no way alarmed by [our] opponents—which is a sign of destruction for them, but of salvation for you" (Philippians 1:28).

If I understand God's sovereignty, I'll know that God has spread His fingers of love to allow these opponents to attack me. My opponents could not get close to me unless they marched through His fingers. So I know God has a purpose in them, and therefore they don't alarm me.

Thus my opponents see me acting calmly instead of reacting in alarm. And they know that this wouldn't be the case if they were to change places with me. So what happens? They see and know that I have something different, a strength, a peace, a confidence they don't have.

Consequently my response becomes a powerful sign, as Paul said, of destruction for them but salvation for me. Their opposition has become my opportunity to demonstrate the reality of my faith, of my belief in the sovereignty of God and His eternal life and values and promises. I have become a living epistle that others can read.

Down through history this has been the heroic and powerful experience and testimony of God's saints. The Roman emperor Nero asked, "Why are they singing?" as he burned Christians at the stake and lit his gardens with human torches. They could sing because they were looking not at things that are seen but at things that are unseen. The world was not worthy of them, but before God's throne a crown awaited them.

Harlan Popov tells the story of when his communist captors said they would kill him because he wouldn't give information on the people in his church. He was marched down a corridor to a place splattered with blood then told that he would be shot on the count of ten.

Suddenly it occurred to Popov that at the count of ten he would die. At the count of ten he would be in the presence of Jesus! At the count of ten he would be freed from his imprisonment.

There was joy, delightful joy, all over him.

His executioner couldn't understand why Popov wasn't quivering or sniveling or somehow resisting. "Why are you smiling?" he asked.

Popov explained the reason. The man in disgust fired the gun—his target the corner, not Popov. He knew his prisoner had something he did not.

Popov was released years later. Much to my delight, he came to Chattanooga on one occasion and spoke at a school, and I had the privilege of hearing him. I went up to meet him afterward and asked, "Mr. Popov, what was it that held you in your trials?"

In broken English he answered, "I don't understand."

I repeated, "What was it that kept you faithful so that you didn't deny Jesus? Was it your knowledge of the Word? What was it?"

He looked at me and said, "When you love someone, you will do anything for Him." I'll never forget his words.

When you truly love God and trust His loving sovereignty, you can bow before Him and say, "If I live, praise the Lord. If I die, praise the Lord. If I live or die, my only cry will be 'Jesus in me, praise the Lord!'"

Your fear of death is gone because you know your God. You know that even death itself, when it comes, has been filtered through His fingers of love. You know that you're counted as sheep for the slaughter. You know you're a living epistle. You know that absent from the body means present with the Lord—which is far better.

NO FEAR OF DEATH

Look with me at Hebrews 2:14-15, where God's Word teaches us about the fear of death. Since we are flesh and blood, this passage says, therefore Christ Himself "likewise also partook of the same." Jesus became flesh and blood because we are flesh and blood. Why?

The purpose was His *death*—so that "through death" Jesus would accomplish two things: first, "that through death He might render powerless him who had the power of death, that is, the devil"; and second, that He would "deliver those who through fear of death were subject to slavery all their lives."

The ultimate earthly punishment is to take away a person's life. But when you really know and understand that you have eternal life because your sins are forgiven, then death and the fear of death have no power over you. You know death is not the end but the beginning.

Satan had the power of death over us because of our sin. *Sin* gave him that control, because the soul that sins will surely die (Ezekiel 18:4). *Sin* gives death its sting; sin gives the devil his power over us. So when your sin is forgiven, Satan no longer has power over you because you no longer face the penalty of death. It's been taken away, for Jesus Himself paid the penalty.

Therefore we can now say with Habakkuk, *"We will not die."* Under the fear of death we were subject to slavery, but now we know that to be absent from the body is to be present with the Lord. To die is only to fall asleep in Jesus and then to immediately awaken in the presence of the Lord.

We will not die, and we will not fear.

Wall of Fire

Marie Monsen was one of God's instruments to bring revival to China in the first decade of the twentieth century. Her story is told in the book *A Wall of Fire*, which she wrote to show how God is like a wall of fire in protecting us in His sovereignty.

While she was in China, God told her to book her passage on a ship bound for another port city where she was to minister. It would be an overnight voyage. She booked her passage, but on her departure day she was told the ship was full. "Now Father," she prayed, "You brought me this far. I know that if it's Your will, You'll find me a place on that ship." Then she was offered a small cabin that one of the crew members was willing to give up, for an extra fee.

She examined the cabin, which was extremely small and smelly. But she told herself, *For one night I can endure it.*

Before the ship departed, Marie had a strong impression from the Lord to go buy some apples. She dismissed the thought at first, but the Lord kept pressuring her, "Go buy apples. Go buy apples." So finally she found a fruit stand on the city's streets and bought several pounds of them.

Then she sensed the Lord telling her to place the money she had with her in a bank in the city rather than carrying it with her on the voyage. So she did.

She also picked up some mail that had been accumulating for her there, among which was a large number of newspapers. She sensed the Lord telling her to take the newspapers with her.

Finally she boarded the ship, and it set sail. But out at sea the ship was boarded and seized by pirates. The one-day voyage was to last twenty-three days.

The pirates demanded that Marie leave her cabin. But she sensed the Lord telling her not to leave. "I'm sorry," she told them, "I'm under higher orders than yours, and I've been told I'm not allowed to leave this cabin."

The pirates came in to rob her, but she had no money for them. They took her watch, but she asked God to cause them to give it back—which they did.

Throughout those days, the apples supplied her food and the newspapers were her bedding. Day after day she saw God sustaining and protecting her. She knew she was in the hands of a sovereign God who ruled over all and who loved her, and He kept her in perfect peace.

She prayed God would let others on the ship see that He is alive and real and better than their own gods. And this was indeed their testimony when the ordeal she had faithfully endured was finally over.

THE GREATEST TESTIMONIES

In my teaching, when I want an illustration to spur people on to holiness, I don't tell about people who had miraculous deliverances or healings. To me the greatest testimonies are of those who faithfully endure under their afflictions when God has not granted their requests for deliverance—people like my dear friend and godly example, Joni Eareckson Tada. If anyone understands the sovereignty of God, it's Joni. She's a woman of the Word and a woman of prayer, and you can see the evidence of it in her life as for decades she has faithfully used her paralysis as a platform for ministry.

An equally compelling story of endurance is told in the following letter, another one that I treasure:

> We found out in late October that the child I was carrying was anencephalic—his brain tissue and skull did not form adequately in the early months of pregnancy, and he would not live more than a day or so at best. It came as quite a shock, and the grief we experienced was intense.
>
> The doctors gave us the option of an early C-section at four months (which technically would be abortion) or to carry the baby full-term. . . . We knew from previous study of the Bible that God values any life and that He is the giver and taker of life. . . . So we knew, in obedience to God and His Word, that we would carry the

child full-term or until God took his life in the womb. And we began to cling to His Word and the promises of His faithfulness.

I can't tell you how tenderly and faithfully God has kept us during these past four months. A favorite verse on this thought is Psalm 145:20—"The Lord *keeps* all those who love Him." We took every question and fear and doubt to the Lord and He graciously came alongside us and answered what needed to be answered and comforted when we needed that.

I had one really low point that lasted almost a week. I kept reading my Bible and praying and knew God would have to be the One to lift me out of it. He did. As I was reading one night, He said to me (in my thoughts): "Don't think that because I've allowed you to suffer, I don't love you. I loved My Son—and I allowed Him to suffer most of His life on earth. I had a higher purpose for Him, and I have a higher purpose for your life too!"

What a comfort! He lifted me out of despondency, and I've been "stable" ever since. Only the Lord can do that. . . .

I went into labor four days before schedule (which I really was hoping to do). It's so wonderful to know God's timing is perfect. My husband was able to be with me. . . .

Our son was born at 12:55 on March 4th. He was precious! He weighed only five pounds, one ounce, but had the biggest hands and feet—just like his Dad. He had the sweetest, most kissable mouth, and Stew and I couldn't seem to get enough of holding him and loving him. We had no idea how many hours he would be with us, so we passed him back and forth to each other—talking to him, singing to him, telling him of our love.

He lived 24 hours and 30 minutes, and what a wonderful day it was with our son. I could see how our love sustained his life hours beyond what was expected. He perked up at the sound of our voices and would "coo" back at us. He was nothing but a blessing and we have *no regrets* from carrying him full-term.

We named him Adam (which means "created by God")

Christopher ("follower of Christ"). In one day he touched so many lives of observers (doctors and nurses) in the hospital. We were able to share with so many our faith in Christ and the strength and joy He infuses in our lives during times like these. . . .

One thing we can both say has been true for us is from Job 42:5—"I have heard of Thee by the hearing of the ear; *but now* my eye sees Thee."

Where God's will leads, God's grace keeps . . .

Whatever your pain, people are watching. You're in this painful trial not just for your own benefit, to be made like Jesus, but also to show the world the sufficiency of Jesus Christ.

People are watching to see if you really believe in this eternity you speak of and if you truly are looking forward to it. And you have *now*, this moment, to show them, to demonstrate the sufficiency of His grace.

WE ONLY HAVE TODAY

God especially brings this home to us in the example of the apostle Paul. Even for women, when we really get to know Paul we truly admire him. We admire his consecration, his dedication. In 2 Corinthians 11 he recalled how he was imprisoned, beaten, stoned, shipwrecked, hunted down; he was in danger from every direction, he was often sleepless and hungry and thirsty and cold. Paul went through all this. And yet he lived with the anticipation of death as a friend and not as an enemy—not because he wanted to escape but because he knew the glories to come. He looked to the future. He lived in the light of eternity.

"We look not at the things which are seen," he said, "but at the things which are not seen; for the things which are seen are temporal, but the things which are not seen are eternal" (2 Corinthians 4:18).

The prophet Jeremiah wept over Jerusalem because "she *did not consider her future*" (Lamentations 1:9). We are a society today that doesn't consider our future. We live for the here and now, and because of that the future is painful. We don't perceive that there's a harvest coming, that what we have sown is what we will reap, that if we sow to the flesh we reap corruption but if we sow to the Spirit then from the Spirit we reap eternal life (Galatians 6:8).

Do you want to reap what has eternal value, or what is temporal and will only fade away?

Imagine it—consider it: Someday I'll stand before Him. Someday I'll see Him face to face. And on that day, nothing else is going to matter except my relationship to Him. That's why it's so key, so absolutely crucial, that we understand His eternal ways *now*—including His loving sovereignty over every detail of our lives that's leading up to that day.

One of the prayers I keep praying is that God will stamp eternity on my eyes so that I keep the eternal perspective ever before me.

So often all that seems important right now is that we be relieved from this pain or delivered from this situation where we feel unsuccessful or uncomfortable or unfulfilled or unappreciated or unaccepted. We look at it that way because we can't see the future, we can't see what God has in the space that's added when we change disappointment to His appointment. And because we can't see what's in that space, we so easily focus back on the disappointment, that one incident, that one situation, that one shattered dream.

But someday we must all stand before the judgment seat of Christ, "that each one may be recompensed for his deeds in the body, according to what he has done, whether good or bad" (2 Corinthians 5:10). There will be a compensation, a reward for what each of us has done in the body here on earth.

But this isn't a negative anticipation, something to dread—not if we have eternity stamped on our lives and our hearts. Look at what Paul said in the verses just before this.

"We are of good courage" he said. Here in this life, in this body—"this earthly tent which is our house"—Paul said we groan and are burdened. But we long for what awaits us in heaven, where "what is mortal may be swallowed up by life." We look forward to our future. We "prefer rather to be absent from the body and to be at home with the Lord." And so "we walk by faith, not by sight," and "therefore also we have as our ambition, whether at home or absent, to be pleasing to Him." And we know by pleasing Him here and now, we'll be rewarded later.

When tax time rolls around every April 15, we know it's financial accountability and assessment time, a time to render to Caesar the things that are Caesar's. There's also an accountability and assessment time at the end of every life. We have a Lord—we have a Master to whom we must give account.

Therefore, with gut-level obedience we look at that disappointing and shattering situation and say, "God, You are sovereign. You promise me that this will work together for good. You promise me that this will make me more like Jesus. And I trust You." And then even in our trials we fill our lives today with hours of trust and obedience, awaiting our reward.

SPIRITUAL ASSESSMENT TIME

I like to compare it to the time-card system in a factory or office, where you get paid only for the hours logged in on your card. The minute I choose to walk in faith and obedience (because true faith generates obedience), then I'm logged in, and I'll be "paid," in a sense, for that time; those hours will be rewarded. So today I may log in three hours or eight hours, depending on my faith's obedience.

The reward will be for my deeds, for whether they are good or bad— whether good or good for nothing. Only what's good will be rewarded. And since only God can do what is good, then it's only what I allow Him to do through me that is good and worthy of reward. The minute I do something from self and for self, then it's no longer good.

If I'm looking toward the future, I'll stay aware of this. It's so freeing, so emotionally liberating to live today in the light of my accountability I'll surely give on some not-too-distant tomorrow. And in that trust, in that faith, we log in quality time with the Lord.

"Behold," Jesus told us, "*I am coming quickly*, and My reward is with

Me, to render to every man according to what he has done" (Revelation 22:12).

This is our *hope*—our looking forward to His appearing. And it's a refining hope, a purifying hope: "We know that, when He appears, we shall be like Him, because we shall see Him just as He is. And everyone who has this hope fixed on Him purifies himself, just as He is pure" (1 John 3:2-3).

In that hope we stay accountable to God. Just as we render to Caesar what is Caesar's, so we render unto the Lord what is the Lord's—everything on His terms and in His way.

In light of this, beloved, and in light of God's perfect sovereignty, maybe it's time for spiritual assessment in your life. Maybe it's time to think about spiritual taxes you may owe. I urge you to take time—very soon and without fail—to assess what's really important in the light of eternity: how and where you're spending your time, your energy, and your money, and what it will profit His kingdom now. Then when you see the King and give an account, you'll have no regret about whatever it cost you.

If you're truly a genuine child of God, dear one, you're not your own. You've been bought with a price. You live only because God has given you life, and your moments and hours and days are to be lived for Him—above all else, above everyone else. To live in light of this will prioritize where and how you spend all you are and all you have.

That's why we're to live every day of our lives as if it might be the very last.

You have today. You have this minute. And every day and every minute is to be redeemed. "Be careful how you walk," Paul said, "not as unwise men, but as wise, making the most of your time, because the days are evil" (Ephesians 5:15-16). In the Greek this phrase about making the most of your time is literally "redeeming the time"—buying it back.

Paul continued, "So then do not be foolish, but understand what the will of the Lord is. And do not get drunk with wine, for that is dissipation, but *be filled with the Spirit*" (5:17-18). Redeeming the time means walking under the control of the Holy Spirit.

How can we live *now* so that when the God-appointed allotment of our days is up and we see Him face to face we'll hear, "Well done, My good and faithful servant"? How do we live *now* so that *then* we will not be ashamed?

We live in meekness.

We act, rather than react in every trial of life, no matter how painful.

And we willingly and confidently entrust our life into God's complete and total control.

He is sovereign. Whatever my disappointment, He knows—and He's in control.

Be strong, and let your heart take courage.

PSALM 27:14

CHAPTER TEN

STRONG AND COURAGEOUS

Learning Victory over Discouragement

SWINGS AND SLIDES were part of my childhood—trips to the parks with their playgrounds for family picnics. Those were the fun days before McDonald's and fast food. Money was tight for Mom and Dad and picnics were cheap, but they were far more than a cheap meal. They were leisurely family times when we'd enjoy God's wonderful outdoors. We played ball with our parents, who I now know were younger than I thought then. And of course we'd feast on mother's wonderful fried chicken or some great sandwiches made from ground meat mixed with pickle relish.

When the eating and the ball game were over, it was fun to race up the slide, yell at anyone whose attention you could get, and then with great bravado throw up your hands and careen on down. But what was more fun—because it was more dangerous, more bold—was to get the wax paper that Mom had wrapped our food in (baggies hadn't been invented), and at the last minute slip it under our bottoms and really take off. The higher the slide and the waxier the paper, the wilder the ride!

This was when Mom became more "mom" as she shouted for us to be careful. Children had been hurt on slides, she warned—bones broken, faces busted open, bottoms bruised.

When Mom couldn't stop us, my father would enter the picture, enforcing mother's words.

As I think about what happens when we don't pay attention to what our heavenly Father says about dealing with the disappointments of life, it reminds me of what happens when you put wax paper on an already slippery slide. You go down—and quickly!

When you don't handle disappointment with meekness, you'll find yourself sliding right into the second Deadly D: discouragement. Discouragement is the unwelcome fruit of disappointment. It's the enemy's next level of warfare against you.

As we saw earlier, disappointments are inevitable. Yet they are fires governed by our Refiner for the purpose of achieving His will, conforming us into the image of His Son. And while it isn't wrong to be disappointed, we must be careful not to let that disappointment bring us down into discouragement. If we do, we can find ourselves sliding even further down into dejection and despair, and ending up on the ground in utter demoralization.

So what hope is there for us if we've plunged from disappointment to discouragement? Can we still reverse the slide?

Yes, my friend, even though a battle has been lost the war can still be won. It is *not* God's plan for you to be discouraged. But if you ever find yourself there, or if someone you love and can help is there, then it *is* God's plan for you to know His way out.

WHEN YOUR STRENGTH IS SMALL

What is discouragement?

The word is dis-*courage*-ment. To be discouraged is to be *without courage.*

It means being weakened, disheartened. Whatever the adversity we face, we think either *we* can't handle it or *God* can't. So we want to turn and walk away. We tell ourselves, *I can't do it, I can't handle it, I can't bear it.*

We suddenly find it so easy to give up, so easy to throw up our hands and say, "I'll never make it! It's no use. I'll never get out of this one." Our lives are mirrored in the truth of Proverbs 24:10—"If you faint in the day of adversity, your strength is small" (NKJV).

We feel as if we're standing by the bank of a river of impossibility, and we see no conceivable way to cross that rushing torrent. We easily imagine ourselves being washed downstream, smashed against the rocks, or swept over a waterfall and drowned.

We think there's no way to win in this situation. Victory looks totally unattainable.

And in truth, beloved, in that attitude and frame of heart *there really is no victory*—unless we deal biblically with that discouragement, unless we act on everything we've learned and thereby find the courage God freely gives.

Discouragement is especially damaging in our family relationships. You tell yourself you can't handle it anymore with this child or with your mate. Your family life hasn't lived up to your expectations or your marriage isn't meeting your needs the way you anticipated, and now you've let your disappointment deepen into discouragement. You only want out of the situation, because you weren't determined to stick in there and stay strong no matter what. You fail to pray, "God, this is disappointing, but I know You have something You want to teach me in this, some purpose You want to accomplish; so I will trust *You* to meet all my needs according to Your riches in glory in Christ Jesus."

Instead of looking to God, in discouragement you turn to something else or someone else, or you simply "faint in the day of adversity." You lose your fight and quickly raise the white flag of surrender when help is waiting just over the horizon of prayer.

Discouragement comes like a tornado tearing up our homes or lurks like a hidden reef that shipwrecks our relationships.

WANTING WHAT OTHERS HAVE

And even when discouragement doesn't damage our families or break up our relationships, it damages us within. So often discouragement is festered by our falling into the trap of comparison. Have you ever looked at other Christians and thought, *They've got it made! They're so blessed of God!* They seem to have what we so desperately want: a great marriage . . . a mate who loves Jesus . . . children who not only have a great relationship with their parents but also love the Lord and want to serve Him with all their hearts.

Or maybe it's someone else's successful ministry that catches our heart's desire or the material blessings they enjoy without letting those blessings hinder them at all from loving Jesus.

Whatever it is, it's something that seems ideal to us, something we long for but don't have.

If you've felt this way, I have to admit I understand. To be perfectly honest, I've been there. I've had to fight envy in my life at times when I saw my friends in situations and relationships that I longed for. And as I have thought about it, I've seen that envy is really another form of disappointment, isn't it? We're disappointed because God didn't allow us to have what someone else has. We look at the goodness of God in someone else's life and wish we could experience the same. And when we don't, we feel discouraged.

Which brings me to this thought: How often have you heard people say, "The Lord has been so good to us," as they have shared something positive that just happened to them? I've heard it often . . . as a matter of fact, from my own lips. And yet when I say or hear that expression, the thought crosses my mind: *Would it be said if something hard and painful or even evil had happened instead?* Do we still tell others, "The Lord has been so good to me"?

The answer is, "Not likely." We seem to associate only positive blessings—things that are immediately enjoyable—with the goodness of God, a perspective that goes against the grain of everything we've talked about in this book. How deeply earthbound we are! How temporal our perspective!

The same inadequate outlook is betrayed when we let envy overtake us and send us into discouragement.

The fact is, others who seem so blessed of God—those people you might have a tendency to envy—will have to endure their share of trials also if they're genuinely His. But their trials won't necessarily be the same as yours. Our trials are unique, because each of us is God's unique child. You are uniquely you, and I am uniquely me. God has His own individual set of circumstances for each of us, which He'll use to refine and purify us, bringing us through the fire of affliction so the dross of our ungodliness is consumed.

Do you remember the lesson Peter had to learn in John 21? After Jesus explained how Peter would suffer and die, the Lord then said to him, "Follow Me." Peter turned to look at John and asked Jesus what would happen to John. Jesus replied, "If I want him to remain until I come, what is that to you? *You follow Me!*" (John 21:22).

Peter would eventually be martyred—tradition has it that he was crucified upside down. What Peter never knew until he reached heaven was that John too would face persecution and great torture equal to martyrdom. Both Peter and John would be blessed in the trial of their faith, each in a unique way. But first, the right course for both was simply to follow Jesus without comparing their paths with each other's or anyone else's. Wouldn't it be freeing if we always remembered to do that?

God's way out of discouragement—whether that discouragement is bred from envy or any of a host of other causes—is to simply *follow Him*.

Let's explore the Old Testament example of Joshua to see more specifically what that can mean for us.

FACING THE RIVER

There's no doubt about it: Joshua was in a situation where anyone would find it easy to lose courage.

Under God's powerful and guiding hand, Moses had led the children of Israel out of Egypt and then through forty years in the wilderness. But now Moses was dead. Joshua, Moses' servant, was in charge as God's appointed successor. Until now Joshua had been at Moses' side and always had had Moses to depend upon. But no longer.

Now he stood alone with the people facing a flooding Jordan River. Across that river was the land of Canaan, the country God had promised to Abraham, Isaac, and Jacob as an everlasting possession, the land they were to possess. The time had come—but the leader who was to take them forward was dead, taken by God because he blew it with God and in a fit of frustration struck the rock that he was supposed to speak to.

Now Joshua stood in Moses' place.

It had been forty years since Joshua spied out this well-fortified land filled with giants. And those same Hittites, Jebusites, Amalekites, and all the other "ites" who had intimidated the Israelites forty years earlier were still there!

Can you imagine being in Joshua's sandals, having not only to take over for Moses but also to face such enemies? For just as our enemy wants to keep us from possessing what is ours from God—and will so often use discouragement to do it—so also Israel's enemies would do everything they could to keep Canaan out of Israel's hands.

Can you relate, beloved? Have you ever been asked to step in for somebody else in a leadership responsibility? You think, *God, who am I? How can I do this?* Suddenly your knees are knocking, and you're losing your courage.

We don't know whether Joshua's knees were knocking, but we do know God had much to say to him about courage.

As he stood before the Lord in the opening scene of the book of Joshua, God commanded him again to lead the children of Israel into this land and take possession of what God had promised to Abraham, Isaac, and Jacob— a land that lay across a river that was no ankle-deep stream.

God told him,

> Moses My servant is dead; now therefore arise, cross this Jordan,
> you and all this people, to the land which I am giving to them, to the
> sons of Israel. Every place on which the sole of your foot treads, I
> have given it to you, just as I spoke to Moses. (Joshua 1:2-3)

"That's *your* land!" God was saying. "I've given it to *you*." Only a sovereign God can say something like that!

In the next verse God detailed for Joshua the precise borders of this long and wide land He was giving them. Then He added,

> No man will be able to stand before you all the days of your life.
> Just as I have been with Moses, *I will be with you; I will not fail you
> or forsake you.* (1:5)

Here was a promise Joshua could hang on to—just as you and I can. This promise is reiterated in the New Testament, in Hebrews. Listen: "For he hath said, *I will never leave thee, nor forsake thee.* So that we may boldly say, The Lord is my helper, and I will not fear what man shall do unto me" (13:5-6, KJV).

Then God added this instruction:

> *Be strong and courageous*, for you shall give this people possession
> of the land which I swore to their fathers to give them. (1:6)

Don't be *dis*couraged, God was saying—don't be lacking in courage. Don't be weak. Don't be disheartened. No, *be strong and courageous.*

These are words that God would repeat twice more to Joshua in a span of only four verses. "Only be strong and very courageous," He said in verse 7. Again in verse 9 He added:

> Have I not commanded you? *Be strong and courageous!* Do not
> tremble or be dismayed, for the LORD your God is with you
> wherever you go.

It was courage rather than discouragement that would bring the children of Israel into the promises of God.

And courage rather than discouragement will also bring you and me into the promises of God.

THE COST OF DISCOURAGEMENT

Perhaps when God spoke these words to him, Joshua remembered how discouragement at Kadesh-Barnea had brought forty years of wilderness wandering to the children of Israel. *Forty years!*—all because they had focused on the giants in the land and forgotten the promises of God and thereby lost courage. Instead of being strong back then, as Joshua and Caleb had suggested, instead of clinging to God's promises and facing their enemies in faith, the Israelites were swept into deception by the discouraging report of ten of the twelve spies. That story is told in Numbers 13 and 14, recorded there, says 1 Corinthians 10:11, as examples to teach us; "For whatever was written in earlier times was written for our instruction, that through perseverance and the *encouragement* of the Scriptures we might have hope" (Romans 15:4).

By the way, did you notice the word *courage* crouched in the phrase, "the encouragement of the Scriptures"? Courage is found in taking God at His Word and believing Him when we face difficult waters and seemingly impossible tasks.

Forty years of wilderness wandering had followed Israel's failure. But this was their moment to move out of it, to move on.

Oh, dear reader, have you also been wandering in a wilderness of discouragement? There *is* a way of escape. There is a way to move out and move on.

God's path of escape is for you to determine now—in dependence upon Him and upon His promises, His commandments, His Word—to *be strong and courageous*. This is God's constant admonition to us, just as it was to Joshua.

Before Moses died, he stood before "all Israel" to speak these words:

> I am a hundred and twenty years old today; I am no longer able to come and go, and the LORD has said to me, "You shall not cross

this Jordan." It is the LORD your God who will cross ahead of you; He will destroy these nations before you, and you shall dispossess them.

Joshua is the one who will cross ahead of you, just as the LORD has spoken. . . . *Be strong and courageous*, do not be afraid or tremble at them, for *the LORD your God is the one who goes with you. He will not fail you or forsake you.* (Deuteronomy 31:2-6)

On this same occasion,

Moses called to Joshua and said to him in the sight of all Israel, *"Be strong and courageous,* for you shall go with this people into the land which the LORD has sworn to their fathers to give them, and you shall give it to them as an inheritance. And the LORD is the one who goes ahead of you; *He will be with you. He will not fail you or forsake you.* Do not fear, or be dismayed." (31:7-8)

God's repeated command to His people both yesterday and today is that we be strong *and not be discouraged.* Discouragement was not God's path for His people then, nor is it now or ever.

COURAGE TO SPARE AND TO SHARE

We're to be strong and courageous—and we're to help our brothers and sisters do the same.

Look at how the sharing of strength and courage are taught in a chapter I love, Isaiah 35—

Encourage the exhausted, and *strengthen* the feeble.
Say to those with anxious heart,
    "Take courage, fear not.
Behold, your God will come with vengeance;
    The recompense of God will come,
But He will save you."

(35:3-4)

The basis for encouragement on the part of God's people was that they could know what the future holds: The recompense of God *will come.* Therefore they were to encourage and strengthen those who were weak and worn out. In their present situation they could look to the future *and not fear.*

Yes, the judgment of God is coming—*"but He will save you"!* God's faithful ones can rest assured in their salvation and find strength for today because of it.

In the previous two verses, Isaiah had richly foretold even more of Israel's future:

> The wilderness and the desert will be glad,
> > And the Arabah will rejoice and blossom;
> Like the crocus
> > It will blossom profusely
> > And rejoice with rejoicing and shout of joy.
> The glory of Lebanon will be given to it,
> > The majesty of Carmel and Sharon.
> They will see the glory of the LORD,
> > The majesty of our God.

(35:1-2)

All this was coming, Isaiah was saying, in the glory and majesty of God. So what should God's people do as they stood on the banks of the Jordan? They were to encourage and strengthen any who were fearful of heart, any who were discouraged. And they were to remind them of God's salvation and His promise: *I will save you!*

In the last half of this brief chapter, Isaiah looks again to the future, prophesying even more wonders for Israel:

> Then the eyes of the blind will be opened,
> > And the ears of the deaf will be unstopped.
> Then the lame will leap like a deer,
> > And the tongue of the dumb will shout for joy.

For waters will break forth in the wilderness
    And streams in the Arabah. . . .
And the ransomed of the LORD will return,
    And come with joyful shouting to Zion,
    With everlasting joy upon their heads.
They will find gladness and joy,
    And sorrow and sighing will flee away.

(35:5-6,10)

He was showing Israel her end, *and her end is good*. Therefore they could hold on to courage.

What about you, beloved? Have you listened to the world's analysis of your condition or of your future rather than being strong and courageously believing what your God says?

Isaiah's words—"written in earlier times"—are also recorded for our instruction and encouragement. They are precepts and principles you and I can know and apply, along with God's inspiring words to Joshua on the banks of the Jordan.

THE WAY TO CERTAIN SUCCESS

As we return to those banks, we see God had more to say to Joshua and Israel, to help them—and us—to understand a specific and foundational principle for living in courage. God told him,

> Be careful to do according to all the law which Moses My servant commanded you; do not turn from it to the right or to the left, so that you may have success wherever you go. (Joshua 1:7)

In other words—"Obey My Word, live by it, never proceed in any other direction than that—and then you'll experience victory."

And He said,

> This book of the law shall not depart from your mouth, but you shall meditate on it day and night so that you may be careful to do

according to all that is written in it; for then you will make your way prosperous, and then you will have success. (1:8)

"You know what I've told you," God was saying; "you know what I've promised you. Now meditate on it. Don't let it come in the ear and merely 'depart out of your mouth'—don't just quote it—but *think* upon it. Chew it, digest it. Know it and deeply understand it so you're ready to fully *do* it, to really *live* it." It cannot be mere head-filled orthodoxy; it must be heart-embraced truth.

"And yes," God said to Joshua and to us, "I promise you: Do this and you *will* have success. You *will* be prosperous. You *will* have victory."

Once more God told Joshua in verse 9, *"Be strong and courageous,"* and likewise He repeated His most precious promise: "Do not tremble or be dismayed, for *the LORD your God is with you wherever you go.*" We need not tremble. We need not be dismayed, confused, overwhelmed by the situation, for God—the creator of the heavens and the earth—is with us. What greater help could we have?

This is also God's continued reminder for you and me, no matter what we face: *"I'm always there,* I'm the sovereign God, whatever you go through *I am there* to protect you; I will take you through it. *So do not be discouraged."*

This is the essential for success in the spiritual warfare we face.

Joshua was about to lead the children of Israel into war, and no war is won by cowards who want to sit down in discouragement and be captured or retreat in defeat.

And what would bring Joshua victory, beloved, is what will also bring us victory, and we must turn to it especially whenever we battle discouragement: God's Book must not depart from our mouth, but we must meditate on it day and night that we may be careful to do according to all that is written in it. This is why my life and our ministry are devoted to teaching people how to know and appropriate the truths of the Word of God for themselves.

Only then will we make our ways prosperous. Only then will we have success.

The enemy wants to knock out of your hand your one and only offensive weapon, Ephesians 6:17 warns. He wants you to drop *your sword*. If he can get you to do that, you have nothing to battle back with.

Yes, beloved, this is spiritual warfare, and the enemy wants you to buy his lies! Behind all discouragement—anything that causes you to lose courage in your circumstances of life—you will find a thought that has interpreted the situation contrary to the character of God, the will of God, the promises of God, the Word of God.

I'm sure you've experienced it: You find yourself disappointed and discouraged, and you're tempted to stay away from the Word. Or sometimes when you begin reading it, it seems as if someone is tearing up your insides, flooding you and blinding you with thoughts and feelings that are miles away from consistency with anything on the pages of God's Word. The devil is trying to jam your communication with God. He wants more than anything else to put a wedge between you and God. He wants you to listen to his lies and buy them as truth—to look at life's circumstances and think there is no way God can override them.

But if you ask for and depend on His help, God will help bring back your thoughts to Him, and He will speak to you as you hold on courageously to His truth and the promise of His presence.

OPEN COMMUNICATION

Beloved, believe God—no matter what you see, no matter what you think, no matter what you feel. Stay in His Word.

Keeping the communication lines open also means *praying*. When discouragement attacks, you must be consistent in prayer.

"Keep watching and praying," Jesus said, *"that you may not come into temptation; the spirit is willing, but the flesh is weak"* (Mark 14:38).

In the Ephesians passage on spiritual warfare, God reminded us,

"With all prayer and petition pray at all times in the Spirit, and with this in view, be on the alert with all perseverance and petition for all the saints" (6:18).

Bring *everything* to Him in prayer.

As I write this, I've just finished my quiet time in Isaiah 36 and 37, which describes a confrontation between King Hezekiah and King Sennacherib of Assyria. Perhaps even more than Joshua, Hezekiah was a candidate for discouragement in the situation he found himself in as recorded in these chapters and also in 2 Kings 18 and 19. The king of Assyria had already captured and dispersed the northern kingdom of Israel. He was on a conquering rampage. Nation after nation had gone down in defeat to his mighty Assyrian army. Now he wanted to add a defeat over Hezekiah and the southern kingdom of Judah to his list of conquests.

He sent his messenger to the walls of Jerusalem, telling the whole city that God Himself wanted Assyria to destroy Jerusalem (Isaiah 36:10). When this tactic failed to cause the people to overthrow Hezekiah, the Assyrian king spelled out his threats of destruction in a letter.

Hezekiah had every human reason to be overwhelmed with discouragement, for the odds were truly against him—if you looked at circumstances instead of looking to the One who controls them. Humanly speaking, Jerusalem's demise was certain.

But Hezekiah looked to God. With the letter in hand, he went straight to the temple, spread the letter out before the Lord, and prayed: "O LORD of hosts, the God of Israel, who art enthroned above the cherubim, Thou art the God, Thou alone, of all the kingdoms of the earth. Thou hast made heaven and earth. Incline Thine ear, O LORD, and hear; open Thine eyes, O LORD" (Isaiah 37:16-17).

At once God sent His answer to Hezekiah through the prophet Isaiah: "Thus says the LORD, the God of Israel, *'Because you have prayed to Me* about Sennacherib king of Assyria, *I have heard you'*" (2 Kings 19:20). Because Hezekiah stayed in communication with God, an angel of the Lord in one night struck down 185,000 troops in the Assyrian camp. Sennacherib went back to Assyria, where he was soon assassinated by his own sons while he worshiped in a temple of idolatry.

Oh, the power of prayer! Remember that the next time you're tempted to be discouraged. Prayer brings victory. Talk to God and let *Him* deal with the cause of your discouragement.

Pray and stay in God's Word and don't ever doubt His love or concern for you as His child—no matter what you might have done, no matter what circumstances you find yourself in.

Never forget that Satan is exposed in Scripture as the accuser of the brethren and the accuser of God. So don't believe any of Satan's lying accusations that God doesn't love and care for you and won't protect you and provide for you.

Remember that this attitude is what brought defeat to the children of Israel at Kadesh-Barnea. They got it into their heads that God didn't care about them and wouldn't protect them. They cried out, "Why is the LORD bringing us into this land, to fall by the sword?" (Numbers 14:3).

Be careful, beloved, who you tune in to.

Listen for God, and watch for Him.

When we're like the disciples on the sea, straining at the oars with the wind against us, the Lord will come and say to us, *"Take courage*; it is I, do not be afraid" (Mark 6:50).

And when others we know are in need like blind Bartimaeus, and they're crying out for God's help as Bartimaeus did—we can know the Lord has heard and wants communion and communication with His children, and we can say to them what was said to Bartimaeus, *"Take courage,* arise! He is calling for you" (Mark 10:49).

Let's go back one more time to Joshua on the riverbank. Joshua now had a choice, just as we do. He knew God's calling on his life, he knew God had called him to be the leader, he knew God's promise to give them that land to possess it, and he knew that only discouragement could keep him from victory.

And now . . . he had to cross that river.

That next step would be the true test of his courage.

But with the rich provision of God's guiding Word and the sure promise of victory and most of all the unshakable assurance of God's continual presence—how could Joshua do anything other than boldly step out and step forward in courage and confident faith?

Likewise, how can you and I do anything else, since we too have the promise of just as much?

Let us run with endurance the race that is set before us.

HEBREWS 12:1

CHAPTER ELEVEN

A CALL TO COURAGE

Learning Endurance—in Good Company

THE PEOPLE WE ADMIRE MOST are those who have suffered most and yet endured with grace. We may at times have an infatuation with others who are wealthier or more glamorous or talented or popular. And we may for a while be captivated by some who have experienced an awesome miracle in their lives—they were blind and now they see, or they were lame and now they walk, or they had cancer and now they're cured.

But those who bear with continued suffering capture our deepest respect, and in their suffering we find ourselves drawn to the Jesus who dwells within them—the Jesus they love more than self, more than blessing and benefit; the Jesus they have chosen to follow no matter the cost. Our hearts are stirred, our spirits inflamed, our eyes filled with tears as we listen to those who in faith's courage say with Job, "The LORD gave and the LORD has taken away. Blessed be the name of the LORD" (Job 1:21). In the midst of pain they say, "But it is still my consolation, and I rejoice in unsparing pain, that I have not denied the words of the Holy One" (6:10).

One of my greatest joys in our ministry is reading letters from ordinary people the world doesn't know about but who are "abiding under" unbelievable circumstances. They manifest the joy of valiant warriors, the joy of those who are becoming more than conquerors. They've learned what God's Word has to say, and they walk in the light of it. They believe God, and their stories are the ones I like most to hold up in my teaching as illustrations and examples for all of us.

One woman wrote to say she had a wheelchair-bound husband, a victim of Agent Orange. He also had lupus and rheumatoid arthritis. She said they received no government financial assistance, so she worked both night and day. "I sometimes wonder where the next meal will come from," she wrote, "but my God supplies."

On top of all this, she said they had a child with tremendous problems plus another child who had been sexually molested by a relative. Yet after listing all these problems, she wrote, "Praise God. Jesus reigns." And she told how much she was looking forward to beginning a new Bible study.

Another woman wrote to tell me she had listened one day to a taped message I'd given on the sovereignty of God. The verse standing out to her from that message was Deuteronomy 32:39—"See now that I, I am He, and there is no god besides Me; it is I who put to death and give life. I have wounded, and it is I who heal; and there is no one who can deliver from My hand." On the following day, her eighteen-year-old daughter was killed. In the days that followed, she said this passage rang over and over in her mind.

She persisted in studying God's Word, and then her husband suddenly died. Later her own health gave out, and she went through open-heart surgery. But she was excited to tell me of a friend who had asked for her help in Bible study. "It was a joy seeing her understanding being increased," she wrote. "We all so desperately need to be in the Word to learn of it and grow."

How easy it would be to grow bitter in the face of such severe trials as this sister in the Lord encountered. But she *abided* under them. She counted it all joy, and so trials produced in her endurance, steadfastness, *stickability*. Now she was focused not on her suffering but on the joy of equipping another young woman in the Word of God.

A number of years ago I read a brief but inspiring summary of the life of Mae Louise Westervelt. The tribute was written at the time of her death by a good friend of ours, Robertson McQuilken, the president of Columbia Bible College, from which Mrs. Westervelt had graduated in 1938. This is the portrait of endurance that tribute paints:

> She and her young husband dreamed of providing a home for missionary children. She was carrying her firstborn when her husband was crippled in body and spirit in a terrible automobile accident. Partially recovered, he carried on valiantly, but little Mae Louise was destined to carry the spiritual thrust of the family. Her newborn son was hopelessly handicapped, and at age eleven his young life was snuffed out in a drowning accident.
>
> Tragedy again stalked Mae Louise as her daughter, only a few weeks away from graduating with honors from the University of South Carolina, was killed in an automobile accident. But she kept on with bright good cheer, leading the missions program in her little Baptist church, teaching the teenage girls, and shepherding the children of the neighborhood.
>
> She and her husband secured several low-cost homes in a community of modest residences. . . . These she rented to Bible college students and to missionaries on furlough. Mae Louise kept in touch with the missionaries, supporting them sacrificially, and praying.
>
> One day, as her husband changed a tire by the roadside, he was killed by a drunken driver. Undaunted, Mae Louise walked the streets of her neighborhood, selling Avon products to support her adopted son and sharing the good news of life in Christ. On Fridays she visited the sick in the hospital. On Thursdays there was

evangelistic home visitation. At other times there were Bible studies with the unsaved.

Then came surgery. A pace-maker extended her fragile life, but she just kept pressing on. Sunday morning she would gather a load of little boys in her rattly old Plymouth, bring them to Sunday school, and sit with them as they wiggled their way through the worship service. . . .

I am so glad I told her at Christmastime, "you are one of my true heroes!" And she was. . . .

OUR WITNESSES FOR COURAGE

Hebrews 11 is another record of heroes. While reading the last part of this chapter, in my mind I can hear all of Christendom cheering. We want to shout, "Yes, yes!" as we read of those who by faith conquered kingdoms or shut the mouths of lions or quenched the power of fire or escaped the edge of the sword or put foreign armies to flight. And then there are the women who received back their dead by *resurrection*. Yes, here is victory and deliverance!

Then comes the contrast: *"And others . . ."* We find that these others seemingly had no victory, no deliverance: "And others were tortured, not accepting their release, in order that they might obtain a *better resurrection*" (11:35). They were offered release; they had an opportunity to escape their torture. But they didn't take it, because they wanted the resurrection that is better.

This better resurrection means there's a reward for going through suffering without fainting, without retreating, but steadfastly enduring by faith.

As we read on, it seems that evil is triumphing, that God is deaf, or that He isn't doing the God-things He could be doing:

> And others experienced mockings and scourgings, yes, also chains
> and imprisonment. They were stoned, they were sawn in two, they

were tempted, they were put to death with the sword; they went about in sheepskins, in goatskins, being destitute, afflicted, ill-treated (men of whom the world was not worthy), wandering in deserts and mountains and caves and holes in the ground. (verses 36-38)

It can seem like this for us too: that God isn't at work, because He isn't changing some situation of affliction or injustice or evil, even though we've cried out to Him.

But we can take courage and fear not; we can endure, just as these heroes in Hebrews 11 endured. These were those of whom the world was not worthy because they chose suffering. Their eyes were on a better reward than earth holds, a better resurrection. They understood and believed this, and therefore Hebrews 11:39 tells us they "gained approval through their faith."

These same people now make up "so great a cloud of witnesses" for us, as described in Hebrews 12:1. And because this cloud surrounds us, because the witnesses are looking on, there's this encouragement for you and me: "Let us also lay aside every encumbrance, and the sin which so easily entangles us, and let us run *with endurance* the race that is set before us, fixing our eyes on Jesus, the author and perfecter of faith, who for the joy set before Him *endured* the cross" (12:1-2). Because they endured and because Jesus endured—therefore let *us* now also endure.

In whatever affliction we face, we can be strong and courageous because *it's not over.* One of the things I keep telling people is that their book is not finished—the last chapter has not yet been written. There's more to the story. We face a disappointment, and we think this is the end. But it's not the end . . . it's the middle or maybe only the beginning, but not the end. The end is always that this—whatever "this" is—will result in our good and His glory.

How very far this is from where each of us started out: from the fact that I was a sinner and messed up, without hope, ungodly, helpless, and an enemy of God. And though I'm still facing some of the consequences of my sins, even this will all work together for good when the end of the story is written.

A STUDY ON STICKABILITY

Perhaps more than anything else, *courage* means persevering . . . enduring
. . . overcoming.

It means stickability . . . steadfastness.

If there's anything critically lacking in the character of most of those living today in the United States of America, this is it. We turn and run away
from our disappointments and difficulties. We flee into drugs, alcohol, or
adulterous affairs. We escape into fantasy—vicariously indulging our
dreams and desires through television, movies, novels, or now the Internet.

So very often we don't have endurance. But our loving God wants us
to have it and hold on to it, and in His sovereignty He has provided the
way for us to do just that. So let's look closer at what He says.

Do you remember what James said about the purpose of trials? "Consider it all joy, my brethren, when you encounter various trials, knowing
that the testing of your faith produces *endurance*" (1:2-3). The Greek word
for *endurance* here is *hupomeno. Hupo* is the word in Greek for "under."
Meno means "to abide," or "to remain." So to endure a hardship means
to "abide under" that hardship, to "remain under" it. When a disappointment comes, when the Refiner brings the fire, you stay there. You stick with
it. You don't give up and try to run away.

Look again at James 1:3. It's the *"testing* of your faith" that produces
endurance. The word translated here as "testing" is a form of the Greek
dokimos, and it has the meaning of *proof.* It's a word used for proving
something by putting it to the test and demonstrating that it's genuine.

James was telling us that God will take our faith and prove that it's real
by putting us through trials. Do we want our faith to be strengthened and
proven? Do we want our faith to be *real*? Of course we do, if our values
are the same as God's. And that's why we're to count it all joy when by
God's gracious plan we see it happening as we face those disappointments
and difficulties.

He *proves* us. His purpose in our every trial is not to *dis*prove us, not
to show us how awful we are, how weak, how impotent—but to demon-

strate the genuineness, the strength of our faith. When you and I go through a trial victoriously, it strengthens our faith, builds our spiritual muscles.

PERFECT RESULTS

James went on to say,

> And let endurance have its perfect result, that you may be perfect and complete, lacking in nothing. (1:4)

What is this "perfect result" of endurance? What's the finished outcome of abiding under, of staying steadfast, of not running away from a trial but rejoicing in God and thanking Him for it?

The result is that you become "perfect and complete, lacking in nothing." There's a promised blessing of perfection and completion for the one who *wants* it and who therefore endures.

This term *perfection* throws us. Perhaps an easier way to think of it is *maturity*. Maturity is what we're always to seek as Christians.

After all, what is a Christian? Technically, a Christian is any person who possesses Christ. Christianity is essentially "Christ in you, the hope of glory" (Colossians 1:27). Christ is in you, and more and more as He consumes you and you are consumed by Him, it's like a blossoming, a coming out. . . . This is the perfection, the maturity.

We want the *fullness* of Christ.

Paul constantly had this in mind. He always had a vision of that final perfection in Christ as well as the unsurpassed privilege of growing toward that perfection now. And to attain that perfection—to the extent of being "found in Christ" and of fully knowing Christ—he said in Philippians 3 that he counted everything else as loss (verse 8).

And he added, "Not that I have already obtained it, or have already become perfect, but I press on in order that I may lay hold of that for which also I was laid hold of by Christ Jesus" (verse 12). Paul wasn't there yet, but he said he pressed on toward the goal for the prize of the upward call of God in Christ Jesus. Then he added, "Let us therefore, *as many as are perfect*, have this attitude. . . ." (verse 15).

Paul's expectation and his teaching for God's people was that we would press on to become perfect, mature, complete.

In essence, we want to be able to say what John the Baptist said about Jesus: "I must decrease, and He must increase." John was fading away as Christ was coming to the fore. More and more we want who we are only in ourselves to fade away so that, more and more, others will see Jesus in us—and I must confess that I'm ashamed that people don't see more of Jesus in me and less of myself.

PROVING OUR LOVE

Look again with me at James 1, moving ahead to verse 12. James said, "Blessed is a man who *perseveres* under trial"—and this word *perseveres* is also from the Greek *hupomeno*—again James was speaking of one who endures, one who abides under the trial. And how is this person blessed? James said that "once he has been *approved*"—and here is *dokimos* again, the testing that proves genuineness—"he will receive the crown of life, which the Lord has promised to those who love Him."

The crown of life is promised to those who endure . . . and those who endure are the approved ones . . . and the approved ones are those who *love* Him.

If I stay and endure in the trial I'm now facing, if I respond to it in meekness, this demonstrates that *I really love God*. Love doesn't seek its own, we learn in 1 Corinthians 13. Love seeks another's highest good. If I love God then I'm seeking not my own comfort or selfish aims but rather *His highest good*. Therefore I say, "Lord, if it pleases You, it pleases me."

By enduring in this way you'll reach the point where your purpose and mission in life are truly finished and perfect and complete. You can come before Jesus Christ face to face and say as Paul did, "I have fought the good fight, I have *finished* the course, I have kept the faith" (2 Timothy 4:7). And like Paul you will know even now that "in the future there is laid up for me the crown of righteousness, which the Lord, the righteous Judge, will award to me on that day; and not only to me, but also to all who have loved His appearing" (4:8).

By enduring, as you approach the end of your life you can then say to your heavenly Father as Jesus did, "I . . . *accomplished* the work which Thou hast given Me to do" (John 17:4).

You'll receive the crowns of life and of righteousness that God gives to all who love Him and who have loved His appearing, and who *because of that love* have abided under the trials the Refiner sent their way to make them perfect.

THE SPECIAL TEMPTATION OF TRIALS

Let's look again at James 1, and this time notice the close relationship there between trials and temptation. James talked about both in the same context. After talking about enduring trials, asking God's wisdom, and glorying in your circumstances, he said in verse 12: "Blessed is a man who perseveres under trial. . . ." Then immediately in the next verse James transitioned into temptation:

> Let no one say *when he is tempted*, "I am being tempted by God"; for God cannot be tempted by evil, and He Himself does not tempt anyone. (1:13)

When you're in a trial there's always the danger of temptation, and the temptation is this: that you'll face that trial in the reaction and power of your flesh rather than in the power and control of the Holy Spirit. And if you're reacting only in the flesh to these flames, you may well be tempted to escape—to pop out of the crucible and run away instead of enduring, instead of abiding under.

The lessons we learn on temptation from James 1 are crucial, and we don't want to miss them. Here are three that we want to note:

First, temptation is never from God.

Second, just to be tempted is not sin.

And third, to yield to this temptation *is* sin.

I've had women come to me and in essence say, "I know God told me to leave my husband and to marry this other man; God doesn't want me and my children to have to put up with him. And the children will be better off with another father." Or men will say the same thing: "Surely God doesn't want me to live like this, to be so unhappy, unfulfilled." In the midst of our trials, we can be so prone to rationalize our way of escape, our way to get out of the situation! And in the process we convince ourselves that this escape is of God. We buy in to the conclusion that James said we should never reach: "I am being tempted by God."

But *God never tempts us to act contrary to the precepts in His Word.* James made it clear that just as God Himself can't be tempted, so also He does not tempt anyone.

James went on to tell us the source of these temptations:

> But each one is tempted when he is carried away and enticed by his own lust. Then when lust has conceived, it gives birth to sin; and when sin is accomplished, it brings forth death. (1:14-15)

To be tempted is not sin; to yield is. Sin doesn't happen until lust conceives and gives birth to it. Sin doesn't happen until lust takes the bait of temptation and then runs with it.

Remember this, beloved, when you're in a trial and thoughts of running away or worse come to mind. Those thoughts themselves are a temptation from the flesh, but they are not sin. Let me say it again: To have those thoughts is not sin. But to yield to them *is* sin—to yield to them is to mistrust God rather than to trust Him. It is choosing to yield to the desire within—that's when conception takes place and sin is born!

But you have His Spirit within your soul, and therefore you can hang on, *and you need not sin.*

In the midst of any disappointment or trial, our first normal, human reaction will be in the flesh. Our normal first response will be to react rather than act. And though you'll have those temptations, if you walk by the Holy Spirit you won't yield to them—and they won't give birth to sin.

Remember Jesus in the Garden of Gethsemane. Remember how He cried out to God in the midst of His trial, "Lord, if it is possible, remove this cup from Me. Nevertheless, not My will but Thine be done." Three times He wrestled in prayer with that request. He was God, but He was man—God in the flesh. He was tempted in all points as you and I are. And in the midst of His trial He woke up His disciples and told them what you and I must always keep in mind: "Watch and pray, for the spirit is willing but the flesh is weak."

Watch and pray. However willing your spirit is, your flesh is still weak.

Therefore you must remember that in Christ you are more than a conqueror. That's why, no matter how great the disappointment, no matter how painful the trial, you can count it all joy. You can rejoice and abide under it. You can endure. You have the Endurer within you!

Endure, and do not yield to the temptations that come. If you will not yield, God will give you incredible victory, and in the process He will use it all to make you like Himself.

NO COWARDS HERE

So what will we choose, beloved reader—to be cowardly quitters or to be courageous overcomers who endure and finish?

In the opening verses of Revelation 21 we're told about a new heaven and a new earth and the holy city New Jerusalem and God Himself dwelling among His people and wiping away every tear from their eyes and the spring of the water of life for everyone who's thirsty. And God said, *"He who overcomes* shall inherit these things, and I will be his God and he will be My son" (21:7).

Then He gave a list of those whose part will not be in the New Jerusalem but instead will be in the lake of fire, which is the second death. And who's at the very top of this list? *The cowardly.* Next are the "the unbelieving," and then come "the abominable and murderers and immoral persons and sorcerers and idolaters and all liars." So God lumps cowards together with all these evildoers. Interesting, isn't it?

This isn't to say people who are discouraged will go to hell instead of heaven. But this passage is insightful for revealing the importance of courage and for showing us the link between unbelief and wickedness on one hand and on the other, lacking courage so that you don't keep or walk by His commandments.

God wants us to be courageous overcomers. "And who is the one who overcomes the world?" (1 John 5:5). The answer is: "He who *believes* that Jesus is the Son of God." John said, "This is the victory that has overcome the world—*our faith*" (5:4). A cowardly person is someone who isn't believing God, who isn't having faith.

So when you find yourself discouraged, bring it before God: "God, I've been discouraged. I haven't been strong, I haven't been courageous, I haven't embraced Your Word.

"God, I repent. Father, I'm going to rejoice, I'm going to grab Philippians 4:13 and embrace it: I can do all things (bear all things) through Christ Jesus, who infuses His strength into me. I can do *all* things. I can stand, I can be strong, I can be courageous, because I have an infusion of the strength of Christ Jesus in me. I have God's strength and His power."

Because I live, you shall live also.

JOHN 14:19

CHAPTER TWELVE

WHERE COURAGE SHOWS MOST

Secrets of Everyday Endurance

SO WHAT ABOUT those situations where, even for believers, a particular sin seems so entrenched? This, for so many, is a source of deep discouragement.

Do you know someone who's caught in what we often call in the terminology of Hebrews 12:1 a "besetting sin"? A besetting sin is something that has such a hold on a person that he or she can't seem to get free from its viselike clutch. Maybe that "someone" is even you.

Rejoice, my friend; there *is* a way to break free.

OUR DECLARATION OF INDEPENDENCE

Freedom from sin—even nagging, unrelenting sin—is what Jesus Christ's resurrection . . . and ours . . . is all about. The One who died on Good Friday was raised on Sunday, and because in the mysterious economy of God we are foreknown by God, we were identified—united in His death and in His resurrection. Because Jesus was raised from the dead, *we* have been raised and shall be raised.

Christ's resurrection is the declaration and promise of our independence—our freedom from that viselike grip of sin. You know, so often when we think or speak of the gospel of Jesus Christ, we talk of Jesus' death for our sins, yet we speak little of His resurrection, which according to 1 Corinthians 15 is an essential element of the gospel. The practical implications of His resurrection are incredible and liberating. I believe that if we really understood what it means that Jesus Christ rose from the dead, it would forever change the way we live, the way we deal with sin, and the way we help others deal with it.

Let's look at 1 Corinthians 15 together, so we'll be perfectly clear on what the gospel is, for our own sake as well as for explaining it to others.

The fact that Jesus Christ died for our sins is the critical first point of the gospel. In verse 3 of this passage Paul said, "For I delivered to you as of first importance what I also received, that Christ died for our sins according to the Scriptures." Jesus died for a reason: He died "for our sins." Remember how Paul told us in Romans 3:10 that there is none righteous, not one? Then in 3:23 he said that all have sinned and fallen short (missing the mark) of the glory (the correct image, the proper estimate) of God, in whose image Adam and Eve were created. We're all born into this state of sin. David said, "In sin my mother conceived me" (Psalm 51:5).

The point is, we aren't what we're supposed to be, and if something doesn't change our state—and thus our status—we will never enter the kingdom of heaven because no matter how hard we try in one area or another, we'll fall short of the spiritual maturity, the perfection of Jesus Christ.

Why? Because God calls the shots, and He says that the wages—the payment—for sin is death, which is eternal separation from Him in a place called the lake of fire. In other words, every person born will live forever *somewhere*—either in an eternal state of life with the Father, Son, and Holy Spirit on a new earth with a new heaven, *or* in an eternal state of damnation called "the second death." The second death is the lake of fire where the worm dies not and the fire is not quenched.

Whoever doesn't believe this—and I doubt that's the case with you— does not believe the Bible. And whoever doesn't believe the Bible is deny- ing truth. Any person who believes he or she can attain eternal life and escape the consequences of sin apart from the Lord Jesus Christ is deceived and deluded and headed for the second death—not because I say so but be- cause this is the clear yet unpopular message of the Word of God. This is "the word of *truth*, the gospel" (Colossians 1:5).

Anyone who doesn't believe this is embracing a lie. It all boils down to a matter of simple faith; you either take God at His Word about something that hasn't actually happened yet, or you don't. And if you don't, you may not realize the certain truth of it until you are there, and then it will be too late to repent, to have a change of mind.

So the first fact of the good news is that Jesus died for your sins. He paid the wage in full, the wage you owed God. The Lord Jesus Christ, the only begotten Son of God, became a man, born of God's seed through a virgin. He alone among all men was not conceived or born in a state of sin. He was born without inherent sin, and although He was tempted to com- mit acts of sin just as you and I are tempted, Jesus never yielded to this temptation.

HIS CHOICE—AND OURS

Because Jesus was born without sin and because He never sinned, He did not have to die. Yet out of love and obedience to the Father, Jesus *chose* to die in your place, as your substitute. Jesus, who knew no sin, was made to be sin for you so you could have His righteousness, a gift of pure grace— unearned and unmerited favor—and with that righteousness, eternal life.

However, beloved, it did not stop there! The fourth verse of 1 Corinthi- ans 15 tells us that Jesus was indeed buried—the proof of His death—but that He was raised on the third day. The next four verses record all the times Jesus was seen on earth after His resurrection. The varied and multiple witnesses and the surrounding circumstances give proof of the fact that He who was dead, very dead, now lives. For according to Romans 6:9, "Christ, having been raised from the dead, is *never to die again.*"

So what makes His resurrection so profound? When you grasp the whole picture from the New Testament, you can't miss the fact that if you really believe the gospel so as to embrace it in faith, then you, beloved, will live *because Jesus lives* (John 11:25-26, 14:19).

And listen to this, dear believer: You can live as a victor, not only over death, but over sin! For once you genuinely believe, you are set free from slavery to sin. Whoever commits sin is the slave of sin, but if the Son sets you free, you will be free indeed (John 8:31-36). Free indeed! Free from what? Free from sin's power to enslave you, its victim! Free from sin's power to hold you or any other believer in its clutching grip.

Now, this next statement may sound rash, but it's biblical: *No true child of God is involuntarily a slave to any besetting sin. Sin is always a choice for the believer.* It has to be, or the death and resurrection of Jesus Christ was not efficacious—it did not do its job of setting us free from sin's slavery.

This is why God said to His church, "You shall be holy, for I am holy" (1 Peter 1:16). *Holy* means "to be set apart." The work Jesus accomplished on the cross sets apart everyone who believes in Jesus and in what Jesus did. Every time you and I act in faith, which is to walk in obedience to truth, we overcome the pull, the promise, the lure, and the seductive deadliness of sin. We're tempted to sin, but we don't have to yield to it.

This freedom from slavery to sin that I am speaking of is set forth in Romans 6. Therefore, if you're having a hard time believing or grasping what I'm saying, may I suggest, beloved, that you read Romans 6 prayerfully on your knees, over and over, day in and day out until God explains it in all its fullness of truth by the Holy Spirit.

YOU HAVE THE POWER

This is the truth that makes 1 Corinthians 6:9-11 so clear and powerful. Let me quote this passage for you:

> Or do you not know that the unrighteous shall not inherit the kingdom of God? Do not be deceived; neither fornicators, nor idolaters, nor adulterers, nor effeminate, nor homosexuals, nor thieves, nor the covetous, nor drunkards, nor revilers, nor swindlers, shall inherit the kingdom of God. And such were some of you; but you were washed, but you were sanctified, but you were justified in the name of the Lord Jesus Christ, and in the Spirit of our God.

Did you notice? "And such *were* some of you." This is what you *were*. In the Greek, *were* is in the imperfect tense, which refers to continuous or linear action in the past. This is what you were before you were united by faith with Jesus Christ in His death and resurrection. But now you have been *washed*, cleansed by Jesus' blood shed on the cross. You were *sanctified*, set apart by your identification with Christ. Baptism as transliterated from the Greek in Romans 6:3-4 means "to be identified or united with." Thus when *Jesus the Christ* died, *you* died. When He was raised, you were raised with Him to walk in *newness* of life (Romans 6:3-7).

And because of everything Christ accomplished, you were *justified*—declared righteous before God, put in right standing with Him. Romans 4:25 describes Jesus this way: "He who was delivered up because of our transgressions, and *was raised because of our justification*." After Jesus died for your sins, He was raised because God was satisfied with the payment Jesus made for your sins. Therefore God is able to declare you righteous by Jesus' payment. Those who believe on and receive the Lord Jesus Christ are justified and receive the Justifier!

What is the mystery of the gospel, that truth that was hidden from the world and not revealed until Jesus Christ came to earth and died and rose again? Paul says this mystery is "Christ in you, the hope of glory" (Colossians 1:27). If Christ is in you, guaranteeing your glory—eternal life with

Him forever—by the receiving and sealing of the Holy Spirit of God, don't you think you have the power at any given time to say *"No!"* to whatever is tempting you? Whether it's gossip, another bite of food, pills, drugs, alcohol, immorality, stealing, breaking a law, looking at anything pornographic in print or on the Internet—and unfortunately the list goes on—you have the power, the ability to resist, to say *NO*.

You have the power. *You have the power.* Do you get it, beloved? You have the power! For the true child of God, sin is simply and always a matter of choice. The power to obey is there because the Spirit dwells within. In fact, according to John 14:23, both the Father and the Son abide with you as well.

And it is all because of the resurrection!

Isn't this worth celebrating? O beloved, if we really understand what the resurrection of Christ is all about, if we understood what it means to us practically, Easter would become the celebration of celebrations! It would be a celebration calling for new clothes in a biblical sense (putting on the new man—Ephesians 4:21-24, Romans 13:14), a celebration worthy of our most heartfelt worship with others in church, and a time for hilariously wonderful family togetherness because we don't have to yield to the sin that would wound and separate us.

But don't wait till Easter. Celebrate it every day, beloved, every moment of the day by declaring with your mouth what is true of you if you're a child of God. Say it aloud:

> I don't have to _____ because I've been freed from sin's power and I can walk in newness of life. I will not yield the members of my body (including my mind) to be an instrument of unrighteousness. God, I give my _____ (mind, eyes, tongue, hands, feet, body, affections, desires) to You as an instrument of righteousness. I thank You that sin shall not be master over me, because I am under grace, and therefore I have You in the power of Your Spirit living within me.

If you are a genuine Christian—the real thing—then Jesus Christ is your God, the One who is to rule your life and who has a right to rule it, because He *is* God. Jesus Christ is your Savior because He is the only One who can save you from a second death and the lake of fire. This is what you believe by faith—and it's the single most important thing you could ever do, because it determines both the way you live now and where and how you spend eternity.

FINDING YOUR PURPOSE

Another deep source of discouragement for many is experiencing a lack of purpose in life.

Are there ever times when life seems so dull, so ordinary, so routine . . . so void of deep satisfaction . . . that you wonder if it's really worth it all, if there isn't more than "this"?

Or perhaps you're afraid that in the light of history's big picture, you're totally insignificant. Are there ever moments when you feel lost and so incredibly small as you consider the swirling events on this globe? Have you ever wondered, *Will it really matter that I have lived or died?*

Or maybe life simply seems too short.

Or it might actually seem too long, considering the pain and limitations you find yourself enduring.

Let's approach this entire topic first by lifting our eyes on high. Let's think about Jesus: His life . . . His mission . . . His vision . . . His words. Consider these snatches from His teaching and conversation:

"For this purpose I came" (John 12:27).

"We are going up to Jerusalem" (Matthew 20:18).

"For their sakes I sanctify Myself" (John 17:19).

"I glorified Thee on the earth, having accomplished the work which Thou hast given Me to do" (17:4).

As we keep looking up—eyes lifted on high—let's now envision ourselves in this picture. Being able to repeat the last of those quotes I just listed is all that will matter to you and me personally at the end of time, when we stand before our Creator . . . our Sustainer . . . our Father.

And yet, in order to say those words, in order to say with gratefulness and praise, *I glorified Thee on the earth, having accomplished the work which Thou hast given me to do*, it's essential to know that our lives have a specific purpose.

We must know and understand "the hour" of our lives. To be able to say we have accomplished the work He gave us to do will require recognition of "when" our hour has come when it's time for doing whatever is needed.

We must know where we're going and realize that to get there requires steadfastness of purpose. If we're ever going to achieve our calling in life, it will require a "sanctification," a setting apart of ourselves and of certain things in our lives.

THIS IS YOUR HOUR

To think that God would call *us* to such a significant purpose evokes awe, doesn't it! Awe, wonder, and an inexpressible gratitude of heart! And as the reality of His plan and purpose is unfolded and displayed, I'm sure these words will constantly come to your mind: *Whoever would have thought . . . If only I had known . . .*

Yet God doesn't let us know—not in full. Instead, as we are obedient in following Him one step of faith at a time, He just *does* it! And we stand in awe.

Although you may struggle to think or even dream that it could ever be so, all this can be true in your own life, beloved.

I want you to see and understand, precious friend, that your life has a purpose. The breadth of that purpose can be small or great; it matters not. The fact is, you are God's workmanship. Whether you were born legitimate or illegitimate, whether you were raised in your natural family or as an adopted child, you can rest in the foundational truth that God formed you in your mother's womb. Moment by moment He breathes into you the breath of life so you can live all the days He numbered before there was even one of them.

The Almighty God gifted you when He placed you into His body just as He desired (1 Corinthians 12:4-18). As you read Ephesians 1, you see again and again that YOU are His . . . "according to the kind intention of His will," "according to the riches of His grace," "according to His kind intention which He purposed in Him" (verses 5,7,9).

Feel it or not, believe it or not, *you* are linked to the big eternal plan of God. You have an inheritance predestined "according to His purpose who works all things after the counsel of His will" (Ephesians 1:11).

The question is, *Do you know that?* Do you *know* that you have a place, an important purpose, in God's plan, in the furtherance of His kingdom? Do you understand—really understand—the value of *your* life? Has the significance of these words of truth sobered your thoughts so that you think as God thinks in respect to yourself? Do you realize the place you have . . . the purpose for your existence . . . the influence you wield in the way you live and in the way you redeem the hours of your day and in the relationships you form and develop? Do you understand the value and impact of your words?

Or is it hard to believe this, considering the darkness that surrounds you and that surrounds us all? If so, remember that you and I are here to be the light of Jesus Christ in the midst of a crooked and perverse generation. And where is light the most noticeable? *In the darkness!*

Your life has purpose, and if you don't think so, it is because you've believed a lie instead of the truth. You have listened to the whispers of the evil one, whispers which often sound like our own thoughts. But they are not. They are not according to "the mind of Christ," which was given to you as a child of God (1 Corinthians 2:16). They are lies—destructive, insidious lies—lies from the father of lies, the thief who comes to steal, kill, and destroy. Don't believe him; bring every thought captive to the obedience of Jesus Christ. Cast down those imaginations and every high thing that exalts itself against the knowledge of God, the truth of God.

You have been created by God and for God, and someday you will stand amazed at the simple yet profound ways He has used you even when you weren't aware of it. So don't lose your sense of destiny! Make the decision *now* to be His man, His woman, in this hour.

This is His hour—and yours!

DON'T FACE DISCOURAGEMENT ALONE

Remember also that any kind of discouragement seems far worse when you try to face it alone.

God's plan is for others to help you in your discouragement, just as He wants you to help others in theirs.

Remember His command to His people Israel through the prophet Isaiah? He said, "Encourage the exhausted, and strengthen the feeble. Say to those with anxious heart, 'Take courage, fear not' " (35:3-4).

Paul in essence said the same: "Encourage the fainthearted" (1 Thessalonians 5:14).

How truly encouraging it is to see others who are enduring and abiding under their trials. Then we know: *If they can make it, I can make it.*

Whenever you go through a trial and do it God's way, you're mirroring to others the character of Jesus in that trial, and that gives them courage. That's my whole purpose in sharing my own testimony: so people can discover that even though their lives have been messed up, even though they have lived as I once lived, they will find courage to trust God and live for Him, because they see what God has done for me and how He's using me. But if I had been defeated by my past, if I hadn't believed God and taken it by faith that I was a new creature and that old things had passed away, then I wouldn't today have any encouragement for others.

So look at the people of God around you, both to *find* strength and courage and to *give* strength and courage.

So many feel alone today, even in the Body of Christ. But they're not alone, and you are not alone.

I believe this is one of the reasons God lets us know in His Word that we're part of His body . . . members of one another. It's why we're to be part of "the church"—the called-out ones who are to assemble together, not only for the purpose of worship but also for fellowship, which in essence is to share whatever needs to be shared for the common welfare of the believers.

That's why God told us we're to "rejoice with those who rejoice, and weep with those who weep" (Romans 12:15).

We need each other. We need a friend—a friend who is the friend of Jesus, as He says in John 15:14-15: "You are My friends, if you do what I command you.... I have called you friends, for all things that I have heard from My Father I have made known to you."

And consider afresh Ecclesiastes 4:9-12:

> Two are better than one
>   because they have a good return for their labor.
> For if either of them falls,
>   the one will lift up his companion.
> But woe to the one who falls
>   When there is not another to lift him up.
> Furthermore, if two lie down together they keep warm,
>   but how can one be warm alone?
> And if one can overpower him who is alone,
>   two can resist him.
> A cord of three strands is not quickly torn apart.

Yes, it's better when we have each other. It's better when we have each other to lift us up, to take away the chill of being alone, to be there when others would beat us up and leave us for dead, either emotionally or physically.

That "cord of three *strands*" that isn't quickly torn apart represents a friendship in which God is woven in as the third strand—that intimate relationship with the Lord that comes from knowing Him through the Word, from sensing His presence as you, like Moses, have a "tent of meeting" (as we see in Exodus 33:7-11) where you commune with God and come away with the knowledge that His presence will go with you because you are His and you're going to walk in obedience to the precepts of His Word.

How good it is, beloved, when God awakens us to remember that we're part of a threefold cord . . . when we're reminded of the pain and suffering of others . . . when we remember that we aren't alone—that there are others to be concerned about, to minister to, to befriend, to protect, to help . . . when we remember that our lives *do* have purpose: *His* purpose and the welfare of others.

Oh please remember that, won't you?

HIS PROMISES ARE YOUR POWER

And as you faithfully remember, keep in mind how much *God* faithfully remembers as well.

As I read through the Old Testament, I keep seeing more and more the faithfulness of God to stand by His Word in keeping His promises to those who walk uprightly—as well as His faithfulness to judge those who transgress His Word and seemingly get away with it. There may be a delay in blessing or judgment, but the blessing or judgment always comes, *because God is God*.

Oh, how we need to learn that and proclaim it and live accordingly! Ours is not to question God or to choose our own way . . . ours is to trust and obey. And we can trust and obey in the full knowledge of God's perfect faithfulness, remembering:

"Not one of the good promises which the LORD had made to the house of Israel failed; all came to pass" (Joshua 21:45).

"Blessed be the LORD, who has given rest to His people Israel, according to all He promised; not one word has failed of all His good promise, which He promised through Moses His servant" (1 Kings 8:56).

"Faithful is He who calls you, and He also will bring it to pass" (1 Thessalonians 5:24).

Now then, beloved believer, remember the outcome of the war: Jesus is the victor, and all those who align themselves with Him will be more than conquerors.

And remember your military strategy. Be assured that when you're besieged with discouragement, *the promises of God* comprise your concentration of power, the mass of force you need to unload on the enemy. We can be strong and courageous, because He's given us "everything pertaining to life and godliness" and because He's granted us "His precious and magnificent promises"—and because all His promises are ours in Christ, in whom they are "Yes" and "Amen" (2 Peter 1:3-4, 2 Corinthians 1:20).

One of those promises is in Isaiah 42:16—"And I will lead the blind by a way they do not know, in paths they do not know I will guide them. I will make darkness into light before them and rugged places into plains. These are the things I will do, and I will not leave them undone." It's a promise to God's people Israel, another promise that finds its Yes in Christ. The following lines from an unknown author capture the power of this promise:

> Child of My love, fear not the unknown morrow.
>   Dread not the new demand life makes of thee;
> Thine ignorance doth hold no cause for sorrow,
>   For what thou knowest not is known to Me.
>
> Thou canst not see today the hidden meaning
>   Of My command, but thou the light shall gain.
> Walk on in faith, upon My promise leaning,
>   And as thou goest, all shall be made plain.
>
> One step thou seest: Then go forward boldly;
>   One step is far enough for faith to see.
> Take that, and thy next duty shall be told thee,
>   For step by step thy God is leading thee.
>
> Stand not in fear, thine adversaries counting;
>   Dare every peril, save to disobey.
> Thou shalt march on, each obstacle surmounting,
>   For I, the Strong, shall open up the way.

Therefore go gladly to the task assigned thee,
   Having My promise; needing nothing more
Than just to know where'er the future find thee,
   In all thy journeying—I GO BEFORE.

"God, I Know . . . !"

Therefore, my friend, when disappointments come your way, do not run away, and when others seem more blessed of God because they don't have to endure what you must endure, do not be envious.

And don't make the mistake of not recognizing God's goodness in allowing your every trial. Count it all joy.

When you feel discouraged, when you lack courage, when you think you can't do it . . . can't handle it . . . can't survive it . . . then remember that "with God nothing is impossible." Remember that "I AM" is our Lord's memorial name to *all* generations, including yours and mine! He is everything and anything you will ever need.

You can do all things through Christ Jesus who strengthens you; therefore discouragement never comes from God.

As you read all this, are you thinking, *But how can I know that I really belong to God?* You know if God's Spirit is really inside of you. Romans 8:16 says, "The Spirit Himself bears witness with our spirit that we are children of God."

You know if you have an ability to say no to sin in your life so that sin is no longer habitual. Remember that sin can be as simple as walking your own way and doing your own thing.

You know if you want to be totally God's, and the reason you even want to belong to Him this way is because He has drawn you by His Spirit.

Thank Him, beloved, for all this. You might say—

> *God, I know I am really, truly Yours. I know You hear and answer my prayers. Lord Jesus, You are my Lord and Master. I believe You died for my sins. I believe I can have Your*

righteousness. I believe my body is Your temple. Thank You, Lord, that You have brought me into Your family by faith. Father, thank You for giving Your Son for my sins so that I might never ever perish but have eternal life.

God, I believe I am Your child—not because of anything I've done, but because of what Jesus did on Calvary. And I want to bring You glory.

You are God. You are the sovereign God of all the universe. I submit myself to You. Lord, take me, receive me. I cry, "Abba, Father." I trust You. At times I'm a little afraid, but I trust you.

Father, thank You for Your Word. Father, may I now in meekness continue to receive the engrafted Word, the implanted Word. May I allow it to take root in my heart that I might be rooted and grounded and established in the faith.

Because of Your presence and Your power within me, I know I can be an overcomer—day by day, for the rest of my days on earth. For Your Word says, "Whatever is born of God overcomes the world; and this is the victory that has overcome the world— our faith." I believe that Jesus is the Son of God.

Now then, beloved, if you long to say this but feel you cannot, then why don't you simply turn this into a prayer of salvation. Read it again, personalizing it as your request, the prayer of your heart.

If you do this, will you please let me know?

Do not be grieved,
for the joy of the LORD is your strength.

NEHEMIAH 8:10

CHAPTER THIRTEEN

TURN TO THE JOY OF THE LORD

Learning Victory over Dejection

FROM DISAPPOINTMENT to discouragement—the cycle of Deadly D's keeps spiraling downward when we fail at each stage to respond biblically.

In keeping with our enemy's plan, each stage downward is more serious and acute than the one before. In fact, we can easily view all three of the lower levels we'll look at next—dejection, despair, and utter demoralization—as manifestations of depression.

According to a survey cited in the *Harvard Mental Health Letter*, 16 percent of the adult population in the United States (that's nearly one of every six adults) experience an "episode of depression" every year. Depression's annual financial cost is estimated at forty-four billion dollars—consisting primarily of losses due to absenteeism and lower productivity among depressed persons in the labor force, plus the direct cost of medical treatment, plus costs involved with an estimated eighteen thousand suicides each year associated with depression. But the real price tag is actually greater, the report says:

> These figures, of course, exclude the non-monetary costs of death and suffering from depression as well as the associated costs of cigarette smoking, drug abuse, and physical illness. The estimates also exclude the financial cost to family members who lose time from work and must provide household services for the depressed person.

The newsletter reports that of all serious diseases, depression causes more days spent in bed than anything except advanced coronary artery disease, and it causes more pain than anything except arthritis. The report concludes, "In the long run the social cost of depression is in the same range as the cost of AIDS, cancer, or heart disease."

Depression is portrayed as an affliction that strikes early in life (with 70 percent of its victims being under age forty-five) and typically continues over a longer period of time than most ailments but mostly goes untreated by medical professionals.

So what should be done about depression? Let's look first at what the world says.

A nationally known advice columnist published a letter written to her from a man who said he had "suffered through years of manic depression" and was now considering suicide, despite having "a good wife and two lovely children." From his personal perspective he described depression as "a disease that puts its victims through hell and makes death look inviting."

> I have been to at least 20 psychologists, psychiatrists, priests and counselors, but after three or four weeks of feeling fairly normal, the depression returns with a vengeance. I appear to be perfectly normal, but I agonize daily about my wish to die. I know this is a lot to lay on you . . . but with your many years of advice-giving, do you have any for me?

The advice columnist wrote back:

> You say you have been to dozens of psychologists and psychiatrists.
> Didn't any of them suggest that you take medication? There are a
> number of excellent anti-depressants on the market that help people
> like you.

She then listed the names and addresses of two national depression-
awareness groups, wished the man "good luck," and closed with these
words:

> Let me know you followed through. I'm worried about you.

Is that our only solution for depression—medication and awareness
plus the concern and best wishes of others? Does it stop there? And are
these the only "tranquilizers" that can level out a person's depression and
make life livable?

Before I answer those questions, please know that depression is a com-
plex affliction and one that should be handled medically if there is a chemical or hormonal problem. In a recent national television broadcast, many
related how they had been helped by a simple herb, Saint John's Wort,
found in health food stores. Some of my Christian friends say they have
found this herb to be a great equalizer in stress.

While this does seem to have helped, we know also that there is another Equalizer—another Stabilizer—who can sustain us regardless of
what does or doesn't work in the realm of man's medical knowledge and
ability. And that Sustainer is God.

WONDERFUL COUNSELOR

Let's examine a little more closely what we're dealing with in these lower
reaches of the Deadly D's and how we naturally and normally react.

Listen to this letter:

Dear Kay,

I wanted to write you to say thank you. There's a new freedom in my life that my heart yearned for for years.

There's a woman in my church that I asked to disciple me and to help me see and know God. At the time I had truly hit an emotional bottom and knew the only one who could fill my cup was God. Yet the question was how? The God of my understanding loved me, I knew. Yet I thought it was up to me to get rid of the pain from the past.

My friend was not alone; she is like so many of us! We believe God for salvation, but then we think everything having to do with our becoming mature and handling our lives and getting ready for eternity is up to us. And oh, how such thinking bypasses the grace of God—the abounding, lavish, extravagant, all-sufficient grace that's the birthright and inheritance of every child of God without exception!

In her letter this woman outlined her past:

Alcoholic Mom and Dad. I was born addicted to drugs. I was molested for two years by a brother, sexually molested. I began using drugs at 8. I was a junkie by 14. At 18 I was married. At 20 I was divorced and married again. At 21 I got sober. Then I was divorced again. At 25 I got saved. Then at 27, I married again.

This dear woman said she had been in therapy for ten years since becoming sober and that she knew the twelve steps inside out. She had "gotten stuck" she said—

which I see lots of women in therapy get; they get stuck. We do what is suggested to be able to feel free, and find ourselves still in a dark cave that a light shines in, but we just cannot seem to find a way out to that light.

She struggled with bitterness and felt that she "continued to be held by some kind of bondage."

Then came a turning point. With her friend she began studying the Bible through a book I'd written called *Lord, Heal My Hurts*.

> As we got into the book, God became so loving, so healing to me. . . . And I realized that God, El Elyon, my Elohim has already healed me. There was nothing more for me to do. Acceptance of His grace, forgiveness from His heart—that's what was mine, and I had to believe it. In six months there was more healing and freedom than in ten years of therapy.

My new friend had discovered the liberating truth that our hope is not in this life and not in man or in man's solutions. Our hope is in God and all He promises to be for us.

Those who belong only to the world, those who have not yet become true children of God, have only the wisdom, counsel, and support of the world to turn to. And the world, by virtue of willful blindness, is without hope and without God (Ephesians 2:12). God is the God of all hope, all true hope is His, and because unbelievers don't have God's answers, in their pain and despair they turn to the arm of flesh, which is only logical.

But *we* know that's not the solution. The ultimate cure comes always and only from the One whose name is *Jehovah (Yahweh) Rapha*—"the God who heals." The world tries hard to make it without God, but it is the world's very determination to do it without Him that puts them in such a miserable, unhappy state.

Yet what is so distressing is when the children of God so quickly turn to the flesh instead of turning to God. Why do we so easily turn to self in one form or another instead of relying totally and absolutely and completely on Almighty God? I cannot help but wonder: Why, why, why? Why do we fail to trust Him fully?

I think it is that flesh can be seen, it can be heard, it can be touched; it looks like us, and therefore we think man holds the solution. As Jeremiah says, we turn to the arm of flesh and come up dry and barren, when we could have the all-sufficient help of our yet unseen God. And what is the result of trusting in the flesh of man instead of relying on the Lord, the One who by the mere words of His mouth spoke and brought the world and all creation into existence? The inevitable result is always disappointment, then discouragement and dejection and worse.

As you read this, are you thinking, "Do you mean we should never go to human counselors?" No, dear reader, hear me carefully: I am not saying that. But I do want to say that before you go to any human counselor, you should go to God in prayer. Pour out your situation to Him—it would be good to write it out. Then be still and know that He is God. Cease striving, let go, relax and know that because He is God and because you cried to Him for help, He will let you know where, if any place, you are to go and what you are to do. He will impress it on your mind persistently, and He will bear witness to it through the Word and through other godly people.

Just remember the promise of Isaiah 9:6—"His name will be called Wonderful Counselor, Mighty God, Eternal Father, Prince of Peace." Our Mighty God and our Everlasting Father is also our Wonderful Counselor. Jesus Christ, beloved, is our ultimate source of help for all depression. His Book, the one breathed by God—the Bible—has the answers, all the answers for every single situation in life. The answers are there, awaiting our discovery.

As I write this, I think of Psalm 40: "I waited patiently [or *intently*] for the LORD; and He inclined to me, and heard my cry. He brought me up out of the pit of destruction, out of the miry clay." When we wait patiently and intently *on Him*, He brings us out of the mud and mire—and mud and mire are what depression is.

Depression—in the form of dejection, despair, and demoralization—is sure to come when you listen to man instead of God, when you've made the arm of flesh your help instead of God. (So by the way, let me ask you: Where do you focus your devotional time? Is it in a book written by man, or do you get into the Word of God?)

BEATING THE BLUES

Depression can be a depressing topic, can't it? But I want you to know, beloved, how important it is that we understand and see it from God's perspective.

Perhaps it will help if we address this wide-reaching topic by a more common and less threatening name. My good friend and radio broadcast partner Jan Silvious passed along to me a number of good insights for helping us "beat the blues." Many of her thoughts are good reminders of much that we've already been talking about in this book.

First, she mentions that our behavior is determined by our feelings, which are born in our thoughts. Yes, *the mind is the battleground*, just as we've seen. As Jan says, "It's what we *think* about our life's circumstances that causes 'the blues' to stay around."

Second, remember that nobody's circumstances are perfect. There's trouble in every life. We all have to accept that life is not without problems. Life is not without pain. Life is not without heartache and rejection.

Remember what Jesus said in John 16:33? "In the world you have tribulation, but *take courage*; I have overcome the world." Yes, there's tribulation. But yes, we *can* take courage and must take courage, because Jesus Christ has already overcome those tribulations.

Third, it's not the events of the past or the present that make us blue—even events that are difficult and tragic. No, Jan says, "the factor that causes us to be emotionally overwhelmed with the blues is our *interpretation* of those events."

Once again, it all comes down to this: Do we see these events as disappointments or as His appointments?

The blues, Jan says, "usually come from a sense of loss—loss of relationship, loss of status, loss of personal value, loss of the future"—in other words, *disappointments*, ranging anywhere from minor to major.

And finally Jan reminds us that "we are not without emotion. In fact, God has made us with the capacity of great emotion—something from which we can derive great benefit, or something that will destroy us!"

Therefore overcoming depression—dejection, despair, or demoralization—does not mean turning off or turning away from our emotions but rather bringing them into conformity with God's perspective and God's own emotions.

Jan also reminds us of this truth: *I can be content.* It's always my choice, no matter what. As Paul says, "I have learned to be content in whatever circumstances I am. . . . I have learned the secret. . . . I can do all things through Him who strengthens me" (Philippians 4:11-13).

By the way, "I can do" in this verse is the Greek word *ischus*, which is a combination of two words meaning "strength" and "to have." The word means to have the endowment of either physical strength or mental or moral power. Some have translated this phrase as "I can *bear* all things." This inherent power or strength is because Christ is within us. Thus my ability to bear all things is through Him who literally *keeps on* strengthening me—since "strengthens" here is a present active participle indicating continuous or repeated action. We can, as Jan says, beat the blues—we can handle that depression.

DEJECTION

Now then, let's look specifically at the first of these bottom three Deadly D's that represent a trio of depression.

Remember again where we left off in this cycle: It was in discouragement, which means our courage has been taken away, reducing our hope and confidence. And if discouragement isn't brought to a halt by our return to God's pattern for being strong and courageous, it's like riding wax paper from the top of a high slide. It will cause us to slip down into *dejection.*

Or to play with another metaphor, if you've been in the well of discouragement and have listened to the world's analysis of your condition or of your future rather than being strong and courageously believing your God, then you're certain to sink deeper into the mud of dejection. Dejection is the inevitable aftermath of surrendering to discouragement.

What is dejection?

Dejection is *lowness of spirit*. Instead of the joy of the Lord being your strength—the truth Nehemiah exhorts God's dejected people with in Nehemiah 8:10—you experience great tiredness. You become emotionally fatigued. Dejection wrings you out, draining away your strength.

Instead of knowing "the oil of gladness" and "the mantle of praise" (Isaiah 61:3), you feel worn out, ready to faint, unable to put one foot in front of the other. To open your lips for praise is too much; all you can emit are groans.

And your enemy is circling your wounded and weak soul—he's heard your groans and is there waiting to devour you as easy prey.

A STORY TO PONDER

For help in overcoming any of the Deadly D's, one of the best stories in Scripture to stay close to is that of Joseph. Read it in Genesis 37 and 39–50, and consider Joseph carefully. Study the situations he was in and how he handled them. And observe his relationship to God. And at the end of the story, take a good look at how he treated those who once wanted to kill him.

There is much in Joseph's story to ponder in your heart, especially when you see situations in your life that are hard to understand. You'll find encouragement to believe the Word of God regardless of whether your little human brain can explain or rationalize it.

If any man had reason to become dejected, it was Joseph. As we read the account of Joseph's life in the Scriptures, we know that when his brothers put him down into the pit, he cried and wept before them, begging them to get him out. Yet despite their cold insensitivity that landed Joseph in a physical pit, he refused to be bound in a spiritual, mental, or emotional pit. That was something Joseph could control.

As you know, when Joseph was finally lifted out, it wasn't for his freedom but to be sold into slavery in Egypt. In the days ahead he might well have been tempted with deep discouragement, but we see no record of any lowness of spirit. Instead we see him, even in slavery, enjoying the presence of God and achieving success and prosperity and favor with man.

Then came the incident with Potiphar's wife, and Joseph ended up in prison. He stayed there not for a few hours or days but for two years—simply because he stood for the Lord. Joseph remained a man of integrity. Even in the hard and disappointing circumstances of life, he did not become bitter against God and rebel against God's seeming injustices. Rather, without even having someone to hold him accountable, Joseph refused to "sin against God" (Genesis 39:9).

Surely now, having been thrown into prison for doing what was right, he finally had overwhelming reasons to sink into dejection. But we don't see a hint of it. Again, "the Lord was with him" (39:23). Joseph therefore made the best of his situation and used it for his advantage. He became the best prisoner he could be, and God used that experience as a steppingstone to promote Joseph to a position in Pharaoh's court.

So we can think of Joseph going from pit to Potiphar to prison to palace.

The sovereign God was in control, and Joseph knew it. He recognized that what could so easily seem like a series of crushing disappointments was instead a sequence of God's gracious appointments.

UNDERSTANDING GOD'S SOVEREIGNTY

So many times along the way, the world would have told Joseph simply to curse God and die, as Job's wife told Job to do. But we see zero evidence that Joseph ever listened to that perspective. He continued to be strong and courageous in believing God.

How was he able to do this?

Two key passages in Joseph's story show us how: They reveal to us what Joseph understood about God and about life and the difference such knowledge and faith can make.

In Genesis 45, Joseph encountered and eventually revealed himself to his brothers who had come to Egypt for relief from a devastating famine. Finally his brothers were knowingly face-to-face with the brother they had so cruelly treated.

Joseph said to them,

> And now do not be grieved or angry with yourselves, because you sold me here; *for God sent me before you* to preserve life. (45:5)

Joseph thoroughly understood the sovereignty of God. He showed this again in verses 7-9:

> And *God sent me before you* to preserve for you a remnant in the earth, and to keep you alive by a great deliverance. Now, therefore, *it was not you who sent me here, but God*; and *He* has made me a father to Pharaoh and lord over all his household and ruler over all the land of Egypt. Hurry and go up to my father, and say to him, "Thus says your son Joseph, '*God* has made me lord of all Egypt; come down to me, do not delay.'"

The second revealing passage in this story is Genesis 50:20. Their father Jacob had died. Joseph's brothers now feared openly that Joseph might finally seek revenge for what they had done to him. But Joseph responded this way:

> And as for you, *you meant evil against me, but God meant it for good* in order to bring about this present result, to preserve many people alive.

Here was a man whose faith shined as silver refined—so much so that Joseph is often likened to the Lord Jesus Christ by many teachers of God's Word. Joseph understood that by allowing a boy to be sold into slavery, God was saving a nation. How encouraging it is to see that our adversities not only advance our own good and God's glory but also might well serve for the preservation of the lives of others, that those watching might see the sufficiency of Jesus Christ and come to the fountain of living waters and drink of Him and be satisfied.

In the beauty of the Psalms we see again what God was doing for His people and for Joseph himself:

> He sent a man before them,
>> Joseph, who was sold as a slave.
> They afflicted his feet with fetters,
>> He himself was laid in irons;
> Until the time that his word came to pass,
>> The word of the LORD tested him.
>
> (105:17-19)

Joseph was tested—and proven faithful. If you are dealing with dejection, beloved, pass your test!

WANTING TO DIE

What a contrast Joseph's situation provides to the attitude later demonstrated by the children of Israel in Numbers 13 and 14. Moses had sent twelve spies ahead into Canaan, the land God had given them. The spies came back and confirmed what God had promised: that this was indeed a land flowing with milk and honey.

But ten of the twelve spies also reported that the land would be impossible to possess, because of the overwhelming size and power and fortifications of the enemies who were already there.

Of course, Caleb and Joshua contradicted this dismal conclusion. "We should by all means go up and take possession of it," Caleb insisted, "for we shall surely overcome it" (13:30).

But uncontrolled dejection was the people's response:

> Then all the congregation lifted up their voices and cried, and the people wept that night. And all the sons of Israel grumbled against Moses and Aaron; and the whole congregation said to them, "Would that we had died in the land of Egypt! Or would that we had died in this wilderness! And why is the LORD bringing us into this land, to fall by the sword? Our wives and our little ones will

become plunder; would it not be better for us to return to Egypt?"
(14:1-3)

They were so dejected they wanted to die. How could they sink so low?

It was because they were looking at their situation apart from the promises of God. Of course there were enemies in the land ahead! But they did not have to handle that on their own. They thought they did! And they thought this because they refused to take God at His Word. They looked at their circumstances rather than at God—and because they knew they couldn't defeat giants when they themselves were only grasshoppers, their discouragement sank in a moment into helpless dejection.

That's exactly what can happen to us. Our spirits sink into helplessness when we feel *we've* got to do it, *we've* got to solve this problem, *we've* got to face this enemy—and we know we aren't capable of the task. The situation is too difficult, too impossible, too overwhelming. Thus we're frightened of failure or of the consequences of failure.

It was a lowness they could have avoided if they had only listened the next day to the words of Joshua and Caleb, who had torn their clothes in utter grief over what the people were doing.

> And they spoke to all the congregation of the sons of Israel, saying,
> "The land which we passed through to spy out is an exceedingly
> good land. If the LORD is pleased with us, then He will bring us into
> this land, and give it to us—a land which flows with milk and honey.
> Only do not rebel against the LORD; and do not fear the people of
> the land, for they shall be our prey. Their protection has been
> removed from them, and *the LORD is with us*; do not fear them."
> (14:7-9)

Caleb and Joshua were looking to God, and there they found genuine encouragement.

How did the people respond to their words?

"All the congregation said to stone them with stones" (14:10).

They were ensnared—trapped by their own unbelief.

And because of it, they would spend forty years wandering and dying one by one in the desert until only Caleb and Joshua of that generation remained. Of all who left Egypt, these two men alone would enter the Promised Land.

STRENGTH IN THE JOY OF THE LORD

Let's look at one more instance of dejection experienced by God's people.

Even after they finally settled into the Promised Land, the children of Israel again and again walked according to the dictates of their flesh, refusing to believe God and live accordingly. They did not repent. They continued to walk in their own stubborn way. So eventually God dealt with them. He caused the Assyrians to come down and destroy the northern kingdom of Israel, then He caused the southern kingdom to be taken captive by the Babylonians.

This was all God's doing. He had to judge His people. They had forsaken Him, stopped up their ears, and refused to obey the Word of the Lord.

After seventy years, a remnant of the people was permitted to return to the land of Israel. They had plenty of problems when they got back. Jerusalem's walls were torn down and in shambles. Their temple had also been destroyed, and they had no place to really reinstitute their worship.

They were overwhelmed. They thought, *There's no way*. But God raised up leaders; under Ezra the people rebuilt the temple, and under Nehemiah they rebuilt the wall.

One day these returned exiles gathered in the square in front of Jerusalem's Water Gate, and there they listened attentively while Ezra read to them from the book of the law "from early morning until midday" (Nehemiah 8:3). Standing with Ezra on a specially constructed platform were several Levites who "explained the law to the people while the people remained in their place. And they read from the book, from the law of God, translating to give the sense so that they understood the reading" (8:7-8).

But even the reading of God's Word overwhelmed them. They

responded in tears. "For all the people were weeping when they heard the words of the law" (8:9).

Then Nehemiah said a very wise thing to them: "Go, eat of the fat, drink of the sweet, and send portions to him who has nothing prepared; for this day is holy to our LORD. Do not be grieved, *for the joy of the LORD is your strength.*"

The secret to overcoming dejection is to put your eyes back on Jesus Christ and begin to rejoice. If you cannot come up with your own words, then read the Psalms aloud, whether you feel anything or not (and note that I said "aloud"; verbalizing it vocally is crucial). The joy of the Lord will eventually come as you focus on what you are reading, and that joy *will* be your strength.

Therefore, when you realize that you're experiencing dejection, my friend, force yourself to rejoice in the midst of that lowness. Put your eyes back on Jesus Christ, back on God, back on the Word of God, and begin to rejoice. It may be a sacrifice of your feelings, or your emotions, of your reasoning, but bring to Him the sacrifice of praise, the fruit of your lips.

Your spirits *will* change. You'll experience the truth of God's promise to His people Israel in Isaiah 61:3:

> To grant those who mourn in Zion,
>> Giving them a garland instead of ashes,
> The oil of gladness instead of mourning,
>> The mantle of praise instead of a spirit of fainting.

If you're in dejection or headed toward it, then, my friend, it's time to rejoice and praise God in pure, gut-level faith—whether or not you feel it. If you don't, you will continue to weaken.

Now may the God of hope
fill you with all joy and peace in believing,
that you may abound in hope
by the power of the Holy Spirit.

ROMANS 15:13

CHAPTER FOURTEEN

A MESSAGE OF HOPE

Learning Victory over Despair

A FEW MONTHS AGO I was being rushed out of a convention room in Washington, D.C., on the arm of another woman who was steering me through the crowd. I was cohosting a breakfast for the prime minister of Israel, Benjamin Netanyahu, and time was of the essence. Suddenly someone caught me gently by the arm. The woman's smiling face was as soft as her touch as she said, "I can't thank you enough!" She quickly added that what she had learned through our Bible study ministry had saved her life.

As I paused, she dropped her hand but held me captive with her eyes and added, "And I mean that literally." My hand reached up to her face, for though I couldn't stop and talk as I wanted to, I just had to touch her.

As I was rushed onward by the person steering me to my next destination, I threw her a kiss, smiling from ear to ear as tears joyously toppled from my eyes.

This wasn't the first time I'd heard people say that learning to study

God's Bible for themselves had *literally* saved their lives. When others had despaired of life itself and were tempted to end it all—because the pressure seemed too great, more than they thought they could bear—they had found life and the will to go on in the precepts of His Holy Book!

O beloved, can you relate? Have you endured times of affliction and found yourself telling God, *I would have given up all hope had I not known and clung to Thy precepts.*

Or maybe this is where you are now—despairing, troubled, anxious, not knowing which way to turn . . . unsure . . . questioning . . . tempted to run, to forget what you should do and what you should be.

We've talked so much in this book about the battle we're in. Maybe you're weary of the battle, so weary that you wonder how you can go on . . . so weary that you're tempted to surrender, to let the enemy have his way with you.

Maybe you're wondering if you shouldn't end it all, because "if this is life, then life isn't worth living!"

If this is where you are, beloved, or where a loved one or an acquaintance is, then I believe it's because either you don't know "the exact truth about the things you have been taught" (Luke 1:4)—or that even though you know the truth, you aren't believing God, you're not taking Him at His Word. Instead you're allowing yourself to be directed by your circumstances, your emotions, your thoughts, your reasoning.

AN ANSWER FOR SUICIDE

Not long ago on our ministry's weekly live radio call-in program, our subject was grief. The response was so great we decided to take calls for a second hour and tape the program for a later airing.

When Jan Silvious (my cohost on the program) and I had time for only one more caller on the last segment of this second program, we went to a line where a woman named Sandra had been waiting.

"Sandra, hello. Sandra? *Sandra?* Are you there? Sandra?"

Our electronic timer told us Sandra had been waiting for seventy-seven minutes. I thought, *The poor woman has probably grown tired of waiting.*

As we found out later when she called back, Sandra hadn't become tired—she simply couldn't wait any longer to go to the bathroom. Sandra still wanted to speak to us. *But God . . .*

I love those two words—*But God*—spoken together in one breath. It wasn't Sandra that God wanted us to talk to at that moment. It was John.

John was the next caller in line, having waited for over an hour.

"John," asked our program host Jay Johnson, "what is your question for Kay and Jan tonight?"

John responded in his husky male voice, "My question is, is it wrong to commit suicide if you don't have any other alternative?"

John felt there was no way out of his pain and grief. He had done something he knew was wrong and had tried every way he could to get rid of his feelings—but he couldn't. Death seemed his only choice.

As we talked with this sincere, contemplative man, we learned that he'd had a homosexual relationship with a heterosexual man who wouldn't leave his wife for John. Like many others, John figured the only way out of his pain, the only way to assuage his utter despair, was suicide.

What a lie!

What a deception from the murderer, the father of lies, the serpent of old, the devil!

Remember that the devil came only to steal and kill and destroy. He wants to kill. He wants to bring death. He wants us to think, "I might as well end it all." And there are many who are ending it all. Satan incites death. He happily sacrifices those who live under his dominion, all the while knowing that they will suffer eternal destruction, to be thrown into the lake of fire prepared for the devil and his angels. There is not one ounce of compassion within him, for knowing his fate, this self-made enemy of God still wants to take down with him everyone he can.

And he'll use every subtle lie he can to do it.

In our age, with all our technology, we're bombarded with so much information, so many perspectives and viewpoints. How do we know what is true, what is accurate? How can we tell truth from a lie? How can we know whether our thoughts are skewed, twisted, or perverted—or in accordance with reality?

Jesus told us exactly how we may know the truth: "If you abide in My word, then you are truly disciples of Mine; and you shall know the truth, and the truth shall make you free" (John 8:31-32). That is why Romans 12:1-2 urges us to present our bodies to Jesus Christ as living sacrifices and to be renewed in our minds rather than being conformed to the world. And the transformation can come only through getting to know the Word of God, cover to cover. It must become our habit of life, our lifelong pursuit, our daily nourishing.

By living in His Word, we know the truth that sets us free, that sets us apart unto God. Truth sets us free because it not only exposes error, but it dispels lies and the consequent darkness and destruction those lies bring into our lives.

LOVE'S POWER

But John didn't know about this until that Sunday evening, when in the sovereignty of God we took his call instead of Sandra's.

As we talked with him, I asked John about his relationship with the Lord. When it seemed evident that he was not a child of God, I told him that if he committed suicide he would go to hell, spend eternity in the lake of fire, and never know the thing he longed so much to experience: unconditional love. John would not go to hell because he committed suicide; rather, he would go to hell because in essence he had never committed himself to the Lord Jesus Christ.

In the same breath I told John he would go to hell, I told him that I believed God had kept him waiting on the line all that time so he could know how much God loved him while he was still a sinner, ungodly, helpless, and an enemy of God. I explained God's love and what God wanted to do with him—in greater detail than I'm sharing here—then asked, "How does this hit you, John?"

"Like a ton of bricks."

"What hits you like a ton of bricks?"

John's response came immediately: "What you just got through saying."

"About going to hell," I queried, "or that God loves you?"

And he answered, "That God loves me."

His words brought tears to our eyes. As I told John about my own sinful past and of God's unconditional love toward me, I continued crying out in my heart to our Father for His help. I didn't want John to be a spiritual stillbirth but a living soul for God's kingdom.

When I finished sharing what God had done for me and telling John what God wanted to do for him, I asked him, "What do you think of that?"

John replied, "Pretty powerful."

And it was—and is! Oh, the power of the knowledge of the unconditional love of God, of a Redeemer who does not want to polish us off and finish our destruction but wants to buy us from the slave market of sin with the blood of His only begotten Son! He wants to cleanse us, to set us free from ourselves and our hopelessness. Our divine Silversmith wants to refine us, to make us pure silver that all might see the great work and character of the One who redeems us from the pit.

This is the unconditional love that gives us hope.

Over the air, as our program's closing music began, I heard John pray with me. Tears of gratitude to our Lord fell from my eyes as I heard his husky voice repeat after me, "God, I believe that Jesus is Your Son, and I receive Him now as my Savior, and He can have full control of my life.

"And I ask You and thank You for the forgiveness of my sins. I thank You that You have given me life right now. And I'm going to live for You. Teach me how.

"Father, I thank You for hearing my prayer. . . . In Jesus' name."

You know, I see hundreds come to the Lord every year when God leads me to give an invitation after my teaching. But to hear someone come to the Lord in a one-on-one encounter like that is comparatively rare for me. My heart was bursting with joy, for it was such a special experience not only for John but also for me. *Father, O Father* I thought, *this is what it's all about.*

DOWNWARD TO DESPAIR

Because in our ministry we hear from so many men and women who bare their souls I have been exposed to much—and believe me, beloved, the pain people are experiencing is inconceivable. Their expectations have been dashed against the wall of reality, crushing their minds so to speak and damaging their reasoning.

For them, life is so hard, while for others it seems inconceivably impossible. And I want to tell you this, my friend: In the light of all that's going on in our country and in light of what the Word of God teaches about the times preceding the inauguration of Jesus Christ upon His earthly throne, I believe life here is going to get harder—much harder.

Our disappointments are going to become greater and more painful. I am watching it happen before my eyes, even in the lives of many dear Christian leaders.

And if we continue not to hear and believe the truth as we descend the spiral from disappointment to discouragement to dejection, then we'll drop further down—into the hopeless bondage of despair.

What is despair?

Those who have despaired have lost or abandoned *hope.* They're overwhelmed with the feeling that nothing good can happen—ever again.

Despair can leave you totally apathetic; your mind is numb. It can also lead to frantic activity. In a state of despair you may find yourself acting recklessly and not considering the consequences of your actions. You'll do things you greatly regret later because of their lifelong consequences.

Despair is often experienced by people who find themselves confronted by the infidelity of their mate or the demand for a divorce . . . or who find their children caught in some disgraceful situation . . . or who suddenly face an unexpected financial reversal.

Remember the stories from the Great Depression of businessmen who opened the windows of their office buildings and jumped to their deaths, while others bought guns and blew out their brains? That was energized despair.

Very seldom do I have time to watch television, and when I do it's often hard to find something worth watching except on the more educational channels. However, there's one program Jack and I try to carve out time for—and that is *Biography*. This program is a continual witness to me of the fact that fame, money, and worldly wisdom do not bring the peace and happiness that man so longs for. When I think of energized despair, I think of *Biography's* portrayal of the life of Barbara Woolworth Hutton, a woman with incredible wealth who believed the lie her mother sowed in the soil of her young and impressionable mind. It was a lie that became a mighty tree bearing a rich harvest of poisonous fruit. It brought continual despair to her sixty years of life, a despair she tried to drown out through alcohol, drugs, numerous sexual encounters, and extravagant gifts poured out on utter strangers as well as on friends. She attempted suicide several times. My heart grieved as I thought, *If only she had known the Truth. He could have set her free.*

What's the antidote to despair? What can rescue you from the notion that this is all there is to life? What can offer you life—not only eternal life but abundant life? What can make you steadfast, immovable, always abounding in the work of the Lord? What can keep you going on as more than a conqueror? What's going to cause you to walk as an overcomer?

What will lift you up and keep you out of the pit of despair?

The same thing that has sustained God's people through the ages: *hope*.

So many times we talk about hope in only a worldly sense. When we say we hope for something, we actually have major doubts about whether it will ever happen: "I'm hoping to win the lottery." "I'm hoping to lose twenty pounds." "I'm hoping to finish this work by five." But the hope the

Bible talks about is not a hope for something that may or may not come true. Biblical hope means that what you're hoping for is something God has promised and something that will *assuredly, absolutely, unequivocally come to pass in our sovereign God's time and way—which is always the best.*

That's why our hope is *sure*. It rests on God and on His infallible, unchangeable Word. And it applies to the ultimate hope: heaven. When we hope for heaven, it's not, "Well, I hope I'm going to get there." Rather it's "I *know* I'll get there." This assurance is the birthright of every child of God.

THE ENEMY'S WORST SNARE

God's people are hungry for a message of hope—a message of encouragement. Why? Because many are unschooled in the Word of God, and what faith they have is under attack. And their faith is failing because they aren't rooted and grounded and established in the faith, and therefore they are losing sight of their hope.

I believe the greatest coup of the enemy is to cause us to *lose hope*. It's not to cause us to commit overt sin but to snare us by the sin of unbelief. Then unbelief paves the way for overt sin.

If you think back to the Garden of Eden, remember the first thing Satan said to Eve? His opening words were, "Indeed, has God said . . . ?" He didn't whisper, "Just look at the fruit of that tree! Doesn't it look yummy?" No, his first tactic was to cause Eve to doubt the Word of God, to doubt the veracity of God. If he could do that, he could lead her in any direction he pleased. (By the way, we know from Revelation 12:9 and 20:2 that the serpent in Eden was the devil.)

After casting doubt on the truth of God's Word and thus on the sure and just judgment of God against transgressors, the serpent told Eve that by eating the fruit of that tree she would become like God. The implication was that God knew this all along and was holding out on her. If she would only eat the fruit, she wouldn't have to depend on God; she'd have no need to hear and trust and believe Him. She wouldn't have to be under His thumb. She could be her own god.

Satan sought to snare Eve by the sin of unbelief.

I believe the root of all sin is unbelief. And the basis of all sin is a lie.

That's why Jesus said He came to set us free *by our knowing the truth*.

Now if Satan can snare me in unbelief, then he's going to take away my hope, because my hope is in God and in the truth of the Word of God. My hope is in the fact that God never changes, that He's the same yesterday, today, and forever. My hope is in the fact that God loves me even though I've been His enemy and that He loves me unconditionally. I can live in stability because I have Some*one* in my life who is stable and sure, unchanging, Someone who's always there extending His love to me.

However, when the enemy succeeds in seducing us to not believe God, the result is that we become spiritually, emotionally, and eventually even physically impotent. Our hope of ever being used by God and of ever being free from sin is gone. We lose the hope of being heard by God; we think, *God will never pay attention to my prayers.*

Most fundamentally of all, our hope of forgiveness is gone.

We lose the assurance of hearing God say, "Listen, I forgive you, and I'm never going to hold that against you, because you've accepted My sacrifice and because you've believed Me and appropriated My grace and because by faith you've taken Me at My Word. I forgive your sins, because you're coming to Me the way I tell you to come—through My Son, your Lord Jesus Christ."

Perhaps you have believed, "I know I could never be forgiven by God for that. It's an unpardonable sin." I've never met people any more tormented than those who believe they've committed the unpardonable sin. And sometimes they don't even know what it is. But somehow Satan has sown this lie in their hearts, and they believe him instead of running for refuge into what they know about God's character. They focus on this one sin and take it out of the context of the whole counsel of the Word of God.

Then there are those who have been told, "You're addicted, and you always will be." So they think, *I'm an alcoholic for the rest of my life,* or

I'm a sex addict for the rest of my life, or *I'm codependent for the rest of my life*, or whatever—all this sort of stuff. But that kind of teaching leaves us lifeless *for* God and *before* God. It's the enemy's lie that we're forever trapped in our sins, forever imprisoned by our failures.

It's all a lie, and it all goes back to unbelief.

And yet most of us don't realize that if we are *not* believing God then we *are* believing a lie.

KEEP GOD IN THE PICTURE

God is the God of hope, and we are *never* to despair but always to hope in Him.

Hope looks to the future, but it also looks in the right way to the past. In fact, that's where our hope begins. *Never forget that God has come.* Jesus has come. God sent Jesus that you might have life and have it *abundantly*—that you would not just live on the ragged edge but walk in the fullness of life. To lose hope is not to be living abundantly.

Jesus said that the thief—the devil—came only to steal and kill and destroy. He wants to steal your hope, to kill it, and destroy it. He wants to steal from you the Word of God and the promises of God. He wants to cut you off from God. He wants to pulverize you and immobilize you so that eventually you desire nothing except death. And that's where a loss of hope eventually leads.

Despair leads to destruction.

Let me say it again: Satan is the father of lies. He's a murderer and a destroyer. He wants to convince you that God doesn't care, that He's unwilling or unable to answer your prayers.

Even if the devil knows he cannot take you to hell with him, he wants to destroy any kind of daily relationship you might have with God. Not only that, but he also wants to destroy your relationship with your husband or wife and with your children. He wants to destroy your relationship with the church, to cut you off from both the flock and the Shepherd.

Paul said that *Christ within us* is the "hope of glory" (Colossians 1:27), and if you've lost hope, you can always trace it back to unbelief. You can know that somewhere in your life you've chosen not to believe God. Perhaps you chose to look at the circumstances of the moment and to think, *There's no way.* You thought you were in this problem by yourself and that you had to dig your way out by yourself. That's what Satan was telling you—but he's a flat-out liar.

If that's the way you've been thinking, you've left God out of the picture. You forgot that God is a supernatural God with no limitations. And He is the God of all hope.

A Letter in the Night

Not long ago I was in another city taping a television program. After the taping I stayed to talk with the audience and answer questions, until finally the program producers told us it was late and we all had to go home.

The next morning when I woke up in my hotel room, a light on the telephone was flashing, indicating that I had a message. I called the front desk and was told that a letter was waiting for me—having been delivered about two o'clock that morning.

I picked up the letter as I was leaving to catch an airplane flight, and after reaching the airport that morning I took time to read it.

> Dear Kay,
>
> My wife and I attended the show you gave tonight. I wanted so desperately to talk to you, but I knew you were very tired and needed your rest.

Next to those lines he had gone back and written in, "The truth is, I did not feel worthy." The letter went on:

> I know that you are very busy, but I have nowhere else to turn. I'll try to make this as brief as possible.
>
> When I was in my teens, I walked down the aisle of the church camp and made my first profession of faith to Christ. I followed it

with baptism. I received no follow-up, and since I did not know how to study the Word, I fell away from God eventually.

I do remember feeling that all things were new just after my profession of faith. . . . I felt close to the Lord for a short time, but as I said, I grew further and further away from Him eventually.

When I was in college I did some things that I wish I could change. I was sexually immoral and committed adultery and fornication many times over. I knew it was wrong before I did it, while I did it, and especially after I did it. However, the more I backslid, the easier it became.

On top of all this, looking back, I was dating the girl who I was going to marry all the time. Even after we were engaged, I could not control myself, or I would not. I did know in my heart that when I did finally get married, I would be faithful. I guess this was the way I justified it. In the back of my mind, one of the reasons I wanted to marry is so that I would quit sinning so terribly. I remember asking for forgiveness, but I found myself doing it all over again.

When I married I asked for forgiveness again. I thought it was behind me.

About a year into our marriage I found out that I had herpes. It hurts me beyond what I can put into words, knowing the pain this has caused my wife. I've always felt that "those" people would never really be accepted into heaven by God. That's what really hurt me.

It's hard to explain, but I felt that the disease was a form of the number 666 that people will take in the tribulation and by receiving it, they would be barred from heaven.

See how the thief and liar had come to this young man and given him wrong teaching? He had a wrong interpretation on what the number 666 is all about. In Revelation we learn that it's a physical mark put on the bodies of those who are unsaved, because they choose to worship the image of the beast. They take that mark on their right hand or on their forehead so they can buy and sell. It has nothing to do with immorality. But the enemy twists even the Scriptures to accomplish his lying.

The enemy had convinced this young man that he would be walking around in heaven with herpes still marking his body. But that's a lie.

The fact is, for the present we *all* have sinful bodies. We all live in the flesh, and because this flesh has been corrupted by sin, because at times we have believed in the enemy instead of believing God, then we all have the effects of sin in this body. And that's why God will redeem our bodies. He redeems not only our souls but also these sinful bodies made of flesh where even now He puts His Spirit to live.

And someday, the Bible tells us in 1 Corinthians 15, this corruptible flesh will put on incorruptibility. Death will not have the ultimate victory over us because we'll each get a brand new body that is immortal.

In the letter the young man said, "Kay, I have struggled beyond what I can put into words with this. Was I just unlucky by getting the disease? Did God give it to me? If so, what now?"

Of course it wasn't just bad luck. The Bible tells us, "For the one who sows to his own flesh shall from the flesh reap corruption" (Galatians 6:8). The Bible tells us specifically to "flee fornication," because "he that committeth fornication sinneth against his own body" (1 Corinthians 6:18, KJV). And those who sin sexually receive in their own bodies the "due penalty of their error" (Romans 1:27).

And yet when we confess these sins, when we come back to God, He takes care of that for our coming future. He says, "If we confess our sins, He is faithful and righteous to forgive us our sins and *to cleanse us* from all unrighteousness" (1 John 1:9). No, you and I will not carry the effects of sin in our bodies for all eternity. That's not what the Bible teaches.

So we have a choice. And this young man had a choice. Would he believe God, or would he believe what he felt, what he thought, what he'd been impressed with?

FEELING CONDEMNED

I tell you, precious ones, you lose hope when you go by your emotions or your human reasoning rather than God's Word. You lose hope when you focus on your circumstances. You lose hope when you leave God and the truths of God out of the picture. Despair comes. And that's what this young man was experiencing.

His letter continued:

> I guess what hurt the most was knowing that I had sinned against God.
>
> Kay, I thought that my wife would leave me, but she didn't. I didn't understand why not. I felt so dirty, and not worthy or fit to step one foot inside the door of a church. I felt condemned regardless of what I did or could do. My wife wanted us to go to church, but I did not want to be a hypocrite, so I would not go.
>
> I cannot explain the pain and depression I felt. Kay, this pain was not from being caught, but realizing that I had sinned against God.

Those words were precious, and they showed me this man's heart toward God. He reminded me of David's words in Psalm 51: "Against thee, thee only, have I sinned, and done this evil in thy sight: that thou mightest be justified when thou speakest" (verse 4, KJV).

The young man's letter continued:

> I have nobody to blame but myself. Knowing that the sins were wrong before I did them made it even worse.
>
> Well, I finally got down on my knees and truly repented. This repentance turned me to following God. For the first time I felt things which I'd never felt before: things such as brotherly love, etc.

He went on to say that these were feelings he did not even know he was to have until he began studying the Bible.

Then he mentioned again, "I truly had a sorrowful heart not from being caught but from sinning against the Lord." In contrast to his own sorrow, he said he sometimes felt that "all other Christians must feel joyful and thankful."

He concluded his letter this way:

> At times I thank God for the slap in the face, since it turned me to God. . . . He has given me the privilege to lead several people to the Lord.
>
> But Kay, I have a hard time dealing with my affliction. I know God forgives sin, and has forgiven mine, but I have concerns. I feel convicted to serve Him, since I repented. But I feel like a sorry loser when I think about sharing the gospel or serving Him in any way.
>
> If people knew the truth about me, they would have nothing to do with me, much less listen to what I have to say regarding Jesus.

And finally there was this statement and this plea:

> I love the Lord and would serve Him, even if He did not want me. So please consider this letter.

There in the airport I had only about three minutes before I had to get on that plane. But I went to the phone and called this man. I told him, "I just want you to know that you are so beloved. And I read your letter, and I am so touched by your heart for God."

I told him, "Look at how God is using me, and look at the sin I was once involved in." I reminded him of the truth of 1 Timothy 1:15: "This is a faithful saying and worthy of all acceptance, that Christ Jesus came into the world *to save sinners*" (NKJV). Christ paid for our sins. "He's the great Redeemer," I told him, "and He will redeem this."

Then I asked the man: "Are you going to believe God, or are you not?"

We talked about how the enemy had snared him and taken away his hope and cast him into a bed of despair. And now it was time to wake up, to get out of that bed, to believe God, and to go forward.

Our hope is not in this life. Our hope is in God. Our hope is in God's Word. Our hope is in God's *future*, the future He has prepared for us in His presence.

Despair comes when you look at this moment instead of the future—because this moment can indeed be bad, this moment can indeed be evil. But our future is *good*, and all things now, even the evil things now, are working together to achieve it.

And you know, this dear man chose to believe God. Months later—maybe a year or more—I was doing a tour, teaching people how to use the *International Inductive Study Bible.* After the sessions, people would line up to talk. And although they waited patiently, I would become concerned especially for the men in the line. Most women don't mind lines as much as men, because generally their focus is relationships. After one of these sessions, I noticed a tall young man in line who seemed to be totally content with waiting. His face beamed with a big smile. Little did I know what I was in for!

By the time I finished talking with him and his wife, my makeup was streaked by tears. This was the man who had written the letter. He had been set free by truth. Despair was gone, and his precious wife was radiant. She had her husband back from the land of despair.

FEELING OSTRACIZED

I also received recently a letter from a woman who said she had repented of a lesbian lifestyle, alcohol abuse, theft, and more. She wrote:

> Just a few years ago I was dead serious about living a holy life before God. You cannot imagine the ways Satan tried to keep me from victory. People from the old ways seemed to crawl out from every rock. Taking a stand on it was a struggle.
>
> I don't know if you are aware, but the church uses homosexuality, addiction, and theft as examples to their congregations. This is tough to sit through. As soon as the pastor or Sunday school teacher mentions them in the context of the lesson, I

automatically feel a lot of tough emotions: like shame, rejection, feeling less than desirable. I feel ostracized.

It has been so difficult in these past years that I have had a hard time finding a church home. Sometimes the anxiety of what I might hear in the morning is so severe that I leave the parking lot without being able to go into church.

One pastor was so opposed to these people that he regularly used them as despicable examples. I did talk to him about it, but it didn't seem to help. I never felt desired in the congregation, and so I left. I'm presently finding a place in a church where I feel a lot of hope and I can stay and work for the Lord.

One of the things that this person and all of us must deal with is what God says about us *now*, as opposed to what was true of us in the past. So whenever someone mentions homosexuals or any kind of sexual perversion or theft or whatever, we can know: *That's what I was—but that's* NOT *what I am.* We'll embrace what God says: that we've been washed, we've been set apart, we've been justified and declared righteous so we don't have to experience repeated condemnation.

Part of this precious sister's problem was that she wasn't fully believing God. That's why at times the despair would drive her even from church.

At the same time, I can say that some people in church don't have it all together, and at times they will react to people and situations more on their emotions and from their own opinions rather than responding on the basis of the Word of God. But that shouldn't drive us from one church to another.

So the question is always this: Are we going to believe the whispered lies of the enemy or the written promises of God? Are we going to heap upon ourselves unjustified condemnation, or are we going to remember that while these things must be said and taught, there is no condemnation to those who are in Christ Jesus?

Let's look now at three strong passages that help us greatly with hope.

WHERE IS HOPE?

In Romans 5 we see exactly where hope is, where it comes from, and what it does.

Paul wrote in verse 1, "Therefore having been justified by faith"—in other words, having been saved, having been declared righteous—and not because of anything you did, but simply by believing God, by accepting His sacrifice for your sins, the sacrifice of the Lord Jesus Christ, the Son of God. Having done this, Paul said, "we have peace with God through our Lord Jesus Christ."

You say, "I don't have that peace. I know I'm saved, but I don't have any peace." Precious one, that's because you've lost hope, even though you're saved.

Please stay with me here: Paul went on to say in verse 2 that through Christ "we have obtained our introduction by faith into this grace in which we stand; and we exult [which means "we rejoice"] *in hope of the glory of God.*"

Now what is this "hope of the glory of God"? It's that someday you will be absent from this old body that gives you fits, and you will be in the presence of the Lord. There will be no more pain, no more sorrow, no more tears, no more death. It will all pass away. That's the hope of the glory of God. Life will get better. In fact, it's going to get magnificent!

All the distress, the turmoil, will be gone—not because you died and ceased existing, but because you fell asleep in Jesus and woke up immediately in the presence of God. The hope of the glory of God is the fact that you will live in God's presence forever and ever. And in His presence there will be no sin and no effects from sin. Your hope of the glory of God is the fact that you'll have eternal life, and this eternal life will be *wonderful.*

You say, "If that's what will happen, it tempts me to want to take my life." But if you do take your life, you will be ashamed when you see Him because you chose your time and way, rather than waiting upon God. And in the taking of your life you sent out the message that His grace just wasn't sufficient enough to carry you in and through the trial until God was ready to call you into His presence.

"Okay, but look," you say, "I've got a life to live now, and living right now is nothing short of hell on earth. The despair is awful. I'm under it all instead of on top of it all."

So look with me at what Paul said next in Romans 5. "And not only this"—that is, not only do we exult and rejoice in our hope of the glory of God, "but we also *exult in our tribulations.*" That has a tendency to sound crazy, doesn't it? But Paul gave us the *reason* for our rejoicing in tribulation: "knowing that tribulation brings about perseverance; and perseverance, proven character; and proven character, hope."

"Perseverance" here is *hupomeno*, the abiding under. You don't give up or walk away, because that very tribulation and your endurance under it will make you more like Jesus Christ. The proven character that comes from your perseverance means you'll be approved unto God; you'll be shown to be genuine, to be real. You'll have that "perfect result, that you may be perfect and complete, lacking in nothing" (James 1:4). You'll be as refined silver, reflecting the Refiner's face with a pure, clear radiance.

Your endurance will prove that you know these despairing circumstances will not last forever; you'll come out of the miry clay, out of the pit, out of the fire. And you'll be better for it than if you had never encountered the tribulation.

And this hope, Paul says, "does not disappoint" (Romans 5:5). This hope won't fail you. You'll know you're a victor, an overcomer, more than a conqueror.

You'll say, "I made it through this, I survived, I endured. And look at me: I know Jesus better, I understand myself better, and I can spot the enemy quicker."

And even if you have lingered long in despair, you will in victory be able to say, "I know why I fell into that pit, and I can see that *I never have to fall into it again.*"

You will have hope, and your hope does not disappoint.

Why?

Paul said it is "because the love of God has been poured out within our hearts through the Holy Spirit who was given to us" (Romans 5:5). You're alive to the experience of His love because the Holy Spirit has made it real to you.

ASKING WHY

Twice in Psalm 42 and once more in Psalm 43 we come across this question: "Why are you in despair, O my soul?"

The psalmist asked this because he was yearning to have his communion with the Lord restored to all its fullness. Listen carefully to his longing:

> As the deer pants for the water brooks,
>> So my soul pants for Thee, O God.
> My soul thirsts for God, for the living God;
>> When shall I come and appear before God?
> My tears have been my food day and night,
>> While they say to me all day long, "Where is your God?"
> These things I remember, and I pour out my soul within me.
> For I used to go along with the throng and lead them in the procession to the house of God,
> With the voice of joy and thanksgiving, a multitude keeping festival.
>> (42:1-4)

When he's in despair, when his tears have been his food all day long, when he seems to have lost or abandoned hope, the psalmist tells himself to remember what it was like before he abandoned hope, what it was like to go to the house of God with the voice of joy and thanksgiving, to sing and to wear a mantle of praise.

Psalm 42 begins with a cry of desperation, for it is obvious that the psalmist felt separated from God. He was looking back, remembering those days of joy and the intimacy he once shared with other believers and with God . . . and now they seemed to be gone. God seemed to be gone.

Can you relate, beloved believer?

The psalmist then asked in verse 5,

> Why are you in despair, O my soul?
>> And why have you become disturbed within me?

This is what you should do when you're in despair, when you feel removed from God. Simply ask yourself, "Why?" Find out the real reasons for your despair. We'll explore how to do this very soon.

But first, be assured that the psalmist knew what despair was like. And he also knew the cure.

In the rest of verse 5 he told himself what to do—which is also the pattern for you and me:

> *Hope in God*, for I shall again praise Him,
>> For the help of His presence.

What's the answer to hopelessness? It's to hope *in* God, the God of all hope, the God who hears the cry of the desperate and who answers according to His mercy.

Talk to God. Remember, you're in warfare, and Satan wants to cut you off from God so he can sift you as wheat. You must keep your lines of communication open even as the psalmist did. Yes, he was in despair, but he didn't intend to stay there. He was going to be honest with God.

This is especially evident as he determined to settle the matter by asking God some hard questions:

> I will say to my God my rock, "Why hast Thou forgotten me?
>> Why do I go mourning because of the oppression of the
>>> enemy?"
> As a shattering of my bones, my adversaries revile me,
>> While they say to me all day long, "Where is your God?"
>>> (42:9-10)

As the psalmist laid his questions before God, the answers came. God had not forgotten him. Those who were asking where his God was would not triumph with their accusing question. The psalmist knew his God and the character and power of his God. And he realized that He is the same yesterday, today, and forever. He knew His God had not left him. God's very presence was the psalmist's help.

The God of the psalmist is your God also, beloved, if in the obedience of faith you have received the Lord Jesus Christ. Therefore, when you're in despair, when you find yourself abandoning hope, when you feel too weak to fight, follow the psalmist's example.

Get alone with God . . . which you probably don't feel like doing. In fact, you probably don't feel like seeing anyone or talking to anyone, including God. If so, it is even a miracle that you're reading this book. So force yourself, beloved, beyond the destructiveness of your feelings.

Get your Bible, a notebook, and a pen and get outdoors if you can— there's something about sunshine and God's fresh air that helps lift your spirit.

Then ask why. "Why are you in despair, O my soul? And why have you become disturbed within me?" Why am I in despair? Why have I lost hope?

Get out your pencil and paper and *write down* the why—every why you can think of. It may be over your marriage, your children, your finances, your past, your future. Whatever it is, put it down. As quickly as the thoughts come to mind, record them. Whatever comes, just write it down.

I am feeling this despair, I've abandoned hope, because of . . .

    #1 —

    #2 —

    #3 —

    #4 —

When you've written whatever God brings to mind, read it over. Look for any unbelief. When did you start questioning God? When did you stop believing Him? When did you lose courage? When did you panic instead of resting in His sovereignty?

As you ask yourself these questions and seek out the answers, remember that there's also more you must do. You can't stop at this point, for you haven't arrived at solutions. You've simply examined the problems. In fact, maybe writing out this list and examining it has caused you to feel even lower than before. I can understand.

But God's Word has the answers. So the next thing you must do is look in God's Word for a specific promise from Him for each of the *whys* you've written down.

Next to each cause you listed for your despair, write down God's promise that goes with it. Or if you don't know a promise, record something you know about the character or power of God that can handle each reason for your despair.

Then as the psalmist did, tell yourself, "Hope in God, for I shall again praise Him for the help of His presence." Remember God. Go back and remember all the things God has done for you, and know that God has not changed.

Go down the items on your list one by one and talk to the Lord about everything you've written out. Tell the Lord you choose to walk by faith and not by emotion. This is your opportunity to switch over from the tracks of feeling to the tracks of faith, just as a train comes to a juncture and switches tracks. This is your opportunity to stop looking at the situation and start looking at God.

WHEN EVERYTHING LIES IN RUINS

In our final passage for this chapter, do your best to imagine yourself in this setting: The threatened captivity of God's people to Babylon had become a reality. After a prolonged siege that caused a famine so severe that parents ate their children, God handed Jerusalem over to the enemy.

He even allowed His sanctuary to be destroyed, the magnificent temple built by Solomon with the treasures accumulated by David.

Now Jerusalem sat desolate and lonely.

The poor handful of Jews left behind lay on the ground, clothed in sackcloth with dust on their heads. Their eyesight had faded because of their tears. Their hearts were crushed.

This was affliction. This was devastation.

We pick up the painful cry in Lamentations 3:

> He has filled me with bitterness,
>> He has made me drunk with wormwood.
> And He has broken my teeth with gravel;
>> He has made me cower in the dust.
> And my soul has been rejected from peace;
>> I have forgotten happiness.
> So I say, "My strength has perished,
>> And so has my hope from the LORD."
>
> (3:15-18)

That is real despair. Jeremiah, the writer, was lamenting that his strength was gone, and so was his hope.

Then he said,

> Remember my affliction and my wandering, the wormwood and
>> bitterness.
> Surely my soul remembers
>> And is bowed down within me.
>
> (3:19-20)

Everything was bleak, everything was dark. And he spoke of his soul being bowed down. We can picture someone broken and bent over in helplessness.

They knew, there in the rubble of Jerusalem, that *God Himself* had done this. They knew they could have averted the catastrophe by listening to God—but they didn't.

You know, beloved, it's one thing to be in a state of ruin when you did everything you could to prevent it. It's something else to know the ruin is of your own making. That's when I think we experience the greater despair: *I did it, I caused it. It's my fault. If only I had listened. If only . . . if only . . . if only . . .*

But by then it's too late. Or at least we think it's too late.

And with man it *would* be too late, but not with God. Man is man, and to man there's always a limit when self kicks in. But to God, there is no limit.

Look again into Lamentations:

> This I recall to my mind,
>   Therefore I have hope.
> *The* LORD's *lovingkindnesses indeed never cease,*
>   For His compassions never fail.
> They are new every morning;
>   Great is Thy faithfulness.
> "The LORD is my portion," says my soul,
> "Therefore I have hope in Him."
>
> (3:21-24)

When we lose hope, in essence it's because we believe that God's lovingkindnesses have ceased—that there's nothing more we can expect from God, that He's reached His limit.

But there's a choice made in this passage, and there's a *therefore*. It's *because* I recall this to my mind that I have hope. And what have I recalled to my mind, even in this situation of total devastation and grief? That there's no end to the Lord's lovingkindnesses and no failure to His compassions.

"The Lord is my portion," he said, "and therefore I have hope." There is hope because of who God is—unceasing in His lovingkindness, unfailing in His compassion.

Later in this chapter he would say, "I called on Thy name, O LORD, out of the lowest pit" (3:55). When he was as low as he could go, he called on God's name. And look at what he says about God's response:

> Thou didst draw near when I called on Thee;
>   Thou didst say, "Do not fear!"
>
> (3:57)

When we are in the lowest pit, we too need to *call on His name*.

In a recent study of Acts I was struck with the repeated phrases used by the apostles: "In the name of Jesus the Nazarene," or, "In the name of Jesus Christ." What power there is in His name when someone is indwelt by the Holy Spirit of God and is walking in faith's obedience!

In Acts 3, when the lame man begged money from Peter and John, Peter responded, "I do not possess silver and gold, but what I do have I give to you: in the name of Jesus Christ the Nazarene—walk!" (verse 6).

We cannot give what we do not possess, can we? But we can give what we do have, and that's the power of doing things in the name of Jesus Christ.

Think of where the lame man would have been had Peter and John given him only what he was begging for! He would have been crippled for life and doomed for destruction, clutching a little silver or gold. But there is power . . . and salvation . . . and healing . . . and hope . . . in the name of Jesus.

It's never too late to call on His name or to act in His name—opening the door to all of God's hope.

I've said enough . . . now it's your turn. Call, beloved, call!

Thanks be to God,
who always leads us in His triumph
in Christ.

2 CORINTHIANS 2:14

CHAPTER FIFTEEN

ALWAYS IN TRIUMPH

Out from the Lowest Pit

IF YOU HAVE PLUNGED into the lowest and worst of the Deadly D's—the stage we've called *demoralization*—but still you've read this far in this book, then you know, beloved of God, that there's hope. You know that God has a way out for you, a way to lift you up. In His great love and tender mercy God has divinely put this book into your hands to help you turn defeat into victory, and you know what to do. All that's needed now is for you to begin putting it into action—to start *doing* it.

Or quite possibly you are among those who haven't gone beyond disappointment or discouragement; rather you're reading this book to help you not only understand the dangers of not handling disappointment God's way but also to help and to minister to others who are fighting these battles. May I commend you, my dear brother or sister. People like you are needed greatly today in the body of Jesus Christ. How I pray that God has and will use this book to affirm what you already knew—and to strengthen you as you reach out to others.

This is a short but an important chapter, and I trust it will be a blessing to you, wherever you are in your walk with our precious Lord.

Now then, let's look at demoralization.

The weaknesses and disabilities we identified in the other Deadly D's reach their most severe and intense form in this lowest pit. The defeat, the exhaustion, the hopelessness, the total lack of courage are present in the worst possible state in which a person can find himself. There is no place lower. Having sunk to the bottom, the demoralized can manage only to run in circles, if they have the strength to run at all.

Perhaps the word *disorder* best describes their condition. Demoralized people are untrustworthy in spirit and in discipline. There's an abandonment of function and responsibility, an inability to get their act together. They're really basket cases.

If you've been there, or you're there now, then you know that at this point the temptation is strongest to end it all—to commit suicide, the ultimate, irreversible surrender. But DON'T. You're listening to Satan's propaganda. You've been brainwashed. The enemy has penetrated your mind with the thought that God is through with you, disappointed in you, disgusted with you, tired of being bothered by you, weary of forgiving you.

Those are LIES, all LIES! They contradict the character of your God and the truths of His Word.

If ever you feel your only recourse is to wave that ragged white flag of surrender—*DON'T.*

If you've been there, beloved, I want you to know I understand. I've never been demoralized, but I can tell you there were two times that even as a Christian I had the thought come to me, *Why don't you just kill yourself? Then it would all be over—no more worry, hassle, pain. Just rest . . . sweet rest.* On one of those occasions I was feeling horribly wounded, rejected, and unloved, and this additional thought came: *Then they'll know how deeply they've hurt me.*

Fortunately I know self-pity when I see it . . . and I know the tactics of the enemy. I've learned to recognize his attacks. A long time ago, in my early days of knowing Jesus Christ, I volunteered for God's boot camp, and He has trained me as His soldier. I've learned what 2 Timothy 2:3-4 is all about—that we're to suffer hardship as good soldiers of Christ Jesus, that we're to stay on active duty, pleasing the One who enlisted us for that very service, and not get entangled with other affairs.

Yes, beloved, the battle can get intense and fierce. Jesus Himself has made this clear to us, and surely you know it by now from all you've read in this book.

And you've also heard enough truth to know *you're on the winning side.* Jesus has said He'll never leave you nor forsake you, so you can boldly say, "The Lord is my helper. I will not fear what man may do."

Isn't it a privilege to be God's child? It matters not whether you are or have been disappointed, discouraged, dejected, despairing, or demoralized—God is still your Sovereign Father, the God of all hope, the God of new beginnings, the God who has eternity for you. You belong to Him.

So be assured, beloved, that the Deadly D's are *not* God's plan for your future. They are *not* Christlike, and they are *not* a part of what God is transforming you to become. The discouragement, the dejection, the despair, the demoralization—*they need never happen again to you.* Remember, "God hath not given us the spirit of fear; but of power, and of love, and of a sound mind" (2 Timothy 1:7, KJV).

A CAPTIVE'S STORY

One of my favorite stories about a twentieth-century hero of faith is the account of Song Siong Chiet, or John Sung, as he became known in America.

John was intellectually brilliant. When his father recognized this, he sent John to America to be educated. John studied hard, was praised by his professors, and earned a doctorate in chemistry.

But that achievement wasn't enough. John still experienced restlessness and a void that earning a Ph.D. did not fill.

With his quest for knowledge unsatisfied, John went to seminary—but it was a seminary filled with liberal professors. Finding no reality and no peace of mind, John found himself in depression, despairing of any cure for the troubled heart that now held him captive. His severe despondency did not go unnoticed by his professors.

One night a young woman came to speak at a meeting held by some of the seminary students. The joy of her obviously intimate relationship with Jesus Christ touched John's heart so deeply that he decided to shut himself in his room until he could discover how to know God as she did.

Light was breaking in his darkened soul.

Alone before God, John first saw all the sins of his life spread before him. There seemed no way to get rid of them. He tried to forget them but couldn't. They pierced his heart, and he was sure he must go to hell.

He opened the New Testament, reading it for the first time in months, and turned to the account of Christ's crucifixion in Luke 23. So vivid was this scene in his mind that he felt himself standing at the foot of the cross, laden with his sins. The vision seemed as clear and real to him as what Paul experienced on the Damascus road.

Suddenly John found himself pleading to have all his sins washed in the precious blood of Jesus. He continued weeping and praying until midnight. Then he heard a voice: *Son, thy sins are forgiven.* At once the weighty load of sin seemed to drop from his shoulders. John Sung had met his Savior.

The prisoner who had incarcerated himself in his room, locked up in deep depression, now burst forth, running down the halls of the dormitory filled with a joy that could not be contained. He was saved!

But the seminary authorities thought he had gone mad—that he had finally broken under the strain of his depression. Failing to recognize the joy and the reality of salvation in Christ, they committed John to a psychiatric institution.

John was unable to convince them of either his sanity or his conversion, but the authorities promised him he would be in the asylum only six weeks. John reasoned that he could handle it, since he had his Bible with him. He counted on six weeks—and nothing more.

When the time was up, he asked to be discharged, but the request was denied. Feeling he had been deceived, John argued angrily with his doctor. John's fiery temper burst forth. The doctor, convinced that John was mentally unbalanced, committed him to a security ward for violent patients.

WHY GO ON?

Weeks later John tried to escape, only to be found by dogs trained to track down escapees. John's attempt served only to further the authorities' suspicions about him. This time he was locked up in an even worse ward. John found himself surrounded by swearing, fighting maniacs.

It seemed too much for him to handle. The Deadly D's crashed over him, dragging him down like a sucking undercurrent. The joy John had once experienced in Christ now seemed like a lost dream. Rejoice? He could not rejoice. He was consumed by despair over his failure to escape.

He still had his Bible with him, but he would not read it.

Dark thoughts of ending his life bombarded his mind. But then he heard the Lord's voice in the inner chambers of his being, rebuking him for even contemplating so grievous a sin.

"But Lord," John spoke aloud, "I wanted to serve You and repay my debt of gratitude. Instead, here I am shut up where there's never a moment's quiet. What use is there to go on living?"

The answer came back almost as clearly as if it had come through the ears instead of the heart: *All things work together for good to them that love God. If you can endure this trial patiently for 193 days, you will learn how to bear the cross and walk the Calvary road of unswerving obedience.*

John accepted that answer. But he realized how much more profitably those days could be spent in a quieter place.

He requested an interview with his doctor and convinced him that earlier he had acted in anger rather than insanity. As a result John was returned to his original ward, where he at least had an opportunity to study his Bible without interruption.

Little did he realize how great an education he was to gain from God during the 193 days to come.

God's Word became John's delight. From early morning until time for bed, he spent most of his waking hours reading through Scripture. He was able to sit at his Master's feet almost entirely free from distraction and interruption. The Word of God was his only text and the Holy Spirit his only teacher.

In those nearly six and a half months he went through the Bible forty times, each time using a different scheme of study. God seemed to be showing John a key for understanding every one of the 1,189 chapters of the Bible. Theme by theme and chapter by chapter, the Scriptures were unfolded to him. John's stack of notebooks grew higher and higher.

The God of all hope had become John's shield and refuge, a very present help in time of trouble.

Exactly 193 days after this course began, John was released. Later he often looked back at those days to see how God had disciplined him to become His submissive servant and had taken away his bad temper.

John recognized that his greatest disappointment was his heavenly Father's appointment—a critical appointment that prepared him as a thoroughly trained Bible teacher and as one of God's instruments for igniting the supernatural flames of revival in his homeland when he later returned to China.

John faced the full barrage of the enemy's Deadly D's—and he came out more than a conqueror.

And, beloved, so can you.

PREPARE FOR BATTLE

As you know, this has been a book about God—about His sovereignty and His trustworthiness. It's also been a book about battle and *for* battle—not an entertainment or a diversionary escape from reality but a soldier's manual for everyday life as it really is.

So now more than ever, my friend, I want to urge you and challenge you to remember what you have seen and learned about the principles of warfare that I laid out at the beginning of this book, principles that modern soldiers are taught in military academies.

Remember that in war the decisive application of full combat power requires unity of command. The power for victory is there if you'll but listen to and submit in faith to the Captain of the host, King Jesus.

Stay in constant communication with Command Headquarters—stay in the Word of God so you can know the will of your Commander, and pray without ceasing, and obey fully His commands.

Concentrate your forces—and your forces are *all the promises of God*. Strengthen your security by believing those promises, for in your knowledge of Him, God has broadened and strengthened your shield of faith.

You've gained good intelligence about the tactics of your enemy. You know he will come at you with lies and accusations. You know his tactics are deadly, because he's a murderer as well as a liar, a deceiver. Remember all you've learned of your enemy, and be prepared accordingly. Don't be caught off guard by his surprise attacks. And never forget that the end of the battle, the demise of the enemy, has already been foretold. It's as certain as God—and even the devil knows it, according to Revelation 12:12. You are on the winning side. Hold your position . . . and advance.

Take offensive action. Wars aren't won with only defense. God has supplied you with much truth. He has sharpened your sword, the Word of God. Now wield it.

Be strong in the Lord and in the strength of His might. Submit first to God, then resist the devil, and he will flee from you. Draw near to God, and He will draw near to you.

O beloved, there is nothing more exhilarating and inspiring than to stand in the full armor of God and know you are more than a conqueror through Him who loves us.

So get dressed, mighty warrior—and be prepared for battle.

Follow in the footsteps of Jesus Christ, God's point man, for His steps lead surely to victory.

"Thanks be to God, who always leads us in His triumph in Christ" (2 Corinthians 2:14).

Do you love Me?

JOHN 21:17

A FIRE OF REMINDER

❧

LET ME TAKE YOU back again to a time long ago, to a famous scene from the Bible's pages. Imagine with me what might have been stirring in the mind of someone for whom I believe this incident was created: a defeated man who needed to see that the grace of God is sufficient for all his failures. A dejected man who needed to experience the depth of his Savior's unconditional love. A discouraged man who needed to be restored and commissioned to a purposeful future.

A STRANGER'S COMMAND

Early-morning light tinted the shores of the Sea of Galilee bright gold, igniting sparkling flashes around a fishing boat sailing shoreward. The rising sun peeking over the mountains to the eastern side of the sea put a happy touch on the promise of a new day.

But the men on the boat were anything but cheerful. They had fished all night and caught nothing.

Of course this wasn't the first time that had happened. They had known their share of both empty nets and full. They were veterans at their trade. This, however, was their first full night to be out fishing since—well, it had actually been a few years now. But in these recent days of uncertainty and regret, Simon Peter, the group's natural leader, had determined to "go fishing," and the others had decided to join him.

And now, no fish. How discouraging it was to be freshly back at it and yet to fail so completely! A night of failure at an old profession probably only deepened a sense of defeat that had earlier swept upon them, especially Peter.

The men were tired; a night's labor is a night's labor regardless of what it yields. There was much on their minds. After three glorious years of constant companionship, their beloved Leader was gone. Did they sail in silence? Once they swung in from the deep, nets empty, perhaps a solemn quietness enveloped their boat.

Someone was standing on the shore, now a hundred yards away, but their weary eyes did not recognize him. Then the stranger called across the waters, his voice dispelling the quiet. "Children, you do not have any fish, do you?"

"No!" they shouted back.

Apparently the stranger's interest in them was more than just polite curiosity. "Cast the net to the right of the boat," he told them, "and you'll find a catch."

Now that would certainly be unusual.

But why not try it?

Their tired arms lifted the net's outer folds from the deck and dropped them over the side. They splatted on the surface then slowly sank into the sea's dark depths, pulling the rest of the net over the railing until it all disappeared below.

In silence again they watched the waters, squinting their eyes against the blinding sparkles of reflected sunlight.

Quickly, in one motion, the ropes that fastened the net to the boat grew taut and gave out a groan as they strained against the railing.

They had a catch!

PAINFUL MEMORIES

The men gave their all to the work, for what a struggle it was to bring the catch to the surface! As it came into sight, they were astounded. The net was filled to overflowing with fish—*large* fish!

The catch was too heavy to lift out of the water. They knew the net was in danger of breaking. All they could do was drag it with them, hoping to get their catch to shore, which was but about two hundred cubits away.

Peter's heart raced, not from the work of pulling up the catch, but from something more . . . as he remembered a humbling but glorious, momentous morning a few years earlier. In fact, it was the very last time he had fished all night—another night with no catch. But that next morning their nets had been filled to breaking just like this, all because of the word from the—

Suddenly Peter noticed John staring toward the shore. Then John said simply, "It's the Lord!"

Peter's heart gave a leap. It *was* Jesus—the one whom He had denied.

Grabbing his cloak, he wrestled his arms into its sleeves and threw himself into the sea. As his arms cut through the cool waters, he could hear the men on the boat shouting excitedly, in a hurry themselves to meet the Master yet hampered by the net full of fish they were dragging.

Splashing out of the shallows, Peter cautiously made his way over the slippery rocks and onto the grassy shore. Pulling at his clinging wet cloak with one hand, he wiped back his thick, black hair from his forehead with the other, then squeezed the water from his beard. He shivered slightly. The morning air was still cool.

Jesus stood beside a charcoal fire. Peter's eyes fell.

His thoughts turned at once to that night he wanted to forget, when he had stood by a charcoal fire just like this one—but it was in the high priest's courtyard in Jerusalem. He was in a crowd standing around the fire to stay warm, an odd crowd gathered at an odd hour, while inside the house the Lord was being questioned. There by that charcoal fire, Peter three times denied he even knew Jesus. He swore it with an oath, though only hours before he had loudly and boldly stated to Jesus, "I will lay down my life for You."

Now Peter looked at the charcoal fire with the fish and the bread and remembered how zealously he had sworn to his Lord that he would follow Him even unto death.

But he hadn't. Peter ran his hand over his face again.

He had failed his Lord and gone out and wept bitterly—and that's what he wanted to do now. If he started, the banks of the Galilee would probably overflow. Peter wondered: Would this happen every time he saw a fire?

"Bring some of the fish which you have now caught," Jesus said.

Peter turned, walked back into the water, and began drawing the net to shore as the others jumped from the boat to help him. Peter shook his head. All these fish—153, he would find out—and the net wasn't broken!

"Come and have breakfast," he heard his Lord say.

Peter watched as Jesus took the bread in his nail-pierced hands. Again came the memory of the night when his Master was betrayed . . . and he had denied Him. It was a haunting dirge that Peter couldn't get out of his mind. What would he say to Jesus if they had the opportunity to talk privately?

REMEMBER THE COMMITMENT

Surely the Lord knew what such a setting would do to Peter—the memories, the thoughts it would evoke. Yet Jesus staged it all—a fire, not to refine but to remind.

To remind Peter of his failure? No, I believe it was a fire to release him from the past so Peter could go forward to a purposeful future. A fire, not to remind Peter of his denial but to help him recall his commitment and his personal commission from his Lord. In this dramatic and moving passage I believe Jesus was essentially telling Peter the same thing He told the church of Ephesus in Revelation 2: "Remember therefore from where you have fallen, and repent and do the deeds you did at first."

Remember from where you have fallen.

What was Jesus doing in John 21? He was taking Peter back to two things. First He took him back to the place of his commitment. Then He took Peter back to the place of his denial—not to demolish Peter but to restore him.

In the miraculous catch of fish recorded in the opening eight verses of John 21, I believe Jesus was reconstructing a previous event, the time when Peter made his first commitment to Jesus, as recorded at the beginning of Luke 5.

The scene there was the same as here: fishing boats in the Sea of Galilee. Jesus had been sitting in a boat belonging to Simon. From the boat Jesus was teaching a multitude crowded along the shore. When He finished, He told Simon to launch the boat out into deep water and let down the nets there for a catch.

Remember how Simon responded? "Master, we worked hard all night and caught nothing, but at Your bidding I will let down the nets." They obeyed, and the nets went out.

When Simon saw the amazing catch this cast produced—enough that it began to break their nets and sink their boats—"he fell down at Jesus' feet, saying, 'Depart from me, for I am a sinful man, O Lord!'"

Then the Lord gave His call and His promise to the astonished fishermen: "Jesus said to Simon, 'Do not fear, from now on you will be catching men.'"

Peter and those with him that day immediately showed their commitment: "And when they had brought their boats to land, they left everything and followed Him." They followed Jesus, and from that point on there was no turning back.

Years later, the memory of that day must have come back strongly to Peter as he and the others struggled with that morning catch.

Remember the Denial

So Jesus brought Peter back to the place of his commitment. And in the charcoal fire burning on the shore, I believe Jesus was taking Peter back to the place of his denial. He was confronting Peter with that earlier fire, which was truly a refining fire.

Let's follow the scene further, exactly as it's detailed for us in John 21.

When breakfast was over, Jesus did talk with Peter. Whether it was privately or before the other disciples we do not know. We only know that Jesus said to Peter, "Simon, son of John, do you love Me more than these?"

The word He used here for love was *agape*—the highest form of love, a love that desires another's highest good. It's the love God has for us. It's unconditional love, a love that lays down its life for another.

The Lord's question for Peter—and for us, beloved, as we bring this book to a close—is this: "Do you love Me? In light of all I've done for you, all I've taught you, all you've seen of My love and My sacrifice, do you unconditionally, sacrificially love Me so as to meet *My* needs?"

What would you answer, my friend? Would it be the same as Peter's response?

"Yes, Lord," Peter answered. "You know that I love You."

Yes, Peter loved Jesus, but he could not use the word for love that Jesus used. He could not bring himself to say, "I *agape* You." Instead he had to say, "I *phileo* You." *Phileo* is the word for brotherly love, affection. It's a love where two share the same interests.

How could Peter ever again say to the Lord, "I *agape* You"? He had failed Jesus so miserably at that other charcoal fire. He had not loved Him unconditionally—he had denied Jesus in His hour of need despite all his boasting that he would die for Him!

But Jesus made no mention of Peter's choice of *phileo*. Instead He answered Peter with a command: "Tend My lambs."

Then He said to Peter a second time, "Simon, son of John, do you *agape* Me?"

Peter responded once more, "Yes, Lord, You know that I *phileo* You."

Jesus answered, "Shepherd [or feed] My sheep."

Then it happened the third time: Jesus asked, "Simon, son of John, do you love Me?"—and this time Jesus used *phileo*.

This was upsetting to Peter. "Peter was grieved," John said, "because He said to him the third time, 'Do you love *[phileo]* Me?'" Jesus was saying, in essence, "Peter, do you truly love Me with a strong affection? Do you share My interests?" Jesus was bringing Peter face to face with his relationship with the Lord.

"Lord, you know all things," Peter answered. "You know that I love You"—*phileo* again.

Jesus answered, "Tend My sheep." Then at once Jesus alluded to the humbling death of martyrdom by which Peter would glorify God. "And when He had spoken this, He said to him, 'Follow Me!'" (21:19).

Peter received a commission to tend the Shepherd's sheep. The loving concern of His Master was to be his own, his primary interest. And he would follow the Lord with that love and in that commission all the way to the end . . . all the way to his death.

Second Chances

Our God is the God of second chances. He's the Great Redeemer of our failures.

And all He wants as we rise up and press onward from our failures is for us to love Him totally, completely, and absolutely. If we can't say to Him, "I *agape* You," if all we can say is "I *phileo* You," He will still commission us to tend His lambs and feed His sheep. He will still command us to follow Him.

In his answers to the Lord's piercing questions, Peter was renewing his commitment to Jesus. He was saying yes to the Lord. He was saying, "I love You."

But Jesus had asked Peter, "Do you love Me *more than these?*"

More than what? It could have been several things.

There were 153 fish on the shore. Perhaps Jesus was asking Peter, "Do you love Me more than you love fishing? Are you going to be a fisherman of fish or of men, as I once commissioned you? Are you retreating in failure, or will you believe Me—that I love you, that My grace is there to cover you, that I am not finished with you, that I have a purposeful future for you despite your past? Will you make My interests your priority? Even if it costs you your life? And no matter what any of my other disciples do?"

As we hear Jesus ask this of Peter, you know—don't you, beloved?—that you and I must answer the same question. This is why this account was chosen for inclusion in the Word of God—to bring us to a similar "showdown" of faith.

So let me ask you as well: Do you love Jesus more than your occupation, more than your career, more than your means of making a living? Do you? I know many people who are so busy making their mark professionally or so busy simply bringing in income, or even so busy with their service for God that they don't have time for knowing God and serving Him accordingly. But what did Jesus say in Matthew 6:33? "Seek first His kingdom and His righteousness; and all these things shall be added to you." If you have time for work and earning a living but don't have time to sit and talk with Him in prayer, to hear His voice in the Word, and to make His interests your priority, then something is drastically wrong, and you will find yourself in trouble. You and I must love Him supremely, love Him steadfastly, love Him pre-eminently.

And what if Jesus was not referring to fish when He asked Peter if he loved Him "more than these"? Maybe Jesus nodded His head toward the other disciples rather than the fish. Perhaps Jesus was asking, "Peter, do you love Me more than these disciples love Me?"

Remember that as they left the Upper Room and went to the Mount of Olives, Peter had boldly declared, "Even though all may fall away, yet I will not. . . . Even if I have to die with You, I will not deny You!" (Mark 14:29,31). Peter did seem to have a tendency to keep his eye on others. We see this in John 21, for after Jesus said to Peter, "Follow Me!"

Peter looked around and noticed John. And he asked Jesus, "What about this man?"

His response was so human! Exactly what many of us would be tempted to think and to say.

But Jesus responded, "If I want him to remain until I come, what is that to you? You follow Me!"

We're not to compare our own commitment and service for the Lord with that of others. Jesus was saying, "Don't worry about anyone else. I want you to follow Me!" He wasn't calling Peter to speculation but to action.

And just as He individually commissioned Peter, so He's also individually commissioning you. He's calling you, not to speculation but to action, to work. He's telling you, "Follow Me!"

He showed Peter—as He's also showing us in this passage—that the purpose of life is twofold: to love God and to follow Him. Our greatest commandment is to love Him with all our heart, soul, mind, and strength. And then we're to follow Him unto death, until God takes us home. Our commission is nothing short of loving God and following Him all the days of our life and to the end of our time on earth.

So think of it as the Lord asking you—you alone, dear reader—"Do you love Me with all your heart?"

If you answer yes, if you do love Him wholeheartedly, then what are you to do?

Jesus tells us. Jesus is the Shepherd of the sheep, and the sheep are always foremost on His heart. So if you love God, the sheep will be your business. This is how your love for Him will manifest itself.

When you come to Him in faith, God gives you one or more spiritual gifts, and they aren't for your own benefit but for the edification of the body, for building up the body of Christ. Your gift will always manifest itself in tending the lambs, in feeding the sheep. You aren't necessarily to be a teacher, but wherever you are, you're to minister the Word of God to people in deed as well as in word. Wherever you and I go, we're called to be His witnesses. We're to go into all the world, and we're to disciple others.

We have a responsibility. There are sheep to feed. There are lambs who need pasturing.

Do you love Him? Then shepherd those sheep. Meet their needs. Get out of that boat and take care of the sheep.

A Heart Completely His

When Peter came in his failure to Jesus, did Jesus reject him? No, Jesus commissioned him.

When Peter jumped from that boat to hurry to shore, he was running into the arms of a waiting Jesus.

Peter's heart was the Lord's, and "the eyes of the LORD move to and fro throughout the earth that He may strongly support those whose heart is completely His" (2 Chronicles 16:9). When the soldiers came to Gethsemane and Peter drew his sword and cut off that servant's ear, you can't tell me Peter wasn't willing to die with Jesus. I believe he was. But in his dependence on the flesh he was weak, and in that weakness he would stumble and fall.

He forgot what Jesus had told him earlier in Gethsemane: "The spirit is willing, but the flesh is weak; therefore watch and pray." When Peter should have been watching and praying, he was sleeping instead.

So when he had an opportunity to speak up for Jesus by that first charcoal fire, he instead denied Him.

But his heart belonged completely to the Lord. Judas's heart never belonged to Jesus, but Peter's did. Therefore Jesus stood waiting on the shores of Galilee to comfort Peter and encourage and commission him.

The Lord's purpose is always restoration. His purpose is always to redeem our failures and to turn us into a spiritual success for Him. And that, beloved, is what this book is all about—to help you handle life's failures and disappointments in such a way that you will be as silver refined, effective for the Master's use because you more and more reflect His image, His heart, His passion.

Jesus was showing Peter what He also shows us: Whenever you've failed God, remember your own impotence. Peter needed to remember the day he had knelt before Jesus and said, "Depart from me, for I am a sinful man, O Lord!" Why should Peter ever think he would never deny Jesus? What was he trusting in? He was trusting in his own strength and the emotion of his own dedication instead of trusting in Jesus.

But Jesus knew Peter's impotence, just as He knows ours. Jesus didn't choose Peter or any of us because we're strong and could never deny Him. He didn't choose us because we're so talented or loyal or brave or any other good quality. He understands the weakness of our flesh. And He chose us out of pure love. Not love that was prompted by us but unconditional love that flowed freely from His heart. He loved us, and He chose us. We did not choose Him (see John 15:16).

So when you fail Him, don't say, "It's no use, I've let Him down, He doesn't want me, He can't use me," and then go off fishing. No, do exactly what Peter did: Get out of the boat.

Yes, of course you are powerless and impotent in yourself. But that is not the basis of His call.

Maybe you've thought as you've read this book, *All this is for others. Other people can turn around in their failures, but there can't be a turning around for me.*

But if you've failed, precious one, if you've blown it, then go back and remember your place of commitment, and renew that commitment. Go back to the place of your denial and say, "Lord, I made a commitment to You, but I denied You. I failed You. I failed to do what You told me to do. Lord, forgive me."

And do you know what He'll say? He'll say what He said to Israel millenniums ago when it played the harlot and went into captivity: "My lovingkindnesses are new every morning. My compassions fail not" (see Lamentations 3:22-23).

He will ask you to follow Him, and He will lift your life to a higher plane.

Renew your commitment and hear His commission. His commission is for you to go—go and take care of His sheep, take care of His lambs, take care of them until you die. That's your calling.

So love Him.

And follow Him.

And in your hardships and afflictions, in every disappointment, whenever the Refiner's fires are heating up—remember all these inspired words of Peter, the failure whom the Lord restored:

> In this you greatly rejoice, even though now for a little while, if necessary, you have been distressed by various trials, that the proof of your faith, being more precious than gold which is perishable, even though tested by fire, may be found to result in praise and glory and honor at the revelation of Jesus Christ; and though you have not seen Him, you love Him, and though you do not see Him now, but believe in Him, you greatly rejoice with joy inexpressible and full of glory, obtaining as the outcome of your faith the salvation of your souls. (1 Peter 1:6-9)

> Be diligent to be found by Him in peace, spotless and blameless. (2 Peter 3:14)

> *. . . and as silver refined.*